P9-DEE-039

ADRIENNE VON SPEYR

CONFESSION

ADRIENNE VON SPEYR

CONFESSION

TRANSLATED BY
DOUGLAS W. STOTT

IGNATIUS PRESS   SAN FRANCISCO

Title of the German original:
Die Beichte
© 1960 Johannes Verlag
Einsiedeln, Switzerland

Cover by Victoria Hoke

With ecclesiastical approval
© 1985 Ignatius Press, San Francisco
All rights reserved
ISBN 0–89870–040–x
Library of Congress catalogue number 84–80757
Printed in the United States of America

CONTENTS

CONTENTS

EDITOR'S FOREWORD

A glance at all her previous publications clearly shows that Adrienne von Speyr's book on confession is one of her most central works. Not only the great commentary on John, but also the book on prayer, that on Mary, that on the Passion in Matthew, indeed all her books revolve around the act and attitude of confession, around the personal and ecclesial-sacramental encounter between sinner and God, around that total openness that is the prerequisite for all blessing, mission and prayer.

The new element in the author's understanding of confession—an element fully developed in this volume—is its trinitarian and particularly its christological basis. The Cross (and with it the entire Incarnation of the Son) is the archetypal confession, and Christian sacramental confession thus is imitation of Christ in the strict sense. The present volume examines the enormous fruitfulness of this dogmatic basis from many perspectives. The author gives us less a closed system than a wealth of suggestions which both the theological expert and the layman will want to pursue.

This trinitarian-christological basis of necessity broadly discloses the ecclesial dimension. Here the author encounters the contemporary dogmatic and historical discussion, to which her own fundamental ideas enable her to contribute in a fruitful and original way. Her brief concluding chapter concerning one particular *crux theologorum*—the confession of the saints—shows how well-placed her accents are from the very beginning. Considered in the light of her exposition, this problem no longer causes any embarrassment whatever. In two places the editor has pointed out that the actual development of the author's ideas concerning both the "confessional" attitude of the saints and the infinitely diverse manifestations of this attitude within the Church can be found in another work.

Similarly, the relationship between baptism and confession—a relationship not treated here—will find expression elsewhere.

The quality of the present volume is also manifested in its dual character: speculative and profound on the one hand, practical and simple on the other. Its practical aspect, its applicability to one's own confession, emerges from every page.

It is fashionable today to speak of a "sacrament of penance" instead of "confession". In a certain superficial historical sense this may be correct to the extent that in the first centuries confession was present in Christian consciousness primarily under the aspect of penance. However, everyone knows that in reality this was only an initial seed and not the full-grown plant. Indeed, it was a seed that scarcely suggested the dogmatic basis just mentioned, a basis whose center is expressed by "confession" (Augustine's *confessio*, to admit or confess). Thus there is no real reason to dispense with the traditional word.

Hans Urs von Balthasar
Editor

1. INTRODUCTION:
THE SEARCH FOR CONFESSION

In all events which are not inevitable and in whose course freedom and inclination can intervene, a person usually searches for a solution or a way out and often for a reason or cause as well—though the way out usually suggests itself more readily than the cause. He tries to find out what he could do to improve his situation, to have a more satisfying existence and enjoy more success. Only when this success fails to materialize according to his wish does he look for the causes behind the failure, and it is in this search that he first encounters the question concerning the state of his own life. He tries to understand his situation and to justify it, and in doing so he may have to recognize that circumstances are stronger than he and that he can do nothing to change his condition because he must struggle with forces more powerful than he. Yet it is precisely when he justifies himself and concludes that he is innocent that his deeper discomfort—the feeling of a hidden guilt—begins.

Generally he is not able to perform this analysis of his fate on his own. He needs and seeks dialogue, not so much to listen to what the other person has to say—and that person is rarely able to explain his situation to him adequately—as to have the opportunity to express properly what is bothering him. Perhaps he seeks also—and even above all—to allow his own words to strengthen his opinion, as if what is expressed acquired a kind of final correctness by means of some mysterious power of formulation, or as if he were saved by the process of self-expression, or as if his own condition were outlined and stabilized by the words he simultaneously speaks and hears. Even if these words in and of themselves do not change his condition, they at least offer that peculiar kind of relief inherent in order and in the necessity of "this is the way things are."

For many people this self-expression through discussion is so important as a rescue device that they sink into a certain hopelessness once it has been employed. Discussion was their last hope, and its failure proves that they can expect absolutely nothing. Thus, after this discussion has taken place under the wrong conditions, they often become even more indifferent than before by completely running aground in resignation.

Of course, this discussion is often arranged in such a way that, considered objectively, it offers no possibility whatever for success; its outcome is settled in advance because the person speaking, while claiming the desire to change his condition, does not really want to change anything at all. He chooses his partner in such a way that the partner cannot really contribute effectively; his role is merely to nod and to offer mute confirmation. If the partner is chosen in such a way that he is not really permitted to express his own opinion and can only passively accept what is said—if for no other reason than that the speaker has carefully selected what is to be confided, and therefore the image conveyed simply does not correspond to reality—then any discussion naturally remains unsuccessful. Nevertheless, there are people who have perhaps confided in a neighbor or in some other peer, and who then suddenly turn to someone they consider to be of higher rank: to the physician, for example, who is set apart because of his knowledge, his position and his habit of dealing with people. The physician's office is probably the place where most discussion of this sort takes place. What is said to the physician, however, is usually quite one-sided, precisely because only very few of those who speak with him want to hear unexpected advice. Almost all of them want confirmation, and only in the case of the smallest details are they willing to change anything. Indeed, they often only want to use the physician's advice as a trump card against a third person in order to change that person's behavior more than their own.

Most people justify themselves. They like nothing better than to hear someone say, "At some point your daughter really ought to see that . . ." or, "It's high time your husband. . . ." They are grateful for every new weapon offered them in their struggle with their environment, and they interpret their own fate in such a way that one understands: nothing essential can really be changed. Their lives have a kind of necessity. A woman, for example, does not enjoy her husband's company because she is too tired in the evening. She does not like to go to the movies with him because she does not see well. The same holds true for her shortcomings and errors: They are unavoidable because even as it is she is doing the best she can. Such people stand perched on a teetering, precarious scaffold, and if anyone should shake it even a little, they would plunge to their death. "My nerves couldn't stand another confrontation with my husband. . . ." The judgments they make about their surroundings are inevitably false, because they have never gone to the trouble to understand inwardly the lives of others and to share life with them in love. Yet they feel the urge to talk about how badly things are going for them, about how strenuous and difficult their own lives are. They want to be pitied, and they want support precisely in their rejecting attitude toward others. To be sure, they need to express themselves in discussion, but they supply their own norms for this discussion. They speak repeatedly about wanting to talk everything out some time, and they associate this with all sorts of vague expectations of some general improvement in their condition, but they care nothing about real change. Because they subject themselves to no other norm than their own, they feel perfectly free to express their troubles as they see fit without granting their partner any right to interrupt. They speak without first considering what they say, and without being seriously responsible for it. Thus, most encounters of this sort are nothing but so much prattle about oneself and about what one believes to be one's own state of affairs. Talk itself is the most important thing, not responsible dialogue. This is why so many falsely conceived conversations take place and so many people place themselves in the hands of those who are uneducated, incompetent or unprincipled. The result is perhaps a vague relief, but one that in no way corresponds to real change or alteration.

If one were to outline for such people the contours of real confession, with the preparation and interior insight which it requires in order to give rise to genuine guidance, either they would see in confession a mere variation of what they call discussion, or they would be mortally terrified at the prospect of seeing themselves as they really are. After all, this would mean subjecting their entire being to a norm from which an unrelenting and unpredictable challenge might issue. What they call dialogue remains in a sphere external to their own being, and even if the necessity of which they speak is an interior affair, during dialogue it slides to the periphery. Thus this necessity remains unexamined as regards both its source and its content. Their loneliness is one with their incapacity for genuine expression in dialogue.

Anyone who deals with the problems of others as a profession and who in addition treats these problems as something interesting will certainly find a clientele. He may possess simply the art of listening and can elicit trust just because of that, so that people flock to him and tell him the most incredible stories. For them consolation and success are already contained in the time spent on them. They are elated that they were received and were permitted to express themselves. Above and beyond this there are methods and techniques such as those of psychoanalysis which, in the interest of help and relief, reach back to something already present in the person and construct a whole out of the inevitable echo. These methods reveal the life of the instincts and erotic impulses in their more or less conscious expressions, in order to interpret the patient's entire behavior from this perspective and to lend it a significance issuing completely from his impulses, but which leaves behind in the patient the feeling that he has been understood in a completely new fashion. Because this kind of treatment lasts a long time, the patient feels genuinely uplifted for a time; and if the treatment coincides with his more acute difficulties, he will later believe that it helped him in an effective and lasting fashion. People released from treatment as healed are often those to whom *something* about the most primitive things has been explained, and explained in such a way that in the future they will refer back to this explanation whenever conflicts arise. At the same time, however, they have become blind to anything that does not fit into the scheme of impulsive or instinctive factors. Rather than opening up the richness and fullness of the real world to them, this self-expression abbreviates and explains away everything that does not fit into the rigid method of analysis. Not every method or technique has to be as narrow as that of classical psychoanalysis, and there are many ways in which one may try to help people. One can guide them to a more socially oriented attitude, or one can disclose aspects of existence previously hidden to them. In the final analysis, however, all these techniques remain human techniques, prescriptions someone has invented, to be applied in a more or less flexible or rigid fashion to as many cases as possible. They are things invented by human beings, and as such they necessarily can view, comprehend and cure only a very limited side of the human Thou. This would hold equally true of a technique that expressly made use of religious factors, such as prayer, as methodological aids.

Ultimately, only the Creator of the human soul will be able to treat it so that it becomes the soul he needs. Only he can heal it, and he does this in ways that only he knows and discloses and prescribes for healing. Other relationships between those who lead and those who are led are based no doubt on need. But the decisive way of God—confession—is based on obedience: more specifically, on the obedience to God both of the person led and of the person leading. A person may very well feel a need to confess, but if he actually confesses he does so in obedience to God. Even less does the confessor listen to someone else's sins out of some need; he does it primarily and exclusively in obedience to God. God himself has decisively pointed out the locus where he intends to practice psychoanalysis on sinners: the locus of the Cross and of confession established after the Cross. It is a central act of obedience to God to set forth on this path, the path he has pointed out as the only correct one and only really healing one.

This does not mean that every conversation concerning one's own spiritual affairs conducted outside confession and the office of the Church is useless or harmful. But if the need for this conversation arises in the right place and is acted upon properly, that conversation will lead—in the long or short run, directly or by indirect paths—to the act of confession. Of course, peripheral matters can be dealt with quite adequately by means of peripheral techniques.

If a person—in however primitive a fashion—comprehends himself as standing before God, and if he knows that he, like Adam, was created by God and redeemed by Christ and that Christ opens for him the way to the Father and the doors of heaven, then between the two poles of his existence, birth and death, where he unconditionally feels himself to be a sinner, he will expect confession with a kind of necessity. He will expect that God offers him the possibility to return again and again to a center which God himself points out and makes accessible. Every person understands in some fashion that "things can't go on as they are." From this angle of vision he encounters the question of how things might go on, and perhaps of how things ought to go on considered from God's perspective. How has God pictured his life, not only as a whole but at this moment? Does God have any particular expectation which he could and should fulfill in a particular way suggested by God himself? He feels perhaps that if he can rely only on his own freedom, or only on other human beings who live in the same kind of freedom as he, he cannot do justice to God's expectation. He senses that to talk something out according to his own or someone else's formula and to burden someone else with the problem is not enough if he wants to find his way back to that most profound correctness, the straight line connecting his birth and death. Everything he may accomplish outside confession in the way of self-expression and discussion may indeed offer momentary relief; but even the most simple person will see that this moment of relief remains merely one moment among others in life and that it is necessary to comprehend all these moments as a unity.

Let us assume you are my friend, and I say to you, "I can't go on like this." We discuss the situation together; perhaps we discover where I got off the track, and perhaps we even refer to my childhood. What we find will help me to make a new start. In every discussion of this sort, however, the individual is viewed as an isolated person, and it does not become clear that he lives in a community both of saints and sinners. Only God knows the laws both of the community of saints and of the community of sinners. In confession I am, of course, this individual sinner, but I am simultaneously a part of humanity, one of its fallen members. Thus conceptual factors are completely different in confession than in analysis. They are both personal and social; indeed, they comprise a totality that draws into focus the world as a whole, its relationship to God, and the first and last things, even if this larger context only falls into our field of vision momentarily and is experienced only indirectly. And since the situation is different, so also are the means of healing. The truth of God is involved, not the truth of the human being, nor the truth of his soul, his existence or the structure of his deeper being, but decisively the truth of God. None of the human techniques takes this divine truth seriously; at most they save it for the hour of death, and they do not help a man to become the kind of person he will need to be in that hour.

As long as aid for the human being is offered by other human beings and is mobile within the human sphere, it can operate only with human means. Everything approaching a person from external sources can be considered only as accidental and external and be supplied with a positive or negative label; the unity between interior and exterior, however, cannot be effected. The psychological session can offer me only "modes of behavior" applicable to the present, which themselves can and must change under altered conditions. Confession, on the other hand, brings a person face to face with his divine destiny and places him directly within it—within that which is final and ultimate.

As long as a person is not confessing, he feels free to speak or keep silent about whatever he wishes. What he then hates in confession is not the humbling experience of revealing himself, and not the fact that he is a sinner—he already knows that somehow—but the necessity of capitulating before and within total confession, the fact that the freedom of selection has been withdrawn and that the only choice remaining is to reveal everything or nothing. He is sick as a whole person and must be healed as such, and not eclectically. That is the first humbling experience. The second is that he is only one of many and has to accept the same conditions as do the others, even external conditions such as having to appear at the confessional at an appointed hour: a kind of marked condition, the elimination of all external differentiation—the factory owner and the watchman, the lady and her cook, all on equal footing. Precisely when one confesses that which is most intimate, one no longer has a choice or selection, is put on a level with all other sinners and is merely one penitent in the line of other sinners. The peculiarities of my particular "case", which made it seem so interesting to me and which I would so gladly have explained to the listener, do not matter at all any more. Confession [*Beichten*] is above all precisely that: a confession [*Bekenntnis*] not only of my sins but also a confession to God and to God's precepts and institutions, indeed to his Church with her own weakness and her myriad ambiguous, even disturbing, aspects.

The act of "speaking" with someone about my life does not

oblige me further. Afterward, I can experience a certain feeling
of gratitude or of awkwardness toward the person who has
listened to me, but I remain the free person who can detach
himself again. Confession is not an individual act in the same
sense; nothing in it can be isolated. The act of confession
expressly involves the whole person, his whole life, his whole
world-view, his whole relationship to God.

If I mention to a third party that I am discussing various
aspects of my life with another, he will generally agree it is a
good idea: "You're doing the right thing, and I'm glad you've
found someone who can help you along." In a way, this will
elevate me in his eyes. But if I tell him that I am going to
confession and that it redeems me, this lessens my status in his
eyes, for those who do not go to confession always have a
great deal to say against it. It compromises human freedom
and one's legitimate pride; it is antiquated and even medieval
because it involves so many external forms. Those who do not
go to confession feel they are above it; in going to confession I
place myself in a "lower class". At the same time, however,
everyone is familiar with human dialogue; people opt for or
against it at will and make use of it only when and to the extent
that it suits them. For one who confesses, however, any choice
on the basis of "it suits me" has ceased.

If people do come together for the sake of this kind of
dialogue, if some necessity of life prompts them to do this,
they should then persevere until they come face to face with
this necessity, until the motivating factors come into view,
until for at least a moment they are forced out of their illusory
and—in their opinion—immovable position in such a way that
their real guilt becomes visible, or at least until it occurs
to them that there might be a genuine connection between
situation and guilt. Most of the time the case is this: Even if
they know and admit that they have done some things wrong
and that they have done and continue to do things that are not
right, they are nonetheless accustomed to see themselves as a
given unity that is not really affected by their sin. For only

persons who look directly into the face of their own sins will discover that connection which is far more than a mere parallelism between "fate" and "faultiness" that is present in the consciousness of most people. On the one hand they see their distorted situation and their difficult fate, and on the other hand they see themselves, certainly with some short-comings. But we see the unity between the two only when God himself holds the mirror before us—if we have the courage to look into that mirror.

The mirror God holds before us, however, is his incarnate Son who became like us in everything except sin. Thus whoever would learn how to confess must first look at the life of the Son of God; there he will learn what confession is, what the intention of confession is and how confession functions.

2. CONFESSION IN THE LIFE OF THE LORD

Trinitarian Foundation

God stands before God in the attitude that is fitting for God. Analogously, we can designate this as the attitude of confession, since it is the attitude in which God shows himself as he is and since this revelation is expected by God himself; from it emerges each new situation of vision and of love. God shows God what he does, and by revealing his actions he reveals himself, shows the effect of his existence as God within those actions and awaits recognition, affirmation and encouragement in order to proceed further in this exchange of revelation and self-understanding. For God is not a stagnant being; he is eternal, transpiring life.

For God it is bliss to reveal himself before God. The God who sees would naturally have, in human terms, the ability to see without something being shown to him; for example, when God sees the sins of a person who, like Adam, conceals himself. There is in God, however, the bliss of revealing himself and the bliss of seeing what has been shown, the joy of a mutual communication encompassing both revelation and the beholding of something revealed.

In this fashion God stands before himself in the attitude of God, in an attitude perpetually corresponding to and emerging from the perpetual present moment of eternity, in an attitude of trust, of gratitude, of surrender and of acceptance. When the Son institutes confession at Easter, he does so to bring this divine attitude closer to human beings, to mediate to them part of the trinitarian life. To ensure the truth of this attitude, he chooses sin as that which is to be shown. For in the final analysis the human being deceives himself least about sin. At the same time, however, it is that which has separated the human being from God, that to which one always refers if one wants to show where (how far away) the human being stands in relationship to God. Adam alienates himself from God in the first place by succumbing to sin, and God employs this same sin to bring Adam back.

If one understands the Father as the one who begets, the Son as the one begotten and the Spirit as the one who issues from them both, then one also understands that each Person must be wholly and exclusively what he is if this exchange in God's one essence is to be possible. Each Person is wholly himself for the sake of the other two, and for the sake of the others he reveals himself completely to them. For example, out of gratitude to the Father the Son reveals himself to him as the one begotten of the Father, in an attitude that is the prototype of confession. He expects a response from the Father so that he can orient himself toward the Father ever anew. In this confession instituted by the Son we, too, seek to be people who confess completely, who open ourselves in order to experience God totally and to live anew in light of this experience.

The sacrament bequeathed us by the Son, the fruit of his Passion, will then have something of the personal character of the Son himself; it is a revelation of the Father, a part of the Father's gift to us in the Son and the mediation of a basic attitude of the Son toward the Father. The Spirit issuing from the Father and Son, effective in the sacrament, will then reveal something of the characteristics of both and will thus reveal his own identity. What he reveals, he effects; and he is active both in the confessional attitude of the person confessing and in the confessor through whom the Spirit speaks and molds the penitent.

It is not difficult to see and imitate the Son's confessional attitude, first because he demonstrates it to us as a man, second because he is born from the Father alone; he is both an expression of and a response to the Father. The confessional attitude of the Spirit is perhaps more difficult to understand, because he proceeds from both of the other two and his being as a person is not as evident to us. The Spirit becomes particularly visible in the synthesis of the official and the personal in the confessor, indeed in the confessional procedure as such. But one can say that the Father's attitude stands at the source of those of the Son and the Spirit; it is the originating element in the Deity, that primal will or impulse to reveal itself in the begetting of the Son and in the breath of the Spirit and thus to disclose who God actually is.

The Confessional Position of the Son

All the sacraments are reflected in the life of the Lord and have their truth and prototype there. When he institutes the sacrament of confession at the end of his earthly mission, the Lord sees in it in a particular way the fruit of his entire life on earth, for through this sacrament he effects the redemption from sin throughout the ages. Thus from the very beginning his entire earthly life stands in the light of confession. Even his eternal pact with the Father—that he will become man in order to redeem the world—includes confession in a particular way with its confession, contrition and penance by man, and with absolution from God.

One can say that the Lord lives on earth before the Father in the same condition in which the perfect penitent should live before his own confessor, before the Church and before God: in complete openness, concealing nothing, always ready in every moment to expect the intervention of the Holy Spirit, drawing security from the Father and his Spirit instead of from within himself. The Son lives in perpetual contact with the Father, and the expression of this contact is his word, "Not my will, but thy will be done."

From time immemorial he sees the world's sin and its increase; he sees it in all its ramifications. He sees the alienation of men from the Father, the alienation into which they have fallen because of their guilt. Having become a man, he lives among these alienated people as one of them. At first his coming in no way changes the world into which he comes. He is one among those separated from God. If he had wanted only to live as God, then from the very beginning he would have created distance between his own appearance and way of life and those of other men, a perpetually yawning chasm that would have accentuated visibly his total otherness. But he wants to be one human being among others; his appearance is not to be different from ours. He lives in circumstances that are the same as ours. The more he as a human being grows in his recognition of sin—the more he sees and experiences sin among his fellow men—the more he accepts its burden knowingly and in suffering, so that the Father, when he beholds the Son, also sees him bear increasingly this burden of the world's guilt. Thus he who recognizes the truth of sin is also he who confesses it in truth. Recognition and confession cannot be differentiated in the Son, because everything he has and knows belongs to the Father. Because he carries that guilt with full recognition—a recognition of evil which can only be a passive experience because it never becomes active—he suffers, not in isolation from God, but rather in that openness which is of the same nature as the open verbal confession.

Whenever a sinner admits his guilt in confession, a double movement takes place between him and his sin. In recognition and admission, he identifies himself with his guilt and affirms that he is a sinner. In acknowledging that it belongs to him and him only, he puts himself at a distance from it by repenting. Precisely this complete acceptance of his guilt in recognition and repentance leads to complete release. The sinner confesses so that the guilt will be taken from him. He binds himself to this guilt so that he will be released from it.

The Son also accepts the burden of sin by recognizing sin, but he takes it as someone else's property. Taking it upon himself, he does not put himself at a distance from it; his intention is rather to go as far as identification, no further. His ever-closer approach to the Father is simultaneously his ever-closer approach to the human being as sinner, so that in this single approach he can show this sin to the Father and give it over into his hands. When the sinner confesses his guilt and thus puts himself at a distance from it by wishing it away and repenting, it is already separated from him—as if it were already encompassed by the divine grace. At the moment it was committed, on the other hand, it did not stand in grace. But if the Son accepts this guilt, he lends it the radiance of his own grace from the very beginning. And the Father sees from the very beginning in this acceptance of guilt the illuminating love of the Son. The Father can no longer view this guilt borne by the Son as isolated guilt; he can view it only in its connection with the grace of the Son.

When someone confesses, he would like to begin a new life after the confession. He wants to be rid of his sin and be more free for God and for the word of God that he hears in confession. The Son resembles this penitent who yearns for a new life, since the Son has been commissioned by the Father to bring new life, the New Covenant, new human beings. In order to do this, he cannot remove himself from this new life in any way. He must not only avoid sinning (in any case, as God he cannot sin); he must also remain steadfast in the will of the Father in such a way that his human experiences and his experiences of sin and world—things he experiences differently on earth than in heaven—also play themselves out completely within that will. He cannot and may not acquire any human experiences that do not correspond to the experience of sin held by the Father in heaven. As incarnate man he cannot and does not want to appear before the Father as one who "knows better" about things concerning sin. Similarly, the penitent who knows how and why he has sinned may not appear before the confessor as one who "knows" or "knows better"; he rather remains faithful and submissive to the truth of the Spirit that the confessor shows to him. The Son cannot say to the Father: "Now that I have taken on flesh I can evaluate better how many things among human beings can be excused, for your creature is weak." Or: "I could perhaps pass on your truth adumbrated or in pieces, since in their sin human beings are better able to accept truth in this fashion than as a whole." Or as regards the Cross, "It would be better for the time being to take only part of the suffering of the Cross on myself and to proceed to a certain degree of incapacity, so that thereby I could impress my followers and the rest of the world enough to keep them from sinning. I could then continue to live among them and perhaps repeat it all later with more emphasis, should that prove necessary." Or: "It would be better to have one person crucified in every city in which faith arises in order to cause more of a stir . . ."—and whatever other peculiarities the human fantasy can produce. No, the entire sacrifice must be maintained: death without reservations. For the Son, however, this means unreserved submission in listening; and similarly, confession without any tint or stain, in which no human considerations intrude, no attachment to specific sins that may appear interesting or personal or excusable, as is so often the case with the sins of a penitent. The Son wants complete truthfulness before the Father and does not want to be influenced by any maneuvers on the part of sinners. He lets the Father perform all the evaluation, all the appraisal, all the determination and placement of importance —so much so that in the darkest moment the Son will no longer understand him. Yet precisely in this renunciation of understanding he shows how genuine and complete and unbroken his confession on the Cross is. It is not a confession conducted from both sides; he lets the Father alone conduct it.

When on the Cross he finally receives absolution for his entire life and for all the sins he has borne, this absolution takes place at the moment of his death—at a moment when what he has done as a man is no longer clearly present in its entirety before his spirit. He bore our sins in so intense a fashion that he also included the possibility of excommunication; he also bore the sins that are withheld, those that in the present moment have not been absolved. He does not confess the guilt of humanity with the feeling that it will soon be over, and soon everything will be made right again. Part of the terrible burden he carries is that he is not allowed this mitigation in spite of his complete openness toward the Father. Neither does he insist on his right to experience and enjoy absolution to the full. In confession he is indifferent. He does not confess upon the condition that he then also experience absolution. Thus Easter does not follow immediately upon Good Friday; the mystery of Holy Saturday lies between the two.

Sinners very often confess in a way that shows that they understand confession and absolution as a relationship of *do ut des*; they accept the discomfort of the procedure in anticipation of some sort of mitigation owed them in a legal sense. The Church meets these sinners halfway when she demands from them only for quite specific sins that indifference possessed by the Lord. She spares them uncertainty while in confession their sin is weighed and examined. The confessor has the right, indeed the obligation, to examine, to judge, and as a result to retain or not to retain, to bind or to loose. The sinners go beyond this right and demand absolution. Yet in a certain sense the heavenly Father also withholds absolution, since he places the mystery of Holy Saturday between the Passion and the Resurrection. Hanging on the Cross, the Son does not cast off his mortal shell and pass into the glory of the Father, to which he has a right. On the contrary, from the confession of the Cross he passes into the darkness of hell.

The Incarnation

In the Incarnation the Son surrenders himself as the seed of God to the activity of the Holy Spirit. It is as if he accommodates himself to the characteristic of the Spirit to blow where he will. Certainly in the angel's proclamation the Son plays the role of Israel's savior in whom the prophecies are fulfilled; but it is the role of one who is ordained. At the Annunciation it all seems to be a matter between Mary and the

Holy Spirit, mediated through the words of the angel. He speaks of the child to be conceived as if the latter had absolutely nothing to say. And Mary's agreement with the angel is an understanding with God in which there is no discussion at all about her own personal qualification concerning the Son or about her choice of the Son. She surrenders herself in the totality of her being, just as the Son surrenders himself in the totality of his sonship to the will of the Father and the activity of the Spirit. Even if the Son has known everything from time immemorial, this knowledge does not concern him now. He lets the Spirit come to terms with the Mother.

This is the fundamental accommodation that later will become visible again in the whole mystery of confession. The Incarnation is already an anticipation of confession inasmuch as the child who will later make the most all-encompassing confession is in that Incarnation already ordained for the redemption. He is one who is predestined to confess. In this he becomes the same as we sinners who are all conceived and born in order to confess one day both our inherited and our personal guilt. We, however, can choose whether or not to confess. The Son, on the other hand, will do it because he becomes man. He becomes man because he will be the Redeemer and will confess. He is the same as other human beings, however, in that he lets things be ordained or determined for himself, just as a conceived child who does not know what is happening to it is disposed over. The Son's initial attitude will be both constant and final. Similarly, there is nothing in the life of the Lord or of a saint or of a believer that is not simultaneously a part of their lives as a whole, that is not also a sign and cannot be fit into that whole. By accommodating himself to the law of all human existence, the Son impresses his stamp upon the existence of all those who belong to him. The Son acquiesces just as did the bit of earth that in the hands of the Father became Adam, and just as every human being acquiesces who comes into being out of the meeting of two cells. Yet only when this acquiescence becomes the act of the eternal Son does the

acquiescence of a human being to human existence receive
eternal significance.

Immaculata, Conception and Birth

The Son does not come to the world as an adult who suddenly
and briefly undertakes an action in order to take away the
world's guilt. Neither does he come merely for the hours or
days of the Passion to take on the world's sin as a burden to
which—since he does not traverse the human path leading to
it—he has no real human connection. In that case sin would
have stood before him as an immovable object, and he would
have taken it upon himself like a superman and died of it.

He wants instead to be a complete human being, and for this
reason he chooses the entire human path; he wants to be
conceived and carried and brought into the world by a woman,
and as a child to experience his small, human everyday life
until his hour has come. For the mother who conceives him he
is both the Redeemer of the world and the small, growing
child. He is a child like all the others and yet is the eternal Son
who decided in eternity to take the burden of the world
upon himself. This double element also affects the Mother: In
carrying him, she is also—in a way meant and preordained for
her—carrying the burden that will someday rest on the child.
She carries her child as every mother carries her first child,
and yet in spirit she must be prepared for the carrying of
the sin of the world through her son. In faith she knows
what is happening. She is likewise acquainted with sin in her
surroundings, and she has a perfect understanding of insult to
God. When she begins to carry the Son within her, sin is no
longer merely external to her, since he who will carry all sin
dwells within her. It is as if she were carrying the universal
confession of sin within her. With every sin she encounters,
she knows: For that, too, he comes; that, too, he will take
upon himself; and for that, too, he will die. When she gives

birth to him at Christmas, she gives birth to the full power of
absolution; indeed, this act of giving birth is related to the
streaming-forth of absolution, since she suddenly stands
before a superabundance of God's grace in a quite different
fashion than ever before. Until now she has carried grace
hidden within her, and no doubt also active and present
around her in the Spirit; she did not, however, know it then as
she knows it now: as something to be seen with her eyes and
touched with her hands. This new condition is related to the
one into which God wants to place man after confession by
means of the incomprehensible leap away from the sin that was
into the fullness of grace that is, along a path that is at once
fixed and miraculous, just as the birth of the Lord is both
human and miraculous. And just as the sinner traverses the
path through confession and penance, so also does the sinless
Mother traverse it in her assent and enduring obedience. In
this assent she confesses her previous and simultaneously her
subsequent life, and in this assent she becomes acquainted with
sin in a manner corresponding to the sinner's repentance. In
repentance the Mother becomes acquainted with a certain fear:
fear for the Son whose life is threatened by sin.

Yet the Son's existence in her life fills her with the same
happiness as does absolution. The presence of the child whom
she sees and hears and for whom she has waited is for her the
essence of Christian life; it is the maternal happiness that she
will recognize again at Easter in her bridal happiness and
which she will offer in the Church to all those in grace, to all
who have been absolved. It is a happiness which is completely
her own, and which she nonetheless will recognize again in the
confessing penitent: a happiness that is not unacquainted with
the reward of the Cross, since it carries all and includes all
and in this inclusion possesses its own complete unity. Her
happiness cannot be divided; it is the one happiness of the
Church which absolves in the name of the God who is present.
And the Mother's participation in the birth of her child is like

the Church's participation in granting absolution to the world: the participation of those who absolve and of those who are absolved.

One cannot determine precisely the mutual limits in this activity between Mother and Son, particularly since the Father and the Holy Spirit also participate. One can neither divide this happiness among those who participate in it nor determine precisely the roles played by the Father, the Son and the Spirit, and the Mother who also participates in this task of redemption. The limits are withdrawn so that the unity of grace may shine forth out of everything.

The Son, of course, is favored, since he is conceived by an immaculate mother through the overshadowing of the Spirit. This privilege is on the one hand the sign—for the time being visible only to the Father—that he is the eternal Son. On the other hand, it is that which the Father bequeaths to the human being Mary as a gift of grace anticipating her assent; at the same time he bequeaths it to all human beings as a comprehensible yet incomprehensible zone of God's encounter with them, as the place where God can become incarnate. It is the irrational element accompanying the rational features of this birth, the divine element active within what is human. It is also in a way a mitigation of the Son's work, the Son who is to save the world and who in the mystery of his Incarnation possesses several doors through which he can make the mysteries of the Father more accessible to human beings. Simultaneously, however, this privilege is in a way a hindrance, since it immediately places those who are closest to the Son—his mother and Joseph—into the difficult position of having to deal more intensely with the supernatural features of the mysteries, and because in the very manner of his Incarnation it discloses the uncompromising character of his divinity. One can no more come to terms rationally with the mystery of the conception by the Spirit and with the mystery of the virgin birth of the Son than one can with the mystery of his death or of his Resurrection and Ascension. He shows us thereby that anyone concerned with the man Jesus invariably and immediately comes up against his divinity, and that what the Son offers for our comprehension is always imbedded in the incomprehensible.

When a sinner is born, naturally no one thinks about confession; in life itself, however, he will have to orient himself toward it. He is unfailingly confronted with it. The Son is conceived and born as the one who one day will inevitably institute the sacraments. Just as the sinner is born already a sinner, so in the life of the Son, no matter what he will experience later—even unto the "crossfire of confession" on the Cross—one will always be able to refer to his conception and birth. In the course of his life, unto the Cross itself, the Son will increasingly gather sin upon himself. Beforehand, however, the Father plans his birth so that the Son is not surrounded or touched by sin; thus he predestines him to be the one who as a human being can recognize, bear and confess all sin. If he had had a different birth, if he had been weighed down with original sin, then his own sinfulness would have eased his later work of taking sin upon himself. Our own time of protection, our conception, the time spent in our mothers' wombs, our childhood without knowledge of good and evil— all this remains in the context of original sin. The Son is free from this in every respect. And this freedom is not purely divine; it is already visible in his advent as man so that the redeemed—those who will deal with the Son's confession on the Cross by surrendering to him their own sin to carry, and by confessing him as the Redeemer and founder of the New Covenant—will already recognize him in his coming and will be able to perceive in his own divine-human being the confession demanded of them.

Childhood

The Son's childhood, in which he is protected by the spotless-
ness of his mother and the holiness of his foster father, is
otherwise just like that of any other small child. His mother
watches his activity and development as any mother would.
Only when she sees him come into contact with the question
and reality of evil she cannot explain it to him by referring to
his own errors or to the general condition in which human
beings indivisibly both do and suffer evil. Yet it will be clear to
her that he as the Messiah needs a knowledge of evil and
that she is not permitted to conceal anything from him—not
because of the danger of contagion, but rather because he
already needs this perspective and its aid in his mission.
Through the eyes of the Mother, God the Father will see
how the Son perceives sin and how he suffers under it in
a preliminary fashion—for example, how in every new
encounter with human sin he makes the comparison between
his own earthly experience and the experience of God in
heaven.

A Christian mother who shows her child evil and the
gravity of sin is already thinking of confession. When she
awaits and prepares for the child's confession, she does it as
part of her maternal and Christian task. When Mary demands
complete openness from her own son—something he naturally
gives—she also understands that it is the same openness that
the Son has before the Father. Nonetheless, she watches over
the child's openness to her; it is part of her maternal responsibility to the Son, just as when she shows him how to tie his
sandals. She trains him just as she herself is trained by his
being. In the same way it is possible for someone to help an
extremely gifted pupil in a subject the pupil already knows on
the whole better than the teacher, and in the end the one giving
help has profited more than the pupil.

For the Son, being open means showing where he rejoices and where he suffers and what he knows about good and evil. He knows about Mary's natural position as mother, and for that reason he will reveal to her in a childlike fashion how things stand with him. Yet even as a child he will also indicate the sphere in which his solitude with the Father begins. On the other hand, if strangers should ever attempt to goad him into doing something he does not think is good, he will not tolerate this meddling. He will always see that his mother wants what is good; now and then, however, he will encounter her human limitations and perhaps very vaguely and in totally childlike words allude to that which is above and beyond.

He will do this most clearly as the twelve-year-old who draws the boundary quite sharply between the claims of God and those of the parents. When he instructs the scribes, he is already disclosing to them things to which the parents no longer have access—like a human child who goes to confession by himself and stands within the sphere of the mystery of confession: In all probability he will not tell his parents at home all he said and heard in confession. He has learned to stand within that official zone of God which is intended for him personally and which elicits a new tension in his life, but which is also a blessing for the parents even when they no longer have complete access to everything in the child's life. The personal character of confession reveals itself most strongly here, protected by the official character of the Church. Jesus' parents know that he belongs to God, and they cannot expect to find him anywhere except where God is. Even in their natural, humanly limited disquietude they are not permitted to think that something bad has happened to him (for at this point he is standing only at the beginning of his mission) or that he has let himself be led astray to do evil (for he is God's Son).

He stands so much under God's guidance that the first thing he must always do is what God wants. Absolute priority belongs to God. Since his sinlessness is secure, he does not

need to be advised by his parents. Thus a significant conflict
occasionally arises between the two authorities, one not unlike
that experienced by Christian parents regarding the priest's
spiritual guidance of their child (even more so than through
confession). The parents live so deeply within the traditional
sphere that the Son would have been certain of their resistance
had he disclosed to them his plans to remain in the Temple to
instruct the teachers. For them that would have been humanly
incomprehensible, and in spite of their holiness they would
have wanted to prevent him from doing it simply because they
were adults. This would have had two consequences: They
would have struggled against the Son's mission, and they
would have hindered it at a perhaps decisive point. Thus the
Son has no choice. If he shocks his parents, it is because he
suddenly reveals to them the entire scope of his relationship to
the Father, one that is far more binding than his relationship to
his parents. Let us assume that a religiously zealous child of
rather lukewarm parents had to confess things to which the
parents could not be indifferent; they might want to prevent
the child from doing this. Although this analogy is inadequate,
it does offer us a point for comparison. The indifferent parents
would have to come to terms with the situation without
understanding. The same holds true for the pious parents of
the Lord. He has only performed his primary duty.

Jesus' parents are aware of what he knows as a human being,
just as any parents generally are aware of their child's sins and
errors. When the child begins to go to confession, however,
they can probably imagine what facts find expression there,
but they cannot know the interior side of that confession, a
side characterized by the child in his soul standing naked
before God. The confessor in his official position will perhaps
comprehend much more in that child's confession than could
the parents, since he has confessional experience behind him.
Similarly, the teachers who hear Jesus' teaching find out much
more about what he really knows than do the parents, whose
understanding is limited by their lack of education.

The manner in which the Son justifies himself—"Must I not be in my Father's house?"—includes both a defense and a delimitation. It is a defense of his mission. A child's mother might think it useful for his upbringing that she know exactly what transpires in the child's confession. The child, however, is permitted and indeed required to defend his confessional privacy. By his behavior the Lord opens up a sphere for those who come after him. But for the child this confessional privilege means the sudden penetration into a new world. It is now quite proper that he no longer tell his parents everything. The ecclesial sphere of confession is also justified in that the individual becomes accustomed to being more independent and responsible before God. Hence, attempts (such as that of the Oxford Movement) to introduce confession of sins without that officially protected sphere cannot be carried through. Confession of sins is not primarily a matter between human beings, but rather is reserved for God; and the Church, which watches over God's privileges, would not be authorized to keep a child away from confession merely because the child is on such good terms with his parents. Certain institutional things exist which involve and must involve breaking through the human-social sphere, and they arise at a time when the child is able to deal with them naturally.

The sphere of the Father thus emerges in sharp clarity in the behavior of the twelve-year-old. Previously it had been concealed, as it were, in the preliminary knowledge of the Mother and foster father. Despite their disquietude, both parents must be comforted in a deeper sense when they see that these things happen as a part of the mission.

Baptism in the Jordan

The specific time of confession is what is fixed here, something that can be comprehended only with difficulty. When is it time to confess? When is it perhaps time to make a general confession? And when is it time to speak in confession so that the confessor determines accordingly what is to happen next? This time really does exist, the time when one understands confession anew and as a result perceives everything freshly and in a more original and fundamental way and understands everything as God's new and original guidance—even if, like the Son, one has never turned away from God. Indeed, there is even a time to take seriously someone else's confession—in this case John's—and to let oneself be affected by it.

When John the Baptist announces the time, something new enters into the Son's confessional attitude toward the Father. This was the event the Son had awaited, yet which only John the Baptist, and not the Son himself, was to bring about. He, the Son, has only to respond to it. It is as if two people were commissioned to found a new order, and suddenly one of them says, "I want to go out now and see if I can find members", and he goes with his commission and in obedience. Then the hour has come for the other also. The Lord now knows: John has, as it were, confessed. He has come to the end of everything that made up his previous life and has begun to make straight the paths of the Lord in obedience to the Father, who is like his confessor. This obedience cannot be a mistake, and for that reason the Son draws the consequences which follow from it. He takes over the confessional situation of the Baptist in order to bring to an end his own previous life, just as John did in his confession. John has not undertaken a task of which the Son might say, "I did not really commission him with it; let us allow it to develop and then see whether it is right." Rather, the Son is unconditionally obligated by the work John has introduced: because it is a task of confession, and the Son has come to institute confession; because it is a task of obedience, and confession and obedience completely permeate one another, and the Son has come to be obedient to the death. Hence he must join John's obedience in order to accomplish his own obedience unto death.

Let us assume two young people are good friends. One tells

the other in precise terms that he wants to go to a specific, well-known confessor in order to lay out his entire life before him. He knows that something decisive must happen in his life, and since he has heard that this man is able to point out to people the right way for them, and since this man is here now, he wants to see him. This revelation takes place without any indiscretion and without any suggestions being made to the other friend. The young man merely says what he thinks he should do, though in complete openness and in a genuine intimacy of friendship and love. The other friend later learns that the young man has entered an order and had no opportunity to speak with him again; the call was too great, and there was nothing else to discuss. This decision does not constitute an alienation in the relationship between the two; it only means that the one has unconditionally found his way. The other stays behind with his friendship and with the gift of openness he received. He is disturbed; he cannot know what was said between his friend and the confessor, he only sees the result. But from his knowledge of what this friendship was and what kind of openness it involved, he must conclude that there can be nothing divisive between them. He can seek out his friend and ask whether there is not also a place for him there. He can seek advice from the confessor and follow it, whether that advice is the same as for his friend or whether it leads him down a different path. If this path—which perhaps leads into another order—is also God's will, the bond between the two will not be weakened by anything. But the second friend received the sign from the first one, who went forth first, confessed, and changed his own life. Seen both from a human perspective and from the perspective of God, the second friend makes his decision as a kind of acquiescence to the other. The one went forward first, the other followed. And if he is certain that his friend acted out of a necessity grounded in God, how much more certainly does the Lord know this concerning John.

Later it will be the Lord who institutes the Church, the

authority and the institutions, and the sacraments, and by so doing offers humanity a new certainty of being on the proper path. Here, however, the Father allows the predecessor himself to show the Son what it means to walk the path of the New Covenant and to walk it with a sureness that arises because he, John, went forth first in the spirit of confession. What the Lord experiences here of the New Testament, he passes on to the Church.

The Son dies on the Cross in order to atone for all sins; nonetheless, on that same Cross he opens a kind of subsequent discipleship of those who themselves carry the cross. Similarly, in spite of the unique, independent and complete mission of the Son, the Father also opens for him the possibility of following in the mission of the Baptist, who came before him in time.

Suppose someone who has committed mortal sin stands before a decisive confession and cannot bring himself to confess. He sees that he must, but it is too difficult. When he nonetheless suddenly kneels in the confessional and is able to say everything—not only the difficult things he thought he could never say, but even more difficult things that had never even occurred to him—then the question arises whether he, too, is not a successor, whether some saint—a "little soul"—did not pave the way for him with his own confession, and whether the sinner is not able to confess by drawing from a treasury of confessional humility and openness that has been offered him. The same question can be asked concerning the relationship between John and Jesus: The Father might have placed some of the difficult elements of Jesus' own mission into the mission of John beforehand.

A person living a contemplative life is protected by that very life. The regulation of time, the choral prayer, the silence, the meditation, all place him ever anew before the greatness and proximity and consent of God. The active life, which ought to be lived in God, demands that one be able to meet God more quickly, more securely and more often, in order to remain within his will; and it can happen that a slight disloyalty can have devastating consequences for such a Christian mission. The confessional relationship in the two forms of life is accordingly different. The baptism in the Jordan is an intervention of the Baptist's active life into the contemplative life of the Lord, which is coming to a close. The twelve-year-old had gone out on his own initiative—with the Father's consent, of course. The thirty-year-old, on the other hand, goes out at the initiative of John (with the same consent of the Father). The Son opens his catholic spirit to the sign inherent in John's activity, a sign that he perhaps in a purely human fashion did not know John would have to give him. One expects this kind of sign from the saints in the Church; but one can also expect it from every confession in the Church. The two can also occur together, for example, if the confessor offers sound advice with a reference to the example of a saint. John, who began to baptize, did so at the initiative of the Holy Spirit; he had heard and received the word of God, and the word lived in him as it lives in the saints and made him into a sign for the Lord. This sign already intervenes in the contemplative life of the Lord, and the time between the commencement of John's baptizing and his baptism of Jesus is thus an overlapping of activity and contemplation. John already has taken over the activity of the Lord in the will of the Father and thus through it has already interrupted the contemplation of the Lord. One can also say, however, that the full contemplation of the Lord already manifests itself in the commencement of John's work, so that this prayer is itself both contemplative in the Lord and active in John.

This relationship is reflected in the situation of those confessing in the church: one waits in line before the confessional while another kneels inside and makes his confession and the confessor hears it. While the confessor and the penitent appear to do this in an inclusive unity of the two acts, the person waiting appears to be excluded from it. His time has not yet come, since it is now someone else's time. Nonetheless, in the person now confessing the confessor is already anticipating the next one. The same "confessional hour" encompasses all three persons. In the same way the Son's Incarnation also encompasses both his own hour that has not yet come and his recognition of the hour of his predecessor.

This shows that the act of confession is not isolated. Rather, in it one summons and makes visible an attitude that one is never allowed to put aside, just as all activity must contain the effect of contemplation, and all contemplation the willingness to be prompted into action. This is called "indifference": the willingness to receive from God at any moment a sign either to remain in prayer awhile longer or to cease praying for the sake of action. When one waits before the confessional for the sign and prescribed time of the Church, this itself merely manifests a perpetual waiting in the confessional attitude for the proper moment for active confession, for the moment the Spirit will suggest.

In this overlapping period between attitude and act, the receptivity to the Spirit's sign must, if possible, be even more sensitive, since now someone else's mission is at stake as well. Before John begins to baptize, the Son stands within an intensified loneliness before the Father, and this loneliness has a certain enduring color. The Son is always ready and submissive, today and tomorrow just as yesterday and the day before. When the Baptist commences his active mission, however, this mission also enters into the Son's prayer to the Father, since John baptizes in anticipation of the coming Son. This presence in the Son's prayer demands from him an altered awareness into which he must integrate John's mission and office. If one views the Son's openness to the Father as an ongoing confessional attitude, then the inclusion of an office that disposes over incredible faculties as regards the Son will prompt an act or decision of expectation within that confessional attitude.

Baptism is purification, and even the baptism John offers

presupposes a confession of sin. For Jesus this purification will be the complete absolution from sin. When someone steps forth as the authorized official in this purification, however, the Son's relationship to him becomes one in which he, the Son, must confess. Thus when Jesus allows himself to be baptized, he places himself among those sinners who need absolution and in so doing embarks on the path to the Cross, where he will bear and confess all sin before the Father. John, in his official activity, initiates this active movement toward the Cross; he sees the Lord as the sinless Lamb who takes away the guilt of the world.

The Temptation

During the temptation in the desert the Lord knows full well that he *could* overcome the devil by showing him how much more powerful God is than he. In a more profound sense, however, he knows that he can overcome him only if he lets himself be tempted and does not succumb to the evil one in the slightest, but on the contrary proves to the tempter his origin from the Father and his obedience to his mission. To exemplify untainted obedience, even when it is certain that the devil cannot be converted and that both temptation and tempter will persist, is an attitude before and in the Father; it is loyalty to the mission of the Father, a mission that in a fashion only has significance in relationship to the Father. From a human perspective this obedience seems like a waste of energy. If the Lord would yield to the temptation even a little, he could really open the devil's eyes. But this too would be meaningless, indeed doubly meaningless, since one cannot teach the devil anything. The Lord thus chooses the weakness that is strength in the Father. Yet the Father himself does not need this demonstration of the Son's weakness, since he knows the Son will always remain obedient, even unto death. Nonetheless, he will acknowledge this demonstration of obedience, not in order to strengthen the Son's obedience or to secure the mission, but rather so that the Son may become familiar with a certain futility within obedience, so that he may feel at home in it and from this perspective see and bear the will of the Father unwaveringly all the way to the Cross—and so that we who come later, in our own small and smallest temptations, seek strength not in ourselves but in the Son, and not only in the Son but in the Father as well, through the Holy Spirit of divine obedience.

The supporting background of this obedience lies entirely with the Father; at best we can sense it. When we find this divine obedience exemplified in the Gospel, however, we also know that the Son does not simply keep it for himself, but rather has infused some of it into his confession. One can stop short of sin as one stands before God; one can behold the coming path in a vision that derives its point of departure, its comfort and its appeasement from this overcoming of the devil. It is not a victory on the basis of power or might, but rather a calm No spoken equally to the Father and to the tempter. The portion spoken entirely to the Father, however, is taken up into the grace that the Father wishes to offer to humanity in the form of the Cross. This grace is almost completely concealed and veiled, but it nonetheless generates the unity of life within itself. The Father gives the Son his Spirit so that he can accompany him in the Spirit. On the Cross the Son breathes his Spirit back to the Father, but the Spirit remains as if in the background; he is the companion who creates unity.

Before the Lord transmits to his disciples the full authority to bind and loose, he lives through the depth and breadth of temptation and experiences for himself what it costs human beings to persevere in quiet obedience. With this experience he has laid up a reserve for humanity to which everyone can have recourse in hours of weakness. He knows in particular that every person traversing the path of confession—a path that is primarily that of the Cross—will be summoned to pause and reflect before God, and that this reflection in its turn will be able to draw from the reserve of the Lord's temptation. For the sinner must withstand the temptation to sin further, and this cessation and break in sinning is the beginning of the reflection and conversion leading to confession. Only at this point can the sinner be taken up anew into grace; and the path from this point to the grace of absolution leads through the inexpressible experience the Son has before the Father and in the Holy Spirit, between desert and Cross. It is inexpressible because the Father's accompaniment is so discreet and yet so effective and because the Son's obedience passes through every point fixed in the Old Covenant, fulfilling them all, point by point, in the constancy and imperturbability characteristic of his obedience, up to death on the Cross, until the Father resurrects him and thus fulfills the promise for his own part. The constancy of obedience, shunning nothing and desiring to experience everything all the way to death on the Cross, will be the cup he will drink to the dregs, even and especially at the point at which he asks that the cup pass from him. It is the cup encompassing every experience of bitterness, because its form is that of obedience, a vessel whose form accommodates itself to fit all the sins of the world. These sins are where, in the end, God wants them: in a position to be consumed by the Son. The Son's own condition is a reflection of communion. He lets his body die of those sins, so that all who were sinners receive a share in him and in his new life. So that sinners may traverse his path, however, he must know the locus of temptation in order to find the strength for his own life within the weakness of the one tempted—the strength of a plea that becomes the path to confession.

His Public Life

The Son's entrance into public life is similar to an examination of conscience. He always keeps heaven and the Father in mind, the purity of eternal life, and in this light he sees everything on earth that deviates from it: all ignorance of the essence and will of the Father, all willful turning away from him, everything that conceals or extinguishes faith, love and hope. He sees these things in his love for humanity, but this love does not diminish the clarity of his vision. The discrepancy is constantly moving through his consciousness. His acquaintance with sin and its motives and effects makes him like other men who, because they are bound to the body, inwardly know temptation and its ways. Yet he is at the same time the pure, loving one who recognizes alienation from God primarily because of his own closeness to God, one who recognizes withdrawal and turning away from the perspective of self-giving. In this recognition of sin the Son is like someone who comprehends his own sin in the light of the Holy Spirit and who sees where his confession needs to take its point of departure. He is like someone who never tires of searching to find where he has erred so that he can properly confess it. The Son thus goes into and through the world as one who gathers guilt in anticipation of confession. He gathers by continually taking sin on himself and yet at the same time—in parallel to the confessional resolutions of the sinner—continually erasing and extinguishing it. Suppose a sinner has committed a certain sin; he sees very clearly the deviation from the norm, admits the sin, repents and is prepared to confess and to accept penance as a consequence. He can do all this with close reference to the Lord, who knows sin better than any other person, who brings it to the sinner's attention, who perhaps reprimands in order to better a person, who admonishes in order to prevent a lapse into sin, who baptizes or absolves in order to extinguish that sin completely, but who in any case—whether he remits sin or not—takes the burden of that sin upon himself and with that burden confesses it to the Father and accepts the penance.

In the public life of the Lord there is an element of the confession that is perpetually performed and yet perpetually delayed because the hour has not yet come. Let us assume that two friends live together, and one is a priest who normally hears confession on Saturday. At the beginning of the week, however, his friend tells him certain errors and sins he has committed. This takes place outside the sacramental situation, and the one confessing waits patiently until the hour of the official absolution has come. From the perspective of the priest things are such that he (the priest) is already in the picture after the confession has been made, just as the Father knows everything the Son is bearing and yet at the moment does not want to remove the weight of that burden. For the Son has come not to help a few sinners who happen to cross his path, but rather all who have ever lived and will live. Thus he must live even longer, see even more sin, be even more of an aggravation to sinners and finally suffer so much from sin that he dies on the Cross because of it. If the priest heard his friend's confession daily or even hourly because the friend perhaps had a chronic weakness and continually asked for priestly absolution, the time no doubt would come when the priest would have to say to him, "It's too easy this way, my friend! You keep coming, but I see no sign of improvement; in the future we'll have to postpone absolution. Bear your guilt, discover how it burdens you, and accept the penance of not being released from all feelings of guilt. Wait until your confession has matured, indeed, until you yourself have done so."

Thus, the Son lives patiently for the Cross, and this patience grows proportionately with the weight of the burden of sin upon him. He wants to and must bear all sins, the momentary and the chronic ones, the common and the rare ones, and he shows them all to the Father who perpetually watches and accompanies him. Part of his confessional attitude, however, is that he cannot die here and now on the Cross. Just as the consciousness of sin should not be dulled by the postponement of confession but rather sharpened, and just as the postponement should not be a sign of indifference but rather of zeal, so also the Son's burden becomes more and more tangible and differentiated for him. He senses and notices each kind of sin

differently. Each gives him pain in a different way. After all, he
is a man, and man exposes countless vulnerable surfaces to
suffering. He can suffer because of himself or because of his
surroundings, physically or spiritually, from heat or cold,
from exhaustion or hypertension; he can suffer in all his
known and unknown organs, but he also can suffer in places in
his soul he never suspected were there. The Son's exercise in
suffering lays claim to the entire spectrum of his humanity.

Desert and Mount of Olives

One normally views the two great periods in the life of the
Lord as two separate stages of his existence. In the first, he
develops, grows up physically and intellectually, and as a man
becomes acquainted with the Father and learns to grow into
his mission. In prayer and reflection he experiences the heavenly
Father and his own divinity and as a consequence steps out of
this matured consciousness into action. The forty days in the
desert, however, contradict this sharp division. After the
decision to act has already been made and the activity already
set in motion, the Son once again places himself like clay in the
Father's hands and lets the Father mold and shape him. He
submits the brief experience of activity to a new trial in prayer,
exposes himself to the temptation of Satan—and all this in the
weakened condition of forty days' fasting—in order to emerge
triumphantly as this weak man from the struggle with the
devil. As a victor, but also as this weak one, he embarks on the
path of action. He has already experienced all the things that
can keep a person from acting for God and God alone. The
three temptations confronted him with these hindrances in a
concentrated form. Now he embarks on his path, inwardly
altered by this experience which he keeps for himself so that he
can draw it forth again in the hour of his suffering. The Mount
of Olives is contemplation again, no longer with an eye
toward action or to acquire the strength for the right activity,

but rather a contemplation leading into death, a relinquishing
of all active energy to the Father for the sake of being able to
suffer as the Father wishes and of being undisturbed in his
suffering by the powers and thoughts of action.

If one views the Son's entire attitude on earth as one of
perfectly open love of the Father, as an attitude of confession,
then the desert and the Mount of Olives each constitute an
important caesura within this attitude, for here the will of the
Father is accepted in a fresh and explicit way. At other times,
when Christ is living among men in the quiet of the family or
the turbulent apostolate, he takes upon himself whatever sin
he encounters—sin in general—within the context of human
experience. He is the Son of God who bears sin as a human
being. In these two distinct periods he stands alone before the
Father and places himself at his disposal so that the Father can
act upon him directly and give him that to bear which he
thinks is proper.

When one's strengths are exhausted, when one becomes
tired—very tired—human experience easily and almost unconsciously lets itself evaluate and determine what is still
"humanly possible" and what is not. Because the Son who
bears all sins knows of this state of exhaustion and shares it as
he does all human conditions, he withdraws into the desert and
to the Mount of Olives. The preceding moment is "virtue":
One decides to endure, one is willing, one prepares oneself.
Afterwards, in a state of overexhaustion, the tension loses its
power, and one must seek the relationship to God anew. It is
very fine to have courage beforehand and to pray for courage,
for example, before martyrdom or torture; and afterwards,
during the burning or suffering itself, one should simply not
desire to flee, but should rather stay by God and find him anew
as someone who suffers. The Son wants to show the Father
that for him the Father's will is just as unconditionally determinative during the time of action as in suffering. The Son's
active life could appear to be a period during which he loads sin
onto himself with such breathless zeal that the Father cannot

intervene with any objection or interrupting words. But the Son does not act in this way; every one of his steps is predetermined and accompanied by the Father. And he gives the Father particular opportunities to intervene, just as the confessor should always have the right and opportunity to interrupt the confession of sin with a question or comment.

The changes in the Son's confessional attitude are thus not the result of irresolution, but are rather the result of his making fresh contact with the Father. These contemplative periods within periods of activity are like a general confession in which the entirety of one's life is spread out and presented so that God may arrange it in a new way. "Are things as you planned, Father? Am I accepting as you would have me do? Can I continue as before?" The ongoing acceptance and confession of sin is interrupted for a moment in order to be recommenced in an improved fashion. Yet now and then absolution is not granted because one must wait for the hour of the Cross.

The temptation in the desert (and then again on the Mount of Olives, to let the cup pass by) was no doubt partially caused by the Son's long fasting and consequent weakened condition. He wants to demonstrate to the Father in his own life how human temptation looks. Yet in a more essential fashion the temptation of the devil is a kind of response of the Father to the Son's renewed submission. It is now the Father who lowers him into the abyss of that existence determined and shaped by sin, whereby the physical element is the locus and occasion.

3. THE CONFESSION ON THE CROSS

Passion

The moment of the great purification has arrived. The Son has certainly taken sin upon himself during his entire life and has even forgiven sin when it was in order; yet that which was thus extinguished could not simply have disappeared except through the grace of the coming Cross. For the sinner in question the sin was extinguished, but the Lord still had to bear it further to the Cross. In addition there was that large portion which could not be extinguished and which he bore while it was yet unchanged and unbroken in its effectiveness, actively at work in him in a manner similar to that of sin in the sinner. In a certain way it also alienated him from God: not like a sinner whose sense for God has become dulled, but rather as a sharpened suffering. Suffering caused by his feeling of abandonment by the Father is the price he must pay for sin.

It is as if he has to become acquainted with the ultimate subtleties of sin on the way to the Cross and on the Cross—in the physical sense, first of all, through all the various kinds of pain to which he is subjected. Yet the physical is only a symbol of and passageway to his soul, indeed to his unique person, of which he knows and feels that *it* is the real focus in all the suffering. He, and only he, as the legitimate representative of the Father, is intended by every sin. Hence everything in the Passion affects him by heightening his sense of the necessity of the confession on the Cross. If his own alienation through sin were like ours, that is, if he were to grow accustomed to sin and in time come to accept it as something encountered every day and as something he would forgive and extinguish wherever he encountered it so as to continue on his way, simply opening the "spigot of grace" more fully wherever he encountered especially serious guilt or recalcitrance—if he had come to this kind of view and thought that he had the interior power and opportunity to come to terms with each human situation as it arises, then the Cross certainly would have instructed him otherwise. For here he encounters not the individual, but rather that entirety which has been reserved for him and which awaits him; and this entirety that he encounters in the scenes of the Passion makes him recognize anew his destiny as Redeemer. He is certainly never tempted to understand his mission as something merely successive that could be arbitrarily drawn out in time. Yet he needs, because the Father has so arranged it, this kind of final confirmation in suffering in which all his individual acts come together into a whole that encounters and corresponds to the unsettled totality of sin.

The sinner before the confessional never really has the totality together. He has made a list of what he wants to say, but while he waits, while perhaps the woman before him in the confessional keeps talking, while the child kneeling behind him continually chatters, it occurs to him that he has forgotten to accuse himself of impatience and lack of charity and so on. He must return to his contrition, in which he had not included these things. In this way he might always be discovering new and burdensome circumstances in his own sins, and new sins, forgotten ones, might reappear as well. He is still not naked; again and again he must take off another garment.

When the Son is scourged naked and nailed naked to the cross, when the thorns and nails bite into his flesh, he has reassumed the nakedness of the first man—not, however, because of innocence, but rather because of sin, for his arms embrace all that is, was and will be. Everything, completely exposed and in all its truth, is thrust upon the Naked One. For him, the one stripped of all power, the sum of that burden is no longer totally surveyable. It is not the result of an accumulation and summation during the years of his life; on the Cross the totality of the burden can no longer be subdivided in order to be dealt with in this fashion. What he has shouldered in a certain orderly manner now suddenly turns against him in all its weight like an alien external power, and it seems to him that he does not have the slightest thing in common with all that he has taken upon himself. A neutral, anonymous power with no owner breaks upon him. Yet every spearhead of every sin is pointed toward him and wounds him. His confession is now like the cry "Everything!" Here and there something specific appears and acquires contours, and then his cry becomes "That, too!"

When he cries out, "Father, why have you forsaken me?" and "I am thirsty!" these cries are also an expression of his immense confession. They are an expression and answer to the enormous power of sin, which is the resonating response "For this reason" to his own question "Why?" When he spent his life presenting every single human sin to the Father so that the world might really be redeemed, he did so in an understanding with the Father, as when the penitent knows that the confessor listens seriously to him. The penitent has already confessed to this priest many times, and the confessor understands how things are intended; he sees what is sin and how serious it is; he knows what the penitent has already undertaken against it. In the case of the Son, the Father knows how much penance the Son has already done and how much satisfaction has been done. The confessor can often feel as though he has participated in the penitent's sins: he has not given a serious enough warning, has not prayed adequately or has perhaps brought the sinner into a difficult situation with his instructions. The Father, too, is a participant in everything the Son shows him, but on the Cross the Son is no longer aware of this participation. Sometimes it may seem to the penitent that the confessor no longer understands anything. It may even be that at the moment of confession the penitent is so overwhelmed by his sin that his confession seems senseless to him. He could think of much more to say, and the confession could easily go on and on; but the "why" of the confession has been lost. The burden of sin has taken his soul's breath away. Thus the Son wanted to do something meaningful by turning the spearhead of sin—originally directed toward the Father—toward himself. Under the weight of the wounds, however, he no longer comprehends his own intention. He has nothing at all to do with this intention. Perhaps it is this meaninglessness that kills him. Recognition of an intention would mean his rescue from death.

During his entire life of gathering these sins, he certainly felt contrition for each one of them. He was sorry that they had been committed and had offended the Father. He suffered under the alienation of the Father and the sinner, suffered as the mediator between the two. Now, on the Cross, there is no longer any "between". He himself is the man, and on him rests sin. Contrition has, as it were, been submerged in the singular pain that is the direct encounter between confession and penance. That suffering drowns out and swallows up everything, even the act and feeling of contrition. Contrition would imply that there is a correspondence between sin and penance, between the bearing of sin and the evaluation of its gravity. The act of contrition requires an objective state of affairs. On the Cross this state of affairs can no longer be delimited; similarly, the power of sin and the attendant atoning pain have become indistinguishable.

When the Lord meets a sinner on earth, he immediately knows how things stand with him. But on the Cross he experiences that person's sin differently because he must bear it and suffer through it. Beforehand he sees the sin, and the person is transparent to him; he can show the sinner everything and set him right. But his own hour has not yet come. On the Cross, however, he undergoes the experience of suffering, and he puts into the sacrament of confession something of this experience that has been brought before the Father. The movement of a person carrying his own sin to the sacrament of confession is somehow comparable to the movement of the Son carrying all sins to the Cross. The sin is then the coarse, rough, raw element comparable to the beams of the Cross. No one can confess in a "sublime" and ascendant attitude, any more than the sins carried to the Cross were sublime. The priest hears them and accepts them in the commission of the Holy Spirit, in a way similar to that in which the Father accepts them at the behest of the Son on the Cross.

The sacrament of confession has a perfect objectivity guaranteed by the triune God. The confession of sins has a personal character, but the exhortation and absolution are objective. To that extent this sacrament is the reverse of the Eucharist, for there the Lord acts subjectively, in spite of the sacramental character that is independent of human beings and is to that extent objective: in the Eucharist the Lord is the one who offers himself infinitely, while the receiving human person is objective. This double movement with reverse characteristics rounds out a sacramental circle, and one understands how confession and communion belong to one another and answer one another.

The Church also wishes to view the sacraments as connected in this way. Even someone who might find that he has nothing to confess would have to accept the need to confess, since he belongs to the community of sinners. He would need at least to bear part of the burden, subjectively to bring something of the burden of sin into the objectivity of God and receive from God that purification instituted in view of the Eucharist. The reception of communion, in which a human person acts as the objective element, costs him infinitely less than confession: he is really the recipient, not the giver who sacrifices himself. This surrender and submission cost the Lord—who gives himself—everything. Thus the modest effort of confession corresponds in the smallest measure to the infinite effort of the Lord (an effort unto death) to give us his flesh and blood. This shows that human effort here is not, in the final analysis, dependent upon the sin. In confession the human being demonstrates that he has comprehended something of what the Lord did for him on the Cross and continues to do at every communion.

This distinction between the subjective and objective element is grounded in the Lord's twofold recognition of sin. The recognition of sin during the time before the Cross parallels the committing of sin by the sinful individual. The recognition on the Cross itself, where the Lord collapses under the burden of sin, parallels the confession of the sinner, who is also overwhelmed with contrition. For the Lord this recognition of sin is subjective in life (he sees it as a man sees it) and objective on the Cross (he sees it as it is in itself, before God).

Holy Saturday

Seen from the perspective of confession, the mystery of the Lord's descent into hell seems like a summary by the confessor of what has been said and done; it is as if the Father were to present to the Son what has been borne in a form that is a third, mediating element between the confession and bearing of sin and the mitigating absolution. The suffering is over and everything having to do with feeling is withdrawn, but the joy of final achievement has not yet been granted. The sin has become a purely objective entity, free from the evaluation and feeling of human consciousness, empty of and free from the subject that committed it. It is the accumulated aggregate of sheer sin which would precipitate the most terrible suffering if the Lord's suffering had not already accomplished the separation of sin from sinner. Yet the viewing of sin as it is in itself is not a joyous experience. It is only and entirely an objective observation: the mass of sin is this large, this deep, this immeasurably distended. This is how it looks when it is separated from man (simultaneously the sinner and the Lord). The relationship between individual, temptation, sin and difficulty also appears in this objective vision—seemingly measured out, yet immeasurable.

In confession, sin stands thus objectified between the confession itself and the absolution, whether the confessor expressly summarizes and objectifies it or whether he, as the judge in matters of grace, forms an inward image for himself of what has been confessed. Both his own office and the penitent oblige him to carry out this objectification. For the penitent, too, the content of the confession must extricate itself from any subjective points of view and be seen in its unembellished gravity. No longer can one say, "My sin looked like this at the time, my personal circumstances were thus and such, I believe it was a serious sin; I consider this to be a sin, that on the other hand has something to do with it, but I don't know if I was the cause of it; I would like to mention it as well just so it will have been said," and so on. All that is now at an end. In a sense it is like the transition from the muddled layman's description of a patient to the diagnosis of the physician. The penitent is not able to achieve this kind of diagnosis himself, and yet it is a great relief for him. His groping, perhaps fearful understanding receives the answer it sought in vain, and at the same time God's representative has assumed responsibility for that answer. The threads connecting the sin to the sinner have become invisible, even though absolution has not yet been granted; even though the entire affair, from the perspective of the confessor, is perhaps more serious than the sinner had thought; and even though the penitent can neither do away with nor dispute the propriety of this conclusion.

For the Lord this encounter is particularly difficult, since it is the encounter of the totally pure with sin itself. When he as a man absolved someone from sin, as he did for example with Mary Magdalene, he saw in the absolved person the results of his absolution. He suffered under the sin but rejoiced in the purification. Suffering and joy generated one another. Here, however, all subjective feeling is at an end, and there remains only a kind of objectivized experience of the terrible, a kind of suffocation and burial under the fatal burden of world guilt.

Yet the Father allows the Son to go through this experience as well, so that afterward, in the joy of absolution and reunion, he may know that with which he has struggled, so that he may know how that sin he has borne stood before God in its objectivity and how the mystery of the Father appears in the face of this objectivity: the obscurity of the Father. In the state of having died the Son experiences this darkness.

If in the Old Covenant people had tried to confess sins to one another, they would have invariably encountered limitations. One individual would have confessed his sins to another out of a need to speak about this aspect of his life and relationship to God, perhaps in order to attain some sort of clarity or to ask for advice and help or perhaps also to be better understood. It might have taken place in a certain humility and selflessness.

Yet after his Resurrection, when the Lord's first act is to institute confession, he does so on the basis of the reality of his resurrected body, which he has borne through Good Friday and Holy Saturday as the price for the sacrament's institution. Even before his suffering—when he converted people to be his followers, when he cleansed Mary Magdalene from her sins— as a man he was already taking a large portion of their confession onto his own shoulders. He placed his divine knowledge and love in the service of his human knowledge and love; he forgave sins as a man who is simultaneously God and gave the result over to the Father, who preserved it as something preliminary to the Cross.

From this perspective, the Resurrected One as the Bride-groom of the Church imparts the final Christian absolution. From this perspective, confession is wholly a mystery and possession of the Son, his gift to humanity and the Father's gift to him. The Son, who on the Cross "confessed" all the world's sins to the Father, possesses from the perspective of the Cross a new mystery concerning that world, a mystery that remains latent between his death and Resurrection and is borne through hell as the acquired result of suffering. Thus the Son bore sin in two ways. On Good Friday he bore it unto his own death as the personal guilt of every individual; he bore it as an atone-ment with his divine-human person in the most subjective, personal act that the Son could perform for sinners. At that time each sin appeared bound to the sinner and bore the characteristics of the subject that had committed it. On Holy Saturday, on the other hand, in the vision of the world's sin from the perspective of the underworld, sin extricates itself from the subject of the sinner until it is only the hideous, amorphous element that constitutes the terror of the underworld and elicits the horror of the observer. It is sin in its final, eternal ineluctability, and yet sin that has become anonymous, sin whose reality and appearance no longer allow one to conclude anything concerning the individual sinners and their share in it. This path through the underworld thus involves a kind of personal bearing (or an oppressive vision) of impersonal sin.

The Resurrected One knows of this double mystery that shows him how much the mystery of confession belongs to him from now on. The Father has given it to him on the basis of his experience of suffering. The abandonment by the Father on the Cross and the total separation from the Father in the underworld are central to the mystery of the "confession" of the world's sin which he has taken upon himself. His resurrected body arose out of his crucified and buried body, just as his earthly body arose out of the heavenly resolution to Incarnation. The new body that the Father has given him is the body of his pure return to the Father. As regards confession, one can say that his earthly body was his confessional body, the body that was to bear the personal guilt of every individual, as well as original sin and sin in itself. The resurrected body, on the other hand, is the body of absolution which is no longer to bear that sin, since it has already been borne and since satisfaction was made for all sin on the Cross. The first body gathered the total confession into itself, but the second offers itself as pure forgiveness; it stands face to face with sin and is no longer burdened with it, as was the first body. It perpetually offers absolution from within itself; indeed, it gives itself in absolution just as it gives itself in the Eucharist, so that absolution may acquire a final effectiveness and endurance through the most intimate connection with the body of the believer.

Easter

The Son promised that he would rise again on the third day, a promise that no one else believed. During the Passion, this view into the life of the Resurrection was withdrawn even from him. He was, as it were, removed further and further from this knowledge and hope. When he dies and passes through hell, this removal becomes complete. He goes obediently to his death without looking to right or left. There is no way to estimate how long this death lasts or the time remaining until the Resurrection. The latter comes like a bolt of lightning; it is the abrupt absolution.

For the disciples, the history of the Resurrection is characterized by a certain development. First there is their uncertainty and their anxiety, then an oscillation between despair and hope as a result of the women's reports, and then finally the sudden certainty: it is really he, he is here. Here they experience something of the lightning-like character of the Resurrection.

Confession which always anticipates absolution is not an imitation of Christ. During contrition and confession one's attention should be directed only to one's sin. The surrender of the finished confession into the hands of the confessor signifies the renunciation of any initiative in respect to one's own sin. It involves indifference concerning what God's representative may do with the penitent; the latter does not anticipate absolution. It comes to him like a bolt of lightning. Even if psychologically he needs time to grasp it and to let its joy gradually flow into him—that joy of reunion with the triune God—if he needs time to free the entire space inside himself for this joy, this extension of time is unimportant compared with the influx of grace.

The Person of the Son had given himself over to suffering in so complete a fashion that for this Person, too, Resurrection means a reunion with the Father. The Son had deposited his divinity so completely with the Father during the Passion that the Resurrection means for him a reacquisition of all that had been suspended. But because he suffered as a human being, he also experiences this new encounter with the Father in the totality of human joy. He does not give redeemed humanity a joy that he has not experienced himself. Humanity is to receive a share in that joy through absolution; it is the joy in which Adam's inherent capacity for joy fulfills itself and is more than fulfilled, since in the Son it participates in divine joy. This is the will of the Father, who took the Son's mission seriously in every aspect; the Son was to confess sin for all humanity and receive absolution as the representative of all humanity. Thus the Son experiences his own joy not only as existence but also as the joy of all who are redeemed, and for him that infinitely increases the worth of this joy.

Absolution means that sin has been removed completely. For the Son the bearing of sin is over. Its removal does not constitute a *minus*, nor does it leave a gap behind; it is immediately the *plus* of radiant purity within a purified creation. It is the finished possession of the Father, who the sufferer thought had abandoned him. Absolution is much less a turning away from sin than a turning to God. The Son now sees in every individual whom he has redeemed someone filled with joy in whom, as part of the Father's mission, he may dwell. When he thus discovers himself in a person—"No longer is it I who live, Christ lives in me"—this is a guarantee and proof for him that this person belongs to the redeemed of the Father. In the death on the Cross the human being was for him still only the sin he was bearing, for he had breathed his own spirit, the Holy Spirit of love, back to the Father. Now, however, all human beings are again present to him because he now has new powers of disposition over his own love, and all humanity is itself new, mature, fruitful and loving in the triune love.

The disciples participated in the earthly life of the Lord; they learned the mysterious fact that he was the Son of God, and they experienced many of his deeds and encounters that filled them with awe. They never really comprehended his predictions. They took one word or another and interpreted it according to the measure of their understanding. They experienced the death of the Lord as a complete failure, and thus his Resurrection catches them unprepared. The Lord, however, knows the circumstances of every individual. He owes them an explanation that will summarize the meaning of his entire life and finally make it comprehensible within its own context. In this meaning, his meaning, their existence also acquires meaning. From this they receive their commission to proclaim the gospel and indeed to continue his work according to his instructions.

On Easter evening he summarizes the meaning of his life in the words: "Whose sins you remit, their sins are remitted." That is the core of his teaching; there is nothing theoretical about it, since he himself lived it and did it. In this form that he has lived and accomplished he passes on his existence to the Church. His Incarnation was an act of pure love, and during his entire life he never deviated from this act of love. When one views this life in the light of confession, one sees that love and confession converge in him. He so loved the Father's creatures that he gave his own life for them; but he gave it by taking their sins upon himself in confession and obtaining the Father's absolution for them as their representative. He took on life so that he could give it away again. This mission of love is the ultimate glorification of the Father, and its most sublime expression is the Son's glorification of the Father's creation. He glorifies the Father by glorifying humanity in the Father; he takes on human form in order to show the Father the splendor of his creation. The Son, in his own life, so glorifies something that belongs to the Father that the Father experiences the splendor of this something which is his and which has been taken out of him. This glorification, however, depends on man's remaining in the love of the Father, and that means remaining open to the Father. The openness of one's whole life is shown to us by the Son, who does not for a moment relinquish this openness, not even while he is burdened with sin and is dying in abandonment. This openness is the perfect attitude of confession which he passes on to the Church.

4. THE FOUNDING OF CONFESSION

Its Institution

It is striking that the Lord does not ask the Apostles whether or not they want to take on this task. On Easter evening, when they are together, he appears to them and gives them two commands in the midst of their Easter joy: to receive the Spirit and to remit sins. They are at a point where there is no longer a choice. Until now there has been little talk about the Lord bearing sins or about how the disciples should conduct themselves with sinners. They heard the good news that was to deal with sin once and for all and saw the good example to be given, but what the Lord had said about one's behavior toward sin concerned all the faithful as much as it did the Apostles. The Easter command now suddenly changes their position. They no longer merely recognize him or help in the struggle. They have now become judges, judges who are not only to pronounce judgment but are also to carry it out. They have the authority to forgive or not to forgive after confession and to do both within the framework of the power conferred upon them.

They have nothing to say about this authority. The Lord confers this power on them without alternative in precisely the condition in which he finds them. The choice was made already when they decided to follow the Lord, when they could not possibly suspect that this power would one day be bestowed upon them. It constitutes an absolute explosion of their previous relationship to the Lord, a conclusion whose premises they had hardly perceived.

This new power is unconditionally connected to the reception of the Holy Spirit. When the disciples followed the Lord, they wanted to participate in all that was his, and the Spirit is his. Thus this challenge, though unexpected, is logically consistent.

The Lord does not hesitate to bestow upon his followers this unprecedented authority to penetrate so deeply into the fate of sinners. He does not hesitate because he does not give them this power as something they can exercise privately and personally, but rather accompanies it with the competence bestowed by the Spirit. This power will always hold them in tension between two poles. They will always have to reconcile what they comprehend about sin with the incomprehensible aspect of their office; they will have to pass certain human judgments on the seriousness or mildness of guilt, judgments that still are to fall within the framework of their authority. The aid offered them by their own faculty of reason will not be enough, for they will have to draw also from the reason of the Holy Spirit.

The Lord, too, never let himself be guided by purely human motives during his own life on earth, but rather acted and made decisions from within his relationship to the Father in the Holy Spirit. Even when he says, "If it is possible, let this cup pass from me" (which perhaps would have corresponded to his momentary wish), he immediately moves on to the supernatural will of the Father and desires it, so that now, when he institutes confession, he surrenders to the Apostles part of his relationship to the Father. He does not instruct them concerning it; he mediates it to them effectively, so that in their encounter with sin they may make their decisions from within this mysterious obedience of the Son. During his own life on earth they often saw him perform inexplicable deeds by some unknown power. He performs such signs and wonders that his relatives thought he had become demented, and the Apostles' spirit at that time was not so far removed from that of these relatives. And now they are expected to comprehend no longer with their own faculty of understanding, but with that of the Holy Spirit; whenever they have an opinion or insight of their own, they are to refer it to the insight bestowed upon them by the Spirit. And this insight, viewed as a whole, remains incomprehensible to them, but the incomprehensible has changed its position now; it is now precisely what they themselves perform, and in its execution they are to experience ever more deeply their union with the Lord. Furthermore, in their priestly office they are to experience through their own activity the twofold nature of the Son, who is God and man in one person. They are to experience this in the fact that he has placed them, too, into a twofold—yet unified—situation. From within the deepest mystery of the Son there emerges a new mystery adapted to them. The duality that nonetheless must be lived within a unity manifests itself within them like a germinating seed; indeed, at any given moment they should be both seed and fruit. Through their office and through the bestowal of the Holy Spirit there lives in them a tension of fertility that must keep them constantly alert.

On the Mount of Olives they slept. They demonstrated then that they were incapable of staying awake under their own power, even when the Lord's express instructions commanded them to do so. Because of this lack of wakefulness, they could not be present when the whole affair of sin was deliberated between the Father and the Son. Now, however, when the Lord speaks to them and gives them this new form of alertness —for they must now indeed be alert in order to bind and to loose—it becomes a gift of the Holy Spirit.

When the Lord promised the keys to Peter and made him into the Rock, Peter hardly understood what this gift included. It was obscure and went beyond his understanding. He no doubt saw that the Lord was planning something extraordinary for him, but he could not know yet what it would be. The concrete content of the promise remained to be revealed in the future. Things are different at the institution of confession. Although the actual exercise of authority also remains in the future, the disciples must sense how concrete this gift is even in its incomprehensibility. The facts are clear enough: through the reception of the Spirit they are to acquire the ability to forgive sins. They understand that this is to be taken literally, and the shock of incomprehensibility occurs precisely in their understanding of these words. It is the same incomprehensibility that in one form or another is found in every Christian life and that assails the believer time and time again in all the sacraments. The power to forgive sins is no less incomprehensible than the power to change bread into flesh.

When the Apostles celebrate the first Eucharists, no doubt they will be shaken at the thought of being permitted to partake of the Lord's flesh and blood. Yet the process of the consecration lies so much within God and within God's word that they need only to act and not to understand: to act in pure faith, in pure transparency toward the word. When they bind and loose, on the other hand, they must understand in order to pass judgment. And they must pass judgment, even though it be in the Holy Spirit. The tension is greater between the mere instrumentality and one's own effort. They are called into service as those with insight; their understanding and their will are employed as tools within the framework of the Spirit and in union with it. If a priest were to hear a confession merely out of habit, bored and only half-listening, or if he were to evaluate the sinner according to human ethical standards, he would be disregarding the mystery of confession. This would not remain without damaging consequences. A vitality is required of the priest that in its turn should elicit new vitality. The insight he must acquire, an insight assuring him a Christian participation in the penitent's fate, can be acquired only through effort. Office and person must merge into a genuine unity.

Now, after Easter, the victor over sin has the fullness of authority to give his Apostles this kind of power. He has returned to them with the new experience of having suffered and died for sinners. He has acquired for both God and man the experience of redemption in his own person. Any future talk of redemption is talk of him. As the Redeemer he gives his disciples the Holy Spirit. There is no talk of asking or receiving permission from the Father. He gives them the Spirit completely from within himself; and yet in doing so he also surrenders to them a mystery of the divine Trinity, for the Holy Spirit must be ready and willing to be sent by him into his Church. In the service of redemption the Son disposes over the Spirit. The disciples learn of this power of disposition when it is employed for their benefit. It is as if the Son, who before his death was the Father's servant, were now revealing his own glorious independence ever more clearly; yet the emergence of the independence of one divine Person always reveals more clearly the unity of thought and will of all three. The will of the Son is the same as that of the Spirit, and since the will of the Son is always a revelation of the will of the Father, the will of the Father is also that of the Spirit. In the Son's words on this occasion there is no mention of the Father; it is as if he were concealed in the Son and the Spirit and yet revealed along with them in the will of both. But what the Father in his concealment wishes to reveal is the Son's mission. The Son is not just a servant and not just a tool; he expressly participates in the power of the Father, which the Father has unconditionally mediated to him. The Son's disposition now shows clearly that nothing—not even his suffering and death —happened out of weakness or limitation. If the Son were to say, "I have asked the Father for permission to give you the Spirit", he would be an emissary, but not the eternal Son. On the Cross he so fully surrenders to the Father everything he has—even his spirit—that the Father now wishes to reveal the full splendor of the Son's power.

Binding and Loosing

The Son says, "Receive the Holy Spirit." He himself had received it visibly during his baptism: earlier, however, the Spirit had received him [*empfangen*] in order to carry him to his mother at conception [*Empfängnis*]. Everything in God is total surrender, trust and love; every Person stands open to every other. The Son, who became man out of surrender and love, both demonstrated and taught this divine attitude: to be open to the Father in all things, to show him everything that happens within man—not merely that the Father may see it, but rather that he may participate and feel, as it were. On the basis of this openness the Father participated to such an extent in the life of the Son that the Son himself experienced this participation and lived from within it. The Father always gives the Son an echo and response, though also a determinative response: "Not my will, but your will be done!" The Father's determining response here also included the mission to suffer.

In the confession instituted by the Son, then, the sinner is to reveal himself to God's representative in surrender, trust and love, and the response determining remittance or nonremittance lies with the confessor. A person who only hears the words about binding and loosing without a knowledge of the complete context must perceive them as harsh. The sinner must surrender himself unconditionally; the person to whom he thus opens himself, however, can apparently do what he wants with him in the freedom of his own judgement. At best these words might be viewed as a matter of justice, since it may be just to forgive this person but not that one. The Spirit bestowed upon the Apostles would then have to be a Spirit of just consideration. Yet if one understands that the Son's life is one of love, then it becomes clear that the words about binding and loosing can only be the essence of his life and thus an expression of love—and of the highest love, since they are the first words he speaks after dying the death of love on the Cross. This act of love addresses not only every individual, but also the Church as a whole. Redemption does not mean that from now on every person has the freedom to shape his life as he pleases and that God will finally pronounce it all as good in a kind of general absolution. Redemption means that those redeemed should come into a form determined by God—the Church—in order to live in it a life pleasing to God. Following the Son expressly means avoiding sin and assuming a discipline that is at once an education toward the Son and a penance for guilt. The ecclesial organization ordained by the Son issues from his love and is a path to his love, and the authority of binding and loosing corresponds to this origin and goal.

This education toward love—itself an event in love—must include both the possibility of pedagogical discipline (and thus punishment) and the element of penance (which in its turn is part of punishment). There is no education without genuine authority. Since education is a path, however, the authority must be able to evaluate where the one to be educated stands and which is best for him as regards the love he is to attain: binding or loosing. For example, if a person does not understand that the essence of sin is lack of love, he must be educated to this insight. This can be done by having him continue to carry a burden until he sees that it really is a burden. All penitents know of this possibility that of necessity inheres in the authority of love. Even if the confessional secret prevents them from knowing who is refused absolution, it suffices that they are cognizant of this possibility, just as the faithful know about the existence of the treasury of prayer without being able to show who lays claim to it or how. They know that there are people in the Church whom the Church disciplines by means of this possibility, whether these people perceive the imposed measure as justified and serious or not. These are not people who have turned away completely, since apparently they have tried to effect the release from their guilt at least once. They also know that there are others who risk everything in love in order to receive forgiveness. In prayer there is thus a community of those for whom sin has been remitted and those for whom it has not.

The believer deals unhesitatingly with the treasury of prayer; he can take from it and add to it. But if he as someone "loosed" knows that others are still "bound", then he can suffer with them in a fitting conciousness of solidarity; he can atone for them and in a certain way even include them in his confession.

For there is no purely private sacrament in the Church. All the sacraments are a means and occasion for unity; each one unites all believers who are connected with it, whether they receive it directly or not. The sacraments are one of the most excellent powers of unification, since in a very mysterious way they guide all Christians into the unity of the Church. This unity is not just a community and harmony of beliefs, taste or lifestyle; all that can be an expression of unity, and the sacraments provide this form of unity as well. But the real, essential unity lies behind all this, and the sacraments give access to it. The unity of the Church, however, is absolute love; whoever gains access to this love through the sacraments and is educated in it will receive those sacraments—including and especially confession—in the disposition of the communion of saints. Whoever is bound is moving toward love precisely because of that binding. Whoever is released has even greater occasion for being aware of his solidarity with those who are still bound and for behaving accordingly.

In his earthly life the Lord bound some of the sins he encountered and released others; he bound them in the case of the Jews, released them in the case of the disciples and the repentant women who had sinned. Nonetheless he bore all sins and atoned for them all. It is evident that he could not remit the sins of those who, like the Jews, did not believe in him. After all, they desire nothing from him. They are far removed from any thought of making a confession to him or of imitating in their own relationship to him his attitude of openness toward the Father. There are others, however, who would like to confess and who open themselves and who nonetheless do not receive absolution. They have confessed and experienced contrition and yet receive no absolution. How can that be? Are they perhaps the victims of priestly arbitrariness? Do they have to bear penance for the rest? Or is it inherent in the character of certain sins that one knows—even as one commits them—that one is committing something unforgivable? Is there from the very beginning a distinction within sin, not only between mortal and venial sins but also between forgivable and unforgivable sins, between sins against the Holy Spirit and those not expressly against the Spirit? This would lead to untenable conclusions, and therefore there must be another way to explain why the willingness to confess can be present without the confession itself sufficing for absolution. The flaw must lie with the repentance, which appears adequate to the penitent yet insufficient to the confessor. The penitent wants to avoid the sin, but not its near occasion. Or he cannot acknowledge the seriousness of the sin with which the confessor reproaches him. Or he thinks he can master a certain situation in life without seeing what scandal it can give. It is always some sort of reservation which a penitent is not permitted to have; the confessional attitude does not predominate. He is thus caught in an error: he does not take confession to be what it really is, namely, the unconditional submission to God's word for the purpose of approximating the attitude of the Son toward the Father.

Judas lives with the Lord just as the other Apostles do; as one who does not possess the Holy Spirit, he perhaps is not essentially different from them. Yet his sin is retained, since his life within the Lord's circle is not discipleship, is not submission and obedience, is not confession. He has already found and thus searches no more; this finding dispenses him from searching.

In the Church the true saints stand at the top, in the middle the sinners who are absolved and at the bottom those whose sins are still held in abeyance and whose absolution must be postponed. Outside the Church stand those who do not confess at all.

Because he is God, the Lord always means more than we can comprehend, and this "more" also shapes each encounter we have with him. We can never view such an encounter as finished and rounded off, as this way and not that way, and as so large and no larger. It would be unchristian to maintain that by means of numerous definitions and the summary of a great many partial aspects one might comprehend the essence of, say, holy communion. The effectiveness, essence and mystery of the Lord always remain transcendent. The mystery of communion with him lies decisively in him, not in us. The same is true of confession. We know what we have to do when we confess; we are able to distinguish the individual acts such as the examination of conscience, contrition, resolution, confession and absolution. We know that we desire peace with the Lord. But the mystery of that attitude which constitutes a good confession lies in the grace of the Lord, not in us. We are never able to survey our attitude in such a way that we might say that it is good or sufficient. The Holy Spirit confers upon the confessor the grace through which he determines whether our essential confessional attitude is sufficient or insufficient. If absolution can be conferred, we are permitted to know in obedience that it was sufficient. This knowledge, however, also immediately involves the knowledge of our insufficiency, since we—precisely as contrite penitents—know with certainty that we never live up to the purest will of the Father. The happiness of that purity offered us through absolution lies as if suspended within the unhappiness of our awareness that we will never be completely sufficient. If our sin is not remitted, then the ultimate knowledge is no longer merely a vague feeling, but instead is objectified before our spirit with such harshness that it shocks our entire Christian existence in its innermost depths. Then perhaps we immediately see where our insufficiency lies. Even if someone tells us where it lies—in our contrition, our resolve, our consciousness of sin, and so on—we more probably will see the entire yawning abyss of our insufficiency for the first time because a self-satisfied "sufficient" has been unmasked. We did not want to find our sufficiency in God's infinite love, but in ourselves. We confessed as those who think they know better, and thereby dragged the mystery of confession down to the level of a kind of automatic purification that did not stand in grace, because we did not want to submit ourselves to the law of grace. In the

Ever-More of our own failure we discover—with grace—the Ever-More of the divine Master.

Its Prehistory in the Life of the Lord

Childhood. The Lord's early life involves his becoming accustomed both to his existence as a human being and to his mission; it also involves those around him being accustomed to his particular relationship to God. His mother's assent already established her complete willingness, and we learn of Joseph that he recognized and set out upon his Christian path after the appearance of the angel in the dream. One might initially suppose that the overwhelming impression of the two angelic appearances had elicited from Mary and Joseph a single act of consent whose consequences for their whole existence they did not yet sufficiently comprehend. If at the time or even afterward one had asked them how they thought they would demonstrate their fidelity, they might have found it difficult to respond. Perhaps they would have answered that God does not undertake anything for which he does not also supply the means and his help. This means and help reside expressly in the Son. He will spend his entire life being just this for them, but as a child he does so in a special way. In him his parents find the strength to remain faithful in the way of God. As yet he develops no doctrine, calls no disciples and still keeps his relationship to the Father concealed in his inmost being; but the attitude corresponding to all this cannot remain concealed, and he mediates it to his parents when it of necessity appears.

The ongoing attitude of life that he presents to Mary and Joseph as his own is one of complete openness, the attitude of confession. In all important decisions they look to him, for example, in the case of the flight to Egypt, and they look to him in all of life's small concerns as well. They watch over and care for him, and in constant contact with him they practice his attitude.

It was not difficult for the Immaculate Virgin to imitate this posture. One can even say it was "childishly easy" and it was particularly suited to the activity of this child. Joseph, too, however, is a holy man who comprehends the attitude of the New Covenant with almost playful ease while living with this mother and child. The Mother was redeemed from the very beginning and ordained to receive this child so that she might be initiated by him into God's mysteries; Joseph, on the other hand, was chosen from the very beginning to be wed to this virgin and to find in her and her child the center both of his external concerns and of his internal activity. Thus everything radiates from the child. What he will later be and do is already being revealed in a childlike fashion, just as the story is told of a famous architect that even as a child he arranged his building blocks in an amazing way.

Binding and loosing presupposes that one knows the commandments, is familiar with doctrine and has the capacity to live according to it. When the twelve-year-old teaches in the Temple and interprets his Father's teaching, this act is also a preparation for confession. It serves as an aid to recognition of the Father, and this recognition will increasingly deepen humanity's insight into its own sinfulness. The teachers see how the divine law should be interpreted and applied, and at the same time they see what astounding knowledge this child already possesses, a child who will later develop his teaching with the highest authority. He does not yet let himself be recognized as the Messiah; but someone is present among the people who has evidently been instructed by God himself— and evidently with a future mission in mind.

Perhaps those among the listeners who are converted will play a special role in how the Son's confession of self will be understood. One's own confession is the precondition and preparation for acceptance of the confession of Jesus. Those listeners perhaps will be able to offer the proper interpretation and explanation to the people, where the Lord only offers allusions and broad contours. The youth's discourse in the

Temple already involves a substantial clarification of the way sin looks from the perspective of the New Covenant and how it is to be treated. The Son goes there as one who knows in order to instruct those who know, just as he lives in his family's house as a believer in order to demonstrate his child's faith. He is spared any struggle with evil as long as he is still a child; the teachers are astounded to hear him speak as he does, and they question him, but they do not debate him. As a man the Lord will preach in a more apostolic and militant fashion. The twelve-year-old presents the teaching of the New Covenant so that it appears essentially comprehensible and acceptable to the Jews. He shows what the Father's law includes and sharpens the teaching of the Old Covenant by disclosing its profundity.

Entrance into public life. At home the Son lived in a close circle of people who believed in him from the very beginning and thereby created a spiritual home for him. The Child encountered an environment in which he was not only "reared" in a fashion but also received the recognition and love allowing him the complete development of his being. The love he encountered awakened his life, and this life in turn influenced that love. When the Baptist's initiative then opens to him an expanded circle of friends, he will have to love all those he encounters in that new circle the same way he loved those in the original family circle, in the same transparency toward the Father. Yet now the question arises concerning how he must arrange his life so as also to reveal this love effectively to those who are distant and uninitiated. From his own confessional attitude the idea of instituting confession slowly emerges, and the question of how he can mediate his own love to them. The actual act of institution will ultimately be the fruit of his Passion and death, and yet it will be as well the integration and crowning of his entire life's effort.

In the family home, questions are limited by the small number of those present; living with his parents is training for the later encounter with the multitudes. The attitude and point of departure with those initial few people were correct and needed only to be expanded. In the case of the multitudes, on the other hand, an initial conversion is necessary; he sees their insuperable conscious and unconscious hindrances, their aversion, its causes—all differing with each individual. Even if the later institution of confession looks like a unified prescription, it has nonetheless emerged as the result of the Lord's innumerable individual experiences. As such it always contains the possibility of being something different and something special for each individual, something that corresponds to him and yet is able to bring each person to the Father.

The Son could, of course, have shown men his own contemplation of the Father and made it so attractive to them that they would have tried to imitate it. He could have been a kind of theoretician or mystic of divine truth. In his public life, however, he breaks through his own contemplation and theory again and again into the realm of practice and breaks through his vision of the Father into the apostolate of life among human beings. A person who lives only by theory easily forgets to see in his fellow man someone who must be loved in an active, effective way. While living among human beings the Son continually asks himself how he can make the mysteries of triune love accessible to men. The effective mediating elements are not just doctrine and knowledge, but above all the sacraments, and among them particularly confession.

When God first spoke to Adam, he spoke to his own creature standing open before him. He later spoke with a creature who has turned away, and showed him—by continuing to manifest himself—that he was stronger than both Adam and the serpent together. He showed his superior power before any further development took place, and he showed the power of his penetrating voice when he once decided to speak. This power did not lie with Adam, in his stormy demands to hear the word. On the contrary, during flight from God's voice Adam is overwhelmed by precisely that voice. It was humiliating for Adam in spite of everything to have to hear what God said to him. Now, however, the Son takes part of this humiliation onto his own shoulders; he suffers so much for others that everyone acquires as a gift a kind of willingness to speak with God in confession and to let himself be cleansed and set right by God's word. Every time the Son encounters a sinner, he takes part of this humiliation onto his own shoulders. This portion is not intended to be exclusive, as if only his immediate contemporaries concerned him. He wants to redeem everyone, and for that reason he bears all humiliation on the Cross, and after the Cross he opens to sinners the path to God in the institution of confession. Both these acts will be the result of his experience in living with sinners.

Only God can effectively bear the world's sin; when the Son takes it upon himself as a man, this is the efficacious sign that God is turning to those who have turned away and that he is hastening after those who are fleeing. "I know that you are fleeing from me," God says, "but you must know that I am ready to receive you. No matter how grievously you may sin, do not ever believe I have left you. You always have access to me. Never despair of the presence of God; in the Church and in the Eucharist God has erected for you a reminder that he is there, and he has also prescribed the step you must take toward him: confession." In order to create this opening in man, the Son directed and transferred the humiliation to himself, who is God. The step that man still has to take is already situated within grace. The mere existence of this step is itself grace, and yet, if a person takes this step, it is to his merit. Through grace the human being has received the genuine possibility of returning. And the path of grace God has presented has a dual nature: invisible in God and visible in the world, invisible in the divinity of Jesus and visible in his humanity and his Church. He takes humanity's humiliation upon himself and suffers it unto the Cross and unto death, but he also opens for the sinner a path of discipleship leading into suffering as a path of grace-filled return through confession and absolution.

He suffers because people flee from God and do not confess

their sins to him. The result of this suffering for unknown, unformulated sin is the gift that permits its confession. The collective sin Christ bears on the Cross is the sum of all the unspoken, refused confessions. He bears this burden as a man and yet according to the will of the triune God that he take humanity's burden away. Otherwise his bearing of the burden would be incomprehensible and pointless. As it is, however, his suffering as the God-man opens a new path along which God and man can encounter one another. As God's Son he knows how deeply rooted he is in God's will and how God is in perfect agreement with what he is doing; he knows it much better than even the most saintly human being could. Whenever a righteous person suffers in the Old Testament, he views it as a kind of just punishment; the question of atonement, however, remains unresolved. And since the Jew knows of no eternal life, everything is played out entirely within the earthly realm, where the relationship between punishment and atonement can never become transparent. Man can believe, can be oriented toward God and want to tell God how things stand with him, and can experience God's guidance, perhaps even in miraculous ways; but as long as the door to eternal life is never opened, real confession remains impossible. The breakthrough occurs only on the Cross. Only now is God no longer merely the one reigning in heaven who has miraculous powers and who can speak with human beings. He is now the one to whose heavenly throne man can come together with the Son, because the death on the Cross has created a pathway to eternal life. The Son is the way, and in confession he sets sinners upon this way. He opens it to all who want to come to God; he shapes the steps with his own suffering and shows in confession how they can be traversed. He is so much the way and the door that merely getting up and starting toward the Father is already entry into eternal life, separation from personal guilt, communion with all penitents and the new opportunity to hear the Father's voice in the Holy Spirit. Confession is like a reflection of the Cross; yet the Son's act of atonement has made all the various elements so bright and easy that only faith can really perceive that reflection.

The moment the Lord leaves Nazareth, he loses the physical and spiritual protection of home and steps into the perspectives of the Cross. He already sees his own body and soul as the instrument on which will be played all the suffering that extends unto death, that infinite, diverse symphony whose final simplification will be the sacrament of confession. This sacrament reaches back to all the events that begin with the Son's active life when he begins to take the world's sin upon himself in a visible, human fashion. The thousand contingencies of his earthly life finally issue into the totality and completeness of the sacrament.

The Miracles. Whenever the Lord performs a miracle, he sees its effect on men. He sees its ability to generate faith and keep it fresh. Each new miracle brings new people to him or strengthens the faith of those already converted. Within the larger circle there are also many who have questions, who have been moved, who are interested in these events, for whom a new door has been opened. These miracles are also accompanied by "a power that goes out from him", one so intense that the miracles live from it and indeed are made possible by it. Because the Son's every deed is accompanied by the Father and the Spirit, a triune element inheres in each miracle. The purpose of the miracles, however, is to free men from sin and guide them to faith.

After the Passion he knows that his return to the Father is imminent, and that after his Ascension he as an earthly man no longer will perform miracles which require the expenditure of his energy. He also knows, however, that he expended all his energy on the Cross and died weak and powerless. Hence he institutes confession, which nourishes itself from the entire expended energy of his life, and, in its continual repetition, always lends a fresh, relevant element to all his earthly miracles. Confession is the Lord's perpetual miracle, given to the Church, in which all his unique miracles continue to be visible and effective.

As a miracle, confession is above all an event: the presence of that great transformation of a sinner into a saint, and thus the evocation of the act of redemption in every life. Whereas the Eucharist is more the guarantee and mediation of the Lord's continual presence—the presence of his being and essence—confession is the mediation of the event of the Cross, of the absolution of earth by heaven. While the Eucharist is more a pure gift of grace, the act of confession integrates the human event of conversion, the willingness to confess, contrition and confession. During the Last Supper the Lord—in his actions, his mission, his words—controls what is happening, and the Eucharist will always maintain this character. In confession, on the other hand, the fact of sin plays such a role that man in his present and unique situation is invited to participate.

The same is true in the miracles. The deaf, blind, lame, hemorrhaging, dead or possessed man, for example, is considered in his own special situation and then given a gift. The situation is always one of need; the person is always spiritually or physically sick and starving. Through the miracle his situation suddenly becomes the Lord's. He takes it over, assumes responsibility and heals it. He sought out the suffering person where he lay. Now that he has ascended into heaven man must take it upon himself to go to him; but the Lord has said where and how he can be found. Everyone must become aware of this situation of need in his own sinfulness; at the same time he must see that it can be healed by a miracle of the Lord.

Jesus' preaching. When the Lord glorifies the Father in his preaching in order that men can understand him and are moved to imitate that glorification, he never forgets the goal of his mission: that this glorification is to take the form of redemption. Every word he speaks could be viewed from this angle. Every utterance concerning love, every word about the nature of the Father and even the majority of his parables refer to that particular encounter between the sinner and God to which he will later give the form of confession. Men have, on their own initiative, turned their backs on God without cause; they must also begin the journey back to God on their own initiative or at least must make some move on their own initiative for the sake of this return.

There is something in this process that can be compared to the Incarnation, since the Son, too, offers himself to the Father on his own initiative and takes up the work of redemption with complete spontaneity—indeed, so much so that everything he says is marked by it. In his movement away from and back to the Father there is a clear expression of the voluntary nature of his actions and at the same time of the unerring certitude with which he traverses this path and prepares it for us. In his preaching he tries to draw men into this from free certitude; whether he is speaking in parables or in proverbs or is instructing and admonishing his apostles, he is always pointing out the path. His own freely chosen path is a model for those who have freely left the Father and should, through grace, freely return to him. Indeed, in his own departure from the Father the Son took a portion of sin on himself even though he was sinless: that which in the Incarnation is actually God's becoming alien to himself and which reaches its high point on the Cross. His cry of abandonment could just as easily be the cry of a sinner who sees no more hope of return and no rescue. He himself has sold everything in order to buy back from the Father the one pearl of man to be redeemed. In discipleship man himself should sell everything for the sake of returning to the Father.

In life he takes the world's sin increasingly upon himself. This act would remain unnoticed by men, however, if his teaching did not simultaneously expand into a global doctrine extending to all times and all peoples. If the Lord's Cross were considered without knowledge of his teaching, the impression of onesidedness or fanaticism might arise. But if he interprets his essence and his path from every aspect and yet still maintains unity within this multiplicity—indeed, manifests that unity precisely through the multiplicity—then the meaning of the Cross will become evident, even if not comprehensible in its entirety. For all his words, all his parables, lead ultimately to the Cross. Similarly, the confession of every single person—no matter how personally it may be formulated—becomes an expression of the unity of the sacrament, which is itself the expression of the one redemption on the Cross. Confession is the personal gift of redemption, always unique, to each person, just as each person can accept and apply it. For this reason confession is, in all its differentiation, a particularly intensive participation in the communion of saints; every confession, every confessional attitude enhances all the others not only because all sins are connected, but—more essentially—because all confessions are summarized in the Lord and in his sacrament and are made possible in the unity of the two.[1]

Thus there is a compelling necessity for the Lord to speak to us: the necessity lies in the fact that he wants to redeem us. Yet he cannot speak alone without ever getting a response. We cannot always count on the Father taking care of what is lacking, for the Lord wants us to be his brothers and partners. But we can answer only if we are pure. Therefore the Lord chooses to speak with us during moments when he has cleansed us and we are able to hear and speak. He speaks decisively important words, for example, when he has performed a physical or spiritual miracle. The Father then sees in this person the Son's own purity just as it really is given to him. That is why the Son institutes confession, the continuing miracle of purification: in order (through his priest) to enter into genuine conversation with us. The words of contrition and confession, the confessor's exhortation, are all words corresponding to the Lord's own sense and heart, which could

---

[1] Editor's note: Cf. the author's work concerning the prayer and confessional attitude of the saints.

also stand before the Father. In these words the sinner separates himself from himself not just momentarily but rather in such a way that the Lord's grace enters into him and penetrates, purifying, into his innermost interior. The Father sees how what belongs to the Son passes over to the one who confesses; just as grace penetrates him, so also does the Son's word, which is itself a form of grace. All his words are concerned with the event of confession, and all belong to that one act in which he redeems us and the whole world. Even if we do not know all his words, even if we do not understand or comprehend them all, along with his grace something of his own quality as the Word penetrates us; every grace, as his grace, is a grace of the eternal Word, and each one gives us a new capacity for speaking with God. That is why every one of his words has a purifying effect on the listener, for each is grace and redemption.

The Sermon on the Mount, the farewell discourses, indeed every word of the Lord's preaching is able to generate in the listener purity and readiness for God, but for this to happen it is also necessary to confess the Lord. Whoever wants to remain in the Lord's word must confess him and confess his own sins. No one can marvel at the word of God and revere it and at the same time have a closed heart. He must submit himself to the commandment of confession, to the institution that binds and looses. That is the will of the Word, who gave the Holy Spirit to the disciples. Only he who confesses his sin within the Church has access to an understanding of the whole word. Otherwise he would only have a philological, eclectic understanding. The Word of God must be grasped precisely where it simultaneously cleanses and illuminates and is active both as proclamation and sacrament.

The word taken as mere teaching remains a preliminary stage of the full, redeeming Word. If the Lord had not instituted the Church as his Bride, the word of the Gospel itself could be considered his ultimate gift to humanity. As it is, however, he himself stands behind his commandment of love, and we must recognize him in our neighbor not only symbolically but in reality as well. His word and command- ment thus presuppose the transforming, redeeming power of his grace. And just as it presupposes the Church as his Mystical Body, it also presupposes the Church as a hierarchical institu- tion: his word is the divine authority which the Father gives him for governing and which he invests in the Church for the sake of love.

Expressed differently, and more profoundly: the Son lives in uninterrupted communion with the Father, and through this communion he knows that he always recognizes and does the Father's will. He offers believers a model of this communion in the Church and its communion with the ecclesial office. Just as the Son as a divine-human Person is open to the Father through this communion with him, so also a Christian person, through his openness to the office, is in communion with the Lord, and through the Lord in com- munion with the triune God. In his own openness to the Father and to the world, the Son is the one who confesses; he is the Word, and he is this word most intensely on the Cross in the great confession of the world's sin. By confessing our sins in the Church, we participate in the Lord's existence as the Word. Proclamation and confession stand in the same relationship to one another as do the Lord's life and Cross; in a more general sense they are like the Lord's heavenly and earthly life to the extent that the early life as a whole is determined by the law of sin.

The Passion. The resurrected Jesus owes an explanation to the Apostles, who are beside themselves with joy: an explanation of the fact that he died and yet lives, that he failed and yet is victorious, that he suffered and yet is now rejoicing, that he left them and is now among them. He summarizes this justification of his behavior in the institution of confession, as if his entire life, work and death were interpreted sufficiently by this one key word, as if the disciples needed nothing more than this in order to be adequately equipped for their own mission. There is no question they can ask the Lord, no request for explanation, that would not already be answered and even eclipsed by the words of institution. Prior to his suffering he said a great deal concerning the coming Cross and opened a great many doors to the uncomprehending disciples. Yet these prophecies remained tied to specifics—that the Son of Man must be surrendered, that he will have to suffer various things —and the Apostles at most understood these as external events. But the words of institution illuminate the Passion from within and centrally disclose its significance and purpose: so centrally, in fact, that the disciples' faith is the prerequisite for discovering the inner connection between Passion and confession. The Lord no longer speaks directly about the Passion; yet everything in the words of institution is a reference to that Passion and incomprehensible without it. On the other hand, it is through these words, and only through them, that the Passion is interpreted. The disciples are to view and understand death and Resurrection, indeed the Son's entire destiny, from the perspective of confession.

They also understand now that the Lord has taken them into his suffering: those who were actually there as well as those who only knew about it. He took them along by bearing their sins as well, and now he who stands before them so incomprehensibly transformed is therefore the living proof that they, too, are transformed. This, however, is not really the key, but rather the words of institution, that challenge them not merely to comprehend what has happened both to the Lord and to them but to do it themselves. They understand the eternal life they have received through the Passion and Resurrection only by passing it on. Suppose a girl knew nothing about the conjugal act; she does it without really knowing what is happening to her, and later she discovers that she is pregnant. Only then does she understand what has happened; only then does it become a meaningful truth for her. So also do the Apostles understand the death and Resurrection in

administering the sacrament of confession. The man who
performs the conjugal act knows what he is doing. Similarly,
when the Lord takes his Apostles into his suffering, he knows
exactly what he is doing; he acts within the Father and takes
them along. But when he gives them the authority of confession, they know they have performed it with him in the
Father—not out of their own merit and understanding, but
rather because he did it and they were present.

From Easter to Pentecost

When the Lord institutes confession, he sees all its individual
aspects; he sees where it commences, how it develops and
where it ends: in the return of the cleansed person to God and
to his mission in the world. For the Lord himself this return
to God and assumption of his world reign occurs in the
Ascension.

Viewed in the light of confession, the forty days between
Easter and Ascension are a time of hovering, of suspension.
They are like the echo of absolution before the life of mission is
taken up again, a pause between the time of the completed
earthly mission and the imminent resumption of the divine-
human mission in heaven. It is a time void of any difficulty, a
time marked by the consciousness of having done the Father's
will to the end, of having realized, as it were, the ultimate
human potential on earth. On Easter the Son receives the
full power of the Father's absolution; he is like one who
is still kneeling after receiving the words of absolution,
overwhelmed by grace, not yet having stood up again to leave
the church and resume his day-to-day task. It is the conclusion
of the confession, a confession that manifests itself for the Son
as return to the Father, as Ascension.

If this return were the final stage, the Christian would
indeed have received remission of sins, but he would not know
what to do next. He would be without a compass, would be

relieved without knowing what he ought to do with his new power. That is why both for the Lord and for the believer the Ascension merges directly into Pentecost. When the Son sends his and the Father's Spirit into the world, his world reign begins and the Christian world mission begins for the redeemed disciples. Far from being an end, absolution is a new beginning. Rather than releasing the cleansed disciples, the Lord visits them anew by sending them his Spirit. What appears to be a conclusion is actually a prelude; for the Apostles it is the beginning of their hearing of confessions. As long as the Lord himself was among them, there was no reason to confess one's guilt to anyone else. Now his life in the mystical and hierarchical Church begins.

The Spirit and the Church belong together. The Son revealed himself on earth with the twofold intention of pointing backward to the Father and the Spirit and pointing forward to the coming communion of saints. He is essentially a mediator and is always pointing beyond himself. Nowhere does he bind the two ends—Spirit and Church—more inextricably together than in confession, where man encounters man as a penitent sinner and one commissioned by the Spirit to remit sins. On this path, which the Lord himself shaped and traversed, the human being comes to the Father. The Spirit of this path that is Christ and the Spirit of the goal that is the Father are one and the same Spirit.

5. THE CHURCH AND CONFESSION

Bride and Confession

As Christ's Bride, the Church has the task of being continually prepared for the Groom. As Bride she knows the Groom. She not only knows who he is, she knows equally well what he asks and wishes. As Bride she emerged from his hands, which molded her; and because he let her become a bride, and not a maidservant, she also has a certain understanding of the image of her perfection that was in his mind. She does not at first need to pose the question of her worthiness, for she knows that the Lord provided and adorned her with everything this perfection required. When the Lord then returned to the Father and apparently withdrew from her in order to show her his real glory and also to put her through a time of testing, only then did she discover how much he had entrusted to her. As Bride she now has the administration of his concerns on earth and the responsibility for them, and at the end of this time she will be called to account for her stewardship.

One really cannot say that she saw herself while the Lord was shaping her, but she certainly understood what he intended by her shaping. She saw the love that was at work and saw that this love that generated her was to be mediated to humanity. She sees something of her own essence in every Christian and projects her own image into him. Thus she tries to shape every Christian to correspond to the Lord's expectation, not merely to demand it of him but to form it within him so that the image that she is may manifest itself ever more visibly in the world.

By prompting her children to confession according to the Lord's instructions, the Church seeks to allow the bridal element within her to radiate in all her members just as it does in herself. She knows she will not be able to make all her children into perfect saints, and that, just as the Lord foretold, she will always have some black sheep to pasture. Nonetheless, just as the Lord will always make excessive demands of her, so she will make excessive demands of her own members in order to attain the highest possible degree of purity in each. She also knows that in the truly pure there dwells a power to pass this purity on to others in the name of the Church, to awaken new purity among men, to be a compelling factor by means of their own example and intercession, to make love ever more ardent and not only to be converted themselves but also to stand in the place of others.

Because the Lord's image dwells in the soul of every individual, the Church's own offer penetrates to that individual's most intimate sphere. She lets her challenge and admonition resound as fully as possible even in the ranks of the indifferent and those who have turned away, and gives them the Easter confession as a minimum standard. If such a person then really does go to confession, he tries somehow to do full justice to it. The Church pressures him externally in order to elevate him inwardly. At the opposite end of the spectrum—in the case of the saint—she also penetrates to that private sphere. In the case of the sinner she does so by determining the necessary quantity, in the case of the saint through the specific quality she thinks she owes to the entire community.

The Church is concerned not only that as many as possible go to confession but also that everyone experiencing humiliation and elevation in confession knows that he belongs to the communion of saints and is accepted into it anew in order to accept an ecclesial responsibility. Confession is an ecclesial sacrament to such an intensive degree that it really does belong to the Church; thus the individual can no longer view his personal conscience as the highest authority, since his sin and its purification is no longer a private matter between him and God. The Church is the decisive mediator because she has been commissioned by the mediator Christ. She must demand an account from everyone who belongs to her.

Not just the officiating priest but every Christian has

ecclesial responsibility. A good Christian who meets an intransigent sinner in the Church is concerned that this sinner confess. The priest also has to assume his confessional responsibility for the sake of all those concerned—and not just for the sake of the Lord—even if this task of the laity is not expressly formulated. For everyone who senses the love of Christ within understands that this love must always also be a demanding love. Confession is thus not just a private matter for the individual; nor is it a matter of concern only to him and the priest; everyone confesses in the communion of penitents in order to enter anew into the communion of saints. In confession he by no means ceases to be a member of the community—just as the Son does not cease to be part of the triune God even when he, and he alone, becomes man. None of his actions would be comprehensible in itself without the living unity with the Father in the Holy Spirit; none of his actions is without love and responsibility as regards the "divine community". Into his own Church—both into the institution and into the communion of saints—the Lord infuses something of his mission, his consciousness of being challenged to be responsible in an excessively demanding way. He did not come in order merely to live a model life on earth. He wants to be apostolic and to draw others along with him, and those drawn to him should experience their own sense of community.

The Church has received the Lord's Spirit and intent. When she makes difficult demands on the individual by penetrating into his private sphere, she is doing what she saw and learned with the Lord. The best the Church has is what she has received directly from the Lord and what she tries, in pure obedience, to pass on. The energy and decisiveness with which she dispenses the sacraments is a sign of her genuineness and youth. It is an energy full of promise that can fulfill itself in the one receiving it if he senses and affirms the force of the living nature. Things would go badly only if the Church were to accommodate her dispensation of the means of grace to the indifferent members, if an indifferent penitent encountered an indifferent confessor and nothing more could be sensed of the fiery origin, the act of the institution of confession. Only in that act of institution, only in the most personal relationship between the Groom and the Bride can one understand what a sacrament is and intends. Every time the Lord turns to his Church, he also reveals his orientation toward the Father. One should never view the sacrament merely as "something instituted" or as a mere arrangement without also considering the event of Christ instituting it—the institution of an infinitely gentle and ardent love that presses and admonishes, encourages, pardons and helps.

The penitent easily forgets that he is a member of the community and is himself performing a communal act. He believes he must establish order in and for himself. The Church, however, does not forget his status as a member, though she occasionally forgets that she herself stands in a bridal relationship to the Lord and to the triune God, and that the demands she makes, the Lord still makes on her, demands the Father in turn has imposed on the Lord. One can also consider quite simply the act of setting an example by confessing or not confessing. Perhaps two people share a common guilt; one goes to confession, the other does not. The latter will not remain uninfluenced by the former's example. Often it is not so much some great unconfessed fault that has a social effect as the whole indifference of an unconfessed life, the whole lack of guidance and enthusiasm. A person grows lax, egoistic and narrow and does not want to be led by the Church any longer. Perhaps he finds himself unable to put up with some particular manner of expression of the Church; it may well happen that the language of the Church or of some of its representatives seems somewhat aloof or musty because the genuine word—the word that comes from the Lord's own Word and from his triune conversation—is no longer fresh and effective. The person has grown accustomed to accommodating himself to indifference and counts on it from the very beginning; he no longer expects that the word of God can effectively elicit any transformation in man. If the Church no longer believes in the power of the word, how is the individual to hear it in the Church's own speech? When the Church hears the confession of the individual, she should thereby also hear the sound of her own confession to the Lord. In the absolution that she mediates, she herself should receive absolution; she should participate so intensely in this hearing of the confession and in the granting of absolution, in the binding and loosing, that everywhere the individual is meant she should know that she, too, is meant. That is why she needs to let the individual penitent know that he does not stand alone. Precisely in and through the sacrament he is a member of the Church. But then, the Church that accepts the confession must naturally view this person who confesses to her as a portion of herself. Through the Lord she is permitted to dispense the gift of his grace, but this dispensing must take place in the same joy felt by the one receiving it—indeed in an even greater joy, since to give is more blessed than to receive. In a manner similar to that of the Holy Mass, confession is a common meal for confessor and penitent, for priest and layman.

Confession within the Framework of the Sacraments

The incarnate Son distinguishes himself from other men in that he is without sin. Someone who had neither seen one of his miracles nor heard one of his sermons would nonetheless have been able to see his divine mission because of that sinlessness. He lives as the Redeemer among sinners and sees how much sin has alienated them from the Father and continues to alienate them. He wants to intercept the man who has fallen away, create supports for him, throw him the anchor of grace, put up signposts for him that will show him the way back to God. The sacraments serve as such means of interception.

As long as he was on earth, he could indicate these things by means of his own word: He baptized or had someone baptize, he promised and gave his own flesh and blood, he let the sick be anointed and sent the Holy Spirit down upon the Church. He knew, however, that after his departure it would be objected that men are too alienated from God to be reached through these means. Hence he instituted one more sacrament meant exclusively for sinners, one that seizes man from below and grasps him in precisely that guilt and alienation. No one can say confession is too sublime for him. No one can say that alienation from God is not really a burden and that it would not be good to get rid of that burden and lighten himself. Living transparent and without sin before the Father, the Son knows what is good for men. The Son is he who lives in a state of purity. The sinner lives more or less in a state of sin; he does not really believe that he can break with sin, but he feels its burden and yearns—at least in certain moments—to be rid of it. The sacrament of confession is the ever-new moment of purification; if a man's faith is strong and effective, it can encompass whole areas of his life. It brings about—in individual acts and also, increasingly, as a habitual state—an approximation of the purity of the Lord.

Confession catches the sinner in his fall away from God. All the sacraments do this in their own way, and in doing so reveal something of the essence of the Church as a whole, namely, that it can be the means and path of conversion. Confession, however, does this to an especially high degree and is thus a particularly clear symbol for the essence of the Church. It makes visible the fact that the Church turns to all sinners. Communion, accessible as it is to the purified, would have been too exclusive by itself and too alarming for sinners. I as a sinner know that I taint the "communion of saints". I have been baptized, but I do not live according to the rule of baptism. I have been confirmed, but I am no apostle of Christ. I do attend Mass, but it remains incomprehensible to me. The sermon is either too sublime or too flaccid for me; I cannot relate to it. I recognize all the Church's efforts on my behalf;

she encourages, consoles and admonishes me, but it does me
no good. I have a great deal of experience with myself and I
know what I can and cannot do. Saints are shown to me, but I
am simply not one. I live in sin, and as a sinner I can always
have the last word with the Church. But if I am told that the
confessional is reserved for sinners, then I know that here
finally is a place for me; it is precisely I who am meant. The
pew there was made especially for me. Of course, I can also
grumble about confession, but that does not keep me from
knowing that my own situation has been provided for there.
When someone speaks about the communion of saints, it is
clear to me that I do not belong. But if he says to me, "There is
a communion of sinners, who belongs to it?" then I know
infallibly that I do.

The perspective of confession makes the understanding of
ecclesial life accessible to me. When as a sinner I am seized and
freed from my impurity, I know I have been included again. I
was seized as an individual and yet returned by means of
confession, to the community of the Church. Perhaps I felt
quite lonely and singled-out during confession itself. But that
was an illusion, for even there I was already standing within
the community of penitents; no matter how different the
various sacramental communities may be, they all have in
common that they bring one back into the community of the
Church. In returning, the member sees: I was always a child of
this community, even when my sin disturbed the vitality of
that association and my sense for it. I have been baptized, and
the Church has a claim on me.

Confession always involves being thrown back into the
middle. Whether or not I was far away, whether my relationship with sin has now been definitively destroyed or merely
loosened, I am pulled back again and again by the firm hand of
the Church which walks beside the believer so that he does not
fall into the abyss. Everyone who has even a notion of this
grace knows that it would be a discourtesy, indeed a despicable

ingratitude, to sin again with an eye toward the possibility of new confession.

Once I have confessed and have seen the extent to which this means of grace is tailored to me, I suddenly comprehend through this experience the effectiveness of all the sacraments. Confession no doubt seemed to be a lifesaver thrown to me from the ship of the Church, as the special institution for sinners. But as such it is nonetheless still one sacrament among others and is inextricable from the others. To separate it would be just as meaningless as to separate the words with which the Lord instituted confession from all his other words and from the rest of his life. Confession—which is always an "experience"—lends the other sacraments a new plausibility, especially baptism and confirmation, which have mediated a new purity. The one who has confessed knows that he has received something the Lord purchased for him through his own suffering, something commensurate with Christ himself. He will remember that baptism marked him as one who belongs to Christ and that his sin has clouded and even concealed that mark. Confession has now caused his baptismal innocence to shine once again. Baptism, received only once, leaves an indelible mark; it is like a plant that lies dormant during the winter and then blooms and grows anew each spring. It is covered in winter so that in the spring it can bloom again. Confession renders baptismal grace effective again; yet every new confession also revivifies the grace of previous confessions, just as we also encounter the opposite, namely, that new sins revivify old ones. When someone falls thoughtlessly into sin, is then enlightened through confession concerning the seriousness of sin, but falls again, perhaps repeatedly, his guilt can become ever more serious and powerful. In spite of that—and this is a mystery of divine love—each new grace recognizes traces of earlier graces and earlier absolutions, and joins with them and strengthens them.

Revivifying confirmation depends primarily on the resolution made in confession. Contrition brings the penitent to
the point of no longer wanting to sin. A special power is
needed for this. But the strengthening of faith during confirmation bestowed upon the Christian a power of endurance
that was concealed by sin and forgotten. A Christian's life
draws its strength for endurance primarily from the sacraments.
Although sin tears off individual pieces, confession mends
them again so that no "mend" is visible and the original
totality is restored. To the integrity of the soul corresponds
the integrity of all the Church's sacraments. The sacraments
always refer to one another, and in any particular one all the
others are offered. It is as if one were to dry off someone who
was soaked, saying, "You have a raincoat and umbrella, why
don't you use them?" The overall sacramental context shows
the Christian over and over how very much he is cared for and
provided for and that he is not at all cast out.

Communion is instituted before the Passion; as the Mass,
however, it becomes complete only through the Passion and is
accessible to the Church only beginning with Easter. The Last
Supper is thus a promise, while confession on Easter Sunday is
direct fulfillment. At the Last Supper the Lord brought the
disciples into the middle of the Church that is characterized by
the presence of Judas and the necessity of the Lord's suffering;
when confession is instituted, Judas is no longer there. By
rising from the dead and appearing to the disciples the Lord
brings all the members of his Church from their alienation,
flight and denial, their guilt and indifference, back into the
center of his own purity. His appearance itself acts as confession as well as communion, and the word he speaks in
this appearance is both the bestowal of the Holy Spirit (confirmation) and of the power to bind and loose (ordination).
He, however, is the anointed one who died, the one preordained
for death so that as one who died and rose again he unites all the
sacraments in himself as in their source. Marriage is the only
sacrament not yet mentioned explicitly; it lies hidden in the

original mystery between Bridegroom and Bride. The Lord addresses himself expressly to his chosen priests who are to follow him in both life and office. The explicitness of the hierarchy and of the discipleship of the Cross is part of the explicitness of the institution of the sacraments.

Communion and confession stand at the center. Christ himself is communion in the form of his transfigured appearance through which he embodies it. But confession lies at the center of his actions and words and opens up the view of everything else. Communion is what he is, confession what he does.

The visible Church as an institution and the hierarchical element within it manifest a certain character as framework. The sacraments reside in the Church and are mediated by her office as her living content. From the perspective of the framework they, too, admittedly take on aspects of that framework and are in danger of becoming institutionalized. Whoever receives them is aware that he himself must take a step, but it is small compared to what has already been done and what he already finds before him. This is less the case in confession than in the other sacraments. Here it is not enough that a person merely come to church and listen to something or allow something to happen to him. Here his confession, his contrition and his resolution are all required and are required as truth, not as ceremony. Even the reception of confession depends to a far greater extent on his own understanding and reflection than is the case with the other sacraments. There arises a certain state of instability unknown in the other sacraments: one knows that one ought to confess again soon. When? One may have sound reasons for not going again right away. An inner alertness and vitality is necessary to know when the right moment has come, and this already requires a certain Christian maturity and responsibility.

The basic character given the Church by the Lord is an enduring vitality and mobility. And this character has not been bestowed just on the Church as a whole; the individual believers also have a share in it. The Lord became man in order to show us the living nature of the triune God, and the demonstration of this vitality does not end with the Ascension, so that a period of rigid institutionalization follows; it is continued in the vitality of the Church through all ages. This living character is not there for the sake of the framework, but rather the framework is clearly there for the sake of that living element extending through the entire Church into the personal life of each member. This activity manifests itself most clearly in the context of confession, in personal participation in it and in the mutual dependence of Church and believer. Just as the living dialogue with the Father in the Holy Spirit by no means prevents the Son from being a full and perfect man, but rather brings about precisely that perfection, so also a confessing Christian is by no means a diminished person not yet come of age; on the contrary, he is one who has been given adult responsibility. He is as personal and responsible and fully human as the act into which he places himself in order to receive absolution is divine and ecclesiastically institutional.

Original Sin—Confession—Church

The original sin living or active within us gives each of us the predisposition to, facility for and tendency toward actual sin. It often happens that a person resolves to sin no more and falls again anyway, and insight comes to him only afterward; it is as if two egos took turns ruling a person. The one warns him, "Don't do it, it is a sin!" It maintains control as long as the person pays attention to it and takes its advice. But suddenly he turns away from it. Hardly has he prayed, "Lord, I want to do all that you will", when he sinks into a mood of indifference and does precisely what he ought not to do; he forgets the Lord, no longer prays, and loses love for his neighbor. It is as if his love were covered over. When this period of sinful lovelessness with no thought of God is over, the person realizes what it was and regrets it. It is as if a power of evil or a will to indifference were accompanying him. In addition there are a number of sins he commits intentionally, though quite often this predisposition also arises out of a lack of reflection. Basically he does not want to commit them, and yet he does. The flesh is weak because the spirit is not alert enough; it remains alert only if one prays continually. A Christian can know from experience that he finds peace and refreshment in prayer and in reflection upon God; though he knows this, nonetheless he lets it slip again, not as a burden, but out of indifference. He is not concerned. A child who has a jar full of marbles carefully picks up those that fall; he does not think, "One doesn't matter; I have enough." The adult, on the other hand, lets opportunities for prayer pass by; after all, he can always pray at some other time. Often in a particular case one cannot really speak of sin, but merely of lack of interest. Although someone may act like a good Christian who knows and values the "consolations of the Church" and her means of grace, he apparently values one thing above all others: a certain repose of spirit, a certain disinclination to being disturbed or touched, even by grace. Only when the sound of what has fallen from him startles him does he become conscious again of his state of sin, a condition that, in whatever form, always means lovelessness and thus an affront to God.

If someone for some reason had to confess before having had the time and opportunity to forget God again since the last confession, and if for all the world he did not know what to say, nonetheless he would have to admit that even though he did not forget, in a way he really did—he lacked complete alertness and did in fact fall short of the burning demands of grace. This consciousness of falling short would lead one into despair if the grace of confession, the Passion of the Lord and the Church's need for penitence and prayer were not so immeasurable.

Confession has a great many meanings. It does not exhaust itself in the recognition of one's actual sins, their enumeration, the awakening of contrition and the reception of absolution. One of the meanings certainly lies in the insight into the Church's own lack, her need for more, in order in some way to fill out humanity's immeasurable deficit of grace. It is a deficit that is found even in the best people, one that perhaps precisely the best sense most clearly. Yet if we see the Church's enormous neediness, our own neediness is somehow depersonalized into the need to give something to the Church. At this point my own ever-present deficit, associated with original sin, can be revalued as a deficit that stays with me because something was taken from me that benefits the Church. The Church has great need of it, and something must be taken from me so that this gift may be given—though this by no means implies that I now deal with the consequences of original sin as with an indifferent, irrevocable fact and thus increase my own deficit. Quite the contrary, I must try to diminish this indifference so that something is there for the Church to rely upon. What the Church needs is for the discipleship of the Lord to be performed not merely as a kind of triumphal procession but also in toil, sadness and impotence. This insight into our own powerlessness constitutes a small part of humility, because humility in the final analysis does not consist of knowledge; it is more that which the Church gives to the person who knows about his own deficit when the Church accepts his gift. The one praying then opens himself so fully to the Church that there is no more room for reflection upon his own ego. He is, as it were, surrounded by and filled with humility by the Church.

Here again we see that all confession has a social, ecclesial side and that one must oneself be a part of the Church that confesses. The one Church lives and builds herself up through her sacraments. She is by no means only the sum of all Christians or only their order and organization before God.

6. THE PENITENT

False Extremes

Every child learns in preparation for the first confession that he is a sinner and must confess and that everything will not be settled by a one-time confession. He is prepared and trained. He also knows that from the time of his first confession he occupies a special place within the Church and attains a certain maturity as a Christian. At the same time he acquires an obligation, and although he cannot view the entire scope of this obligation, certain moments no doubt reveal something of its essence as an ever-greater challenge. Perhaps the most childlike confessions are among the best, since the child, on the one hand, is aware of his guilt and, on the other hand, experiences his inclusion in something large or even colossal. This experience usually becomes a bit less dramatic later on. The confessions, if they are continued with any regularity at all, gradually lose that element of mystery as regards both sin and the participation in ecclesial life. The adult nonetheless often remains aware that his childhood confessions were the truest, and that with his present degree of insight and perhaps with his loss of self-delusion he needs to try to see the mystery again in a more profound way and to let himself be overwhelmed again by the gift of confession. A good confession, one that has genuinely clarified one's life, has a long aftereffect, not as a memory of things past, but rather as an accompanying presence, a valuable gift that maintains its vitality, a gift that one feels obliged to protect.

Many people admittedly have a relationship with confession that appears as follows. A minimal use of confession is necessary in a completely rational sense that turns this use into a burdensome obligation. When the Church demands the yearly Easter

communion and rests content with an Easter confession, the
mediocre Christian believes that in fulfilling these requirements
he has performed his duty adequately. His practice consciously
or unconsciously has for him the character of insurance. He is
aware of various sins but believes that they are more or less a
part of a normal life, as is the annual cleansing. He does not
want to be overly pious, and he is no saint; he is, however,
prepared to perform this one painful act of humility as long as
it is not required of him too often. He goes to confession with a
kind of cold courage, and it is not as if he does not regret his
sins and does not make a confession that is complete in its own
way. But if he has made this one-time confession the rule, its
after-effect will not be very considerable. This unpleasant act
has one good side; once performed it is over and done with,
and for precisely this reason an after-effect is not even desired.
Confession belongs to the things one does not discuss and
does not even store in one's consciousness. Perhaps this is
particularly a masculine attitude, one that does not understand
the tender mystery of absolution, of its relationship to the
Lord and of the grace that presses to remain active. If confession is only an unpleasant obligation, it acquires a character
of finality; it would be somehow effeminate to "yearn" for it,
to remain open and accessible to what has been received. A
person who thinks like this also shuns or detests any talk about
religion. He speaks as little about it as he does about a small
savings account he might have somewhere. These are private
matters, and the office of the confessor seems so official that
the difference between him and the bank official is inconsiderable. Both perform a function for which in the end the
penitent pays, and both are part of a system of social order. Just
as at year's end one adds up the debits and credits, so one settles
one's account with God and the spiritual official, and then a
new year begins. While the savings account takes care of all
unexpected physical need, confession provides for spiritual
emergencies. One does not expect one's bank to offer any
unexpected dividends; nor does one expect any surprises from

the Church. Everything proceeds within a familiar, fixed, unchangeable framework.

Contrition, also, will correspond to the frugal spirit of such a person. Because confession costs him something, he finds it somehow unpleasant that he really has committed this or that fault. It would be difficult to decide whether he is contrite more because he wants to make an honest confession or because he has offended God. He will not give any great thought to all this, nor probably to love of neighbor or to the tender consideration he owes his wife and child. He examines himself with a kind of dryness and does not let contrition go too far with his bad conscience, since he wants to maintain a certain degree of hardness and principled resolve that he has attained. He expects nothing from the exhortation, which is not one of the essential parts of confession and could just as well be left out. He wants to confess properly, but one should not look too closely at the hand of cards he holds. He does not wish to be pressured by any words or advice to him personally, or to let himself be led anywhere where he is uncomfortable. It is quite possible that earlier he had the experience of taking the confessor's words too much to heart, something that then resulted in difficult situations in his life. Now he wants to be left in peace. He confesses in peace and confesses just as he chooses and as he has planned. His resolutions, if they are even mildly serious, will rather be egoistic in nature. Perhaps he is startled in the middle of his confession and sees that he was farther away than he thought, that he has committed more sins while he thought he had them under control. Then his resolutions will also be rationally calculating: "I cannot afford that anymore, I'll have to watch out. . . ." If confession means insurance to him, then he wants to pay his premium on time, not be overdue, not do anything that might make things difficult when it is time to collect on the premium. Any insurance involves a certain degree of uncalculated risk. Here, if he had sinned too seriously, he would not have been covered by last year's absolution. That must not happen again. The thought suddenly startles him, and he sees that the economic conditions look a bit different than he had imagined.

The confessor feels a certain resignation in regard to these "Easter penitents" and can see them in their numerous variations as the norm of the average sinner. Precisely because he has so little time at Easter and so many people come to confess, he will easily dispense himself from trying any profound conversion experiments. But he really ought to try to hook into them somewhere in such a way that the insurance system collapses. Often in doing so he will encounter rejection. His words are not heard, are understood within these mass-produced confessions as routine measures and only seldom have any after effect.

The other extreme is the person with scruples, who is never done with the consciousness and confession of sin. He, too, can view confession as insurance, but as insurance with whose conditions he is not really familiar. He is fearful because he does not see God's grace; he underestimates grace because he thinks there is such a thing as human sufficiency and adequacy. He overestimates himself because he thinks he is capable of lending his own words the proper weight, whereas God is not able to hear the right thing in an always incomplete, stuttered confession and to make straight what is not straight. He believes one explanation is not enough for God, that every explanation needs further interpretation, and also that he as a penitent is certainly incapable of properly understanding the words of exhortation. Misunderstandings lurk at every corner. He trusts God as little as he trusts himself. In contrast to the Easter penitent, he knows no finality. There is no conclusion. In reality he persists in the position of one who always knows better, one who through the very nature of this one-upmanship repeatedly insists that he has understood nothing and that God can make no use of such a confession. Only with great difficulty, however, can he be brought back to see his main sin, namely, his lack of trust. That he is guilty he knows very well, but even here he knows better and is unable to distinguish the real from the imagined guilt. Hence he slips from one confessional to another and seizes every opportunity to confess, but he is never able to understand and accept absolution as liberation for a new and better life.

How should the confessor treat the scrupulous? If during the first or second confession he is uncertain as to the reason for this scrupulosity, then he had best be generous for a time, since such symptoms can under certain conditions be part of a conversion experience. But if the confessor is certain this is genuine scrupulosity, then only decisive firmness will help, a firmness that never gives in and is coupled with a great deal of kindness. The confession that is a bit too frequent does less damage on the whole than the one that is too infrequent. The appointments should be fixed so that they appear somewhat too frequent to the confessor and somewhat too infrequent to the penitent; the appointments agreed upon should not be missed or changed. Strong emphasis should be placed on God's ever-greater grace. The confession should not be so trivialized that the penitent gets the impression his sin is not being taken seriously. Sin is to be taken seriously in all its forms. Although it may seem paradoxical, the confessor might even enlarge the possible scope of sin even more and thereby show that the penitent need not necessarily have the last word. For this inclination to have the last word manifests itself clearly in the penitent's habit of always having to make an addendum, of referring to earlier confessions and of requesting shorter periods between confessions. Hence it is sometimes better to increase the number and gravity of sins so that the penitent may understand that it is sinful always to claim to be right and repeatedly to relativize the position of the confessor. After the confessor has "adequately examined" sin, however, he must show God's overflowing grace and thereby reserve the last word for himself, since the Holy Spirit is speaking through the office. The final accent must rest on the grace that always surpasses all.

Confessors repeatedly make the mistake of considering a

too-scrupulous person to be too soft. But he is also too hard to the extent that he holds fast to his own insistence that he knows better in such a way that it constitutes a rock-hard resistance. Under certain conditions the confessor might give him a brief, unambiguous written statement to the effect that grace is stronger than everything else. One also might pose the question of the real reason that the penitent confesses, out of love for God or rather perhaps for himself. If he confesses out of love for God—and that is indeed what the penitent wants to claim —then God's overflowing love would be visible to him. Although the confessor must be patient during the confessing of sins, he must draw firm lines in the exhortation.

The healing may come about suddenly, and in that case it is pure grace. But this happens only seldom. It is more usual that it takes place gradually. In general, scrupulosity is a symptom indicating that other things in the person's attitude are not right. Perhaps it is the expression of a genuine neurosis or addiction in which he must continually be concerned with himself, a neurosis that otherwise can find no satisfaction and here at last has found a way to make itself interesting.

In the case of the confessions of such overly scrupulous people the confessor must have as good a memory as possible. One of the maneuvers is to catch the confessor on something inconsequential. As unschematic as the exhortation should be for a normal confession, for this kind of confession it should be as schematic as possible so that the penitent feels reassured by the recurring similarity. It would even be good if the various confessors could pass the word to one another up to a certain point, for the overly scrupulous love to go on to the next confessor if they make no progress with the first, and they should hear the same thing everywhere. Many of the scrupulous change until they find a confessor they can impress, since this motivation plays a considerable role.

But if this excessive scrupulosity is the beginning of a special grace and mission, then the period between the first and second confessions will be decisive. Even if in confession the penitent's self-description is a bit more verbose than the priest would expect, the obedience to grace becomes more visible each time. The readiness for such obedience acquires ever-sharper contours, even if the second confession ends up being more profuse than the first.

The Proper Relationship to Confession

Whoever has recognized that confession is the Lord's unconditional demand and that he instituted it as the fruit of his suffering, whoever tries to be a faithful Christian and to love the Church, will maintain a living relationship to confession. Whenever he thinks of it, he will understand its parts—confession, contrition, exhortation and absolution—as a living unity with a place in his own existence, a place both personal and ecclesial. He will try to guard against seeing the sacrament of confession as a mere means to his own relief and will try to find the proper balance between the serious and light side, between the character of penance and that of joy. He should not only think about the bitter aspect of contrition but should also see the absolution behind it; yet in the joy of that absolution he should not forget how alienated he was and how much reason for penance still remains.

Every Christian is conscious of his sins and errors. He knows them as being specifically his, as emerging almost daily out of his own particular inclinations and weaknesses and out of his lack of alertness and presence of mind. He knows he is capable of even greater sins, even though he commits them only rarely. When he has not been to confession in a long time, he senses that he has strayed. He is able to point to the places where he has erred in greater or lesser degree; even if he has not committed any specific sins, he is aware of his laxity which clearly shows him that he is always able and in a certain sense even prepared to sin and that it is perhaps only a question of some particular protection, grace or lack of the near occasion that has kept him from it. Others who are his brothers have been less favored in this respect; he knows he is in solidarity with them and, in the final analysis, with all sinners. If the "circumstances" of his own life had been the same as those of any other sinner, he would most likely have committed the same sins and crimes. Yet the guilt of the others cannot serve to excuse his own or enable him to view it as a general social phenomenon. On the contrary, it will sharpen his awareness of his own sinfulness and show him, as in a mirror, the things of which he would be capable if he had no protective grace. Something of this "communion of sinners" should become visible in every confession, even though there can be no talk of confessing sins one has not oneself committed or for which one is directly responsible in others by virtue of one's own behavior. Through his own laxity a person sinks ever deeper into the atmosphere of general sinfulness. If he is alert as a Christian, he senses this and feels a heightened need for purification and confession.

It also happens, of course, that a person may fall inadvertently into a serious sin and then go to confession before the appointed time. In this as in the previous case he should always remain aware that the sacrament is anything but an automatic institution and that he is submitting himself to an authority that can bind and loose. He should not forget completely that absolution may for good reasons be withheld. If he does completely forget this, he runs the danger of overlooking the aspect of humility in confession and of setting himself up, to some extent, as the judge of his own sins. In any case, he should always be prepared to do more penance than is strictly prescribed. He is also protected by prayer from the danger of judging himself; the entire preparation for confession should take place in the sphere of prayer. The penitent should examine himself and consider the seriousness of his own guilt, not in his own light, but in that of the Holy Spirit. This is the proper light, and in it his contrition will also be deeper and truly supernatural.

Let him go to confession as humbly as possible and say everything as openly as he can, so that the confessor understands without difficulty what he means and the description of the state of things is not prejudiced in any way. He should accept the exhortation just as openly and try to understand what the confessor tells him. He should so assimilate it that it accompanies and challenges him. After receiving absolution he should say the penance both in humility and thanksgiving, but he should not feel he is a "better person" because of absolution or that he is separated from the communion of sinners. He has been cleansed and strengthened and has returned to the communion of saints, but this does not mean he has withdrawn from his brothers; rather, he has acquired a new, more profound experience of the Church and its catholicity that encompasses all humanity.

When a penitent thinks back on past confessions, he should again view this gift from a balanced perspective of humility and liberation and consider the price the Lord paid for it. The confessional experience should help him become a more alert Christian, reflect more closely on the Lord's own life, and read with more joy the Scriptures, full of confessional motifs and scenes. Like every other sacrament, confession should guide him back to the center of his religion. Let him not believe that all is accomplished with this one confession; it should be rather a ferment that continues to have an effect. For the seed to produce fruit, however, the penitent must also contribute. Confession has led him more deeply into the inner, hidden communion of saints; it is now up to him to let the laws of this communion become visible in his own life.

He should not view confession as a phenomenon that recurs with soul-killing regularity; he is, after all, free to help shape it. He is partly responsible for its proper Christian administration. Yet he is not simply to have control over confession but should let himself be properly instructed regarding it, inwardly by the Holy Spirit and outwardly by the confessor. To do otherwise would be a sign of presumption in the face of the

mystery of the Cross. The Son shows precisely in his openness
to the Father and in his confessional attitude that, in his
orientation toward the Father, he lets himself be guided by
the Spirit and never seeks to control the Father on his own
initiative; yet this does not limit his freedom as the Son. He
himself is one who has been controlled and made use of, all the
way to the abandonment on the Cross.

The frequency of confession can be determined by the
measure of alienation from God that one recognizes if one is
obedient both to the Spirit and to the Church—to the Church
to the extent that she establishes an external order of confession
concerning the days, hours and places when and where one
can confess. This is part of the objectivity of the sacramental
order to which the sinner accommodates himself. If a certain
spontaneity is necessary, one should nonetheless restrain any
excessive self-will or personal "need". By prescinding from
one's own demands and desires one can more effectively align
oneself with the communion of sinners and penitents.

The occasion for confession is one's own sinfulness and
alienation from God and is by no means some sort of sensational
or interesting self-disclosure. No boasting! A childlike spirit,
humility and restraint are necessary. It can happen that someone
feels he cannot hold out until the day after tomorrow when the
general hours of confession are set; it is quite often better not to
press forward at all costs and to consider that under certain
circumstances waiting is a part of salutary penance.

Complete openness notwithstanding, confession also involves a certain discretion. One should confess things just
as one sees them, without any artificial illumination and
without any profound theories about oneself. It can happen
that someone loses the thread of thought during confession
and no longer has everything at his fingertips, that things
come out in a different order or in no order at all, or that
something incidental acquires importance perhaps because
the person is inwardly shaken by the confession or perhaps
because the Holy Spirit wants to push something else into the

foreground. Nonetheless, one should consider oneself bound in obedience to the present confessional regulations and should hold fast to what is there; one should not try forcibly to present things other than in the way one sees them, nor insist inordinately, nor play up or dramatically underscore anything. One should remember that excuses, embellishment and psychological effects are not a part of the confession of sin. Discretion requires that sin be called by its proper name, yet without exaggeration to one side or the other. The priest wants to know what is really at hand; one must not burden him with the product of one's fantasy. Neither ought the sinner to deprecate himself in confession or prostitute himself spiritually. The personal character of sin and confession does not prevent confession from being an entirely objective ecclesial order. If the penitent has an uneasy feeling because what he says is not adequate, it may be that this is simply a result of his most subjective side being accommodated at that moment to the objective sacramental form.

From this perspective written confession is to be discouraged. At most, brief notes may be of use where experience shows that one's memory invariably fails, and perhaps the confessor suggests that one ought to be more precise the next time— whether for the purpose of determining the frequency of sin or of observing its increase or decrease. But if one writes everything down and then just reads what is written, this is no longer a spontaneous confession; one has things literally in hand, presents them as a finished product and then takes them home again afterward. What is written and remains written does not really stand in any living relationship to absolution. Perhaps this constitutes a kind of obstinacy that dulls the event of confession and its grace.

The completed confession yields a fruit: the grace of received absolution, a grace that as their result carries and summarizes within itself all the prerequisites of examination, contrition and confession. Since absolution is pure grace, everything else seems paltry by comparison. Absolution bestows an excess of grace that suffices for the life that follows and, like all grace, is meant to bear further fruit. It was given in order to be passed on. A person coming into contact with it perhaps does not know that it is the grace of absolution; it is enough if it maintains the character of a Christian gift. This grace should be at the disposal of the Church. It comes from the Lord, flows through the Church to the individual, and from him back through the Church to humanity, to every fellow human being in whom the Lord wants to dwell.

The penitent should feel he has been blessed beyond measure with gifts and should behave like the owner of a treasure who can now share it with everyone else. He should show his gratitude particularly to the Church by praying for her and by making her more credible to men by his own behavior.

Belief in the Efficacy of Confession

When the Lord ascends into heaven, it is as if some connection that previously existed were torn asunder. His life on earth among us sinners, his participation in the sinful world, has come to an end. This rupture at the Ascension is a symbol of absolution. We, too, who have been absolved, cease for a moment to be what we were; a connection is torn asunder, a world is left behind us and our souls are freed, for a moment at least, for the ascent to God. The soul no longer knows itself, because the rupture between it and what was is now fully real, because what was once a physical reality interwoven with sinful significance has become unreal and ineffective. We are free with a freedom whose source is the ascending Son, a freedom toward God, better discipleship, becoming a new person. Even if consequences of our sins accompany us, they no longer have the vitality of the sins to which they belong. If we were called by God's judgment to perform more penance for these sins, we could perform it in the spirit of this new existence as children. "The bonds are broken, we are free."

Whoever does not understand this breaking of the cord has misunderstood the primary meaning of confession. Yet it is not our understanding that notices it; it is our loving faith whose visage has been transformed and which enables us to see with new eyes. It opens to us a new awareness of love.

The Lord bore our sins to the Father, and the bearing of this burden brought him death on the Cross. Only in this way was he able to deal with our sins. On Good Friday he held their entire terrible burden once more, and this was the condition that enabled him to experience the lightness of ascension, of a weightless departure to the Father. The Lord gives us the same light, weightless separation in absolution.

How many Christians (priests and religious included) leave the confessional without a trace of elation and relief! They have admitted their small, everyday sins, their disgust, impatience, dissatisfaction, harsh words, all the dust of their daily concerns —petty, paltry things they have confessed because one must, after all, confess. Yet they emerge unchanged because they do not see or do not want to believe the separation of absolution, or have noticed it within the confessional for a minute at most, and then immediately cling again to the disconsolate self-image they have been dragging around with them since time immemorial.

They have not really heard the exhortation, and it is almost as if it were not really addressed to them at all, but merely to an image of them that is then immediately submerged in them again. They sense nothing of the joy of the Ascension, of the joy of being washed that Peter experienced when he wanted to let himself be completely cleansed by the Lord during the washing of feet. For many people confession is merely an annoyance.

For lay people in the world this annoyance is often the general annoyance or irritation with their existence, their chosen path, their narrow unchangeable circumstances. They see the image of their existence as Christians less clearly than do priests and religious; they do not see what is possible for them, where their own sin obscures what is possible, how this image has to endure and the directions in which it can grow. This is what depresses them and what they cannot cast off in confession.

Religious can see this image more clearly on the basis of their Rule. This Rule—through the spirit it embodies and the path it points out—of necessity strengthens the joy in the religious. The Rule already contains the rupture, the separation from the sinful world through the Ascension. Yet this Rule is meant to be lived, striven for and above all attained by confession. That is what so many forget, and that is why the Rule appears so barren and spiritless to them—if it still appears to them at all, if they see at all that the Rule presents itself to them anew with its entire rending power in every confession, so near and real that they need only to reach for it in order for it to transport them up into heaven.

7. TYPES OF CONFESSION

The Confession of Conversion

Two kinds of conversion confessions are possible. Their main characteristic is that grace does not manifest itself only within the narrower temporal confines of confession itself, but rather transforms the entire life of the penitent, reveals the luke-warmness of his entire past, convinces him of the absolute necessity of a transformation from the ground up and always stands within the context of an explicit personal mission.

The first possibility is that a person is seized by grace during confession itself, by an extremely demanding grace that with lightning-like suddenness throws everything into a new light. If this grace is genuine, it is experienced as having robbed the penitent of all rights and taken him totally into its service. It has an abruptness and indivisibility that will not adapt itself to the circumstances, but rather demands a new life free of compromises. The confessor usually perceives this grace as clearly as the penitent, and he understands that he, too, is challenged to take it seriously and to assume the guidance of the penitent according to the intentions of this grace. There are many conversion confessions in which a special mission becomes apparent; indeed, these are the rule. There are others, however, in which what is newly revealed needs to be examined, ordered and shaped, and in which one's state of life in the Church is already a given. This first kind of conversion confession needs no special preparation; it strikes one like lightning, and one cannot say to what extent one's previous life either helped or hindered it. A hardened sinner can be struck as easily as someone who has been striving after perfection. This is the grace that struck Saul on the road to Damascus.

The second form is less abrupt; one can anticipate it, solicit it through prayer and request it. The penitent may have spent a great deal of time preparing himself for such a confession, and may have regarded it as specially significant for some inner reason, or also for external reasons: for example, that he has the opportunity to confess to a well-known confessor to whom particular grace and illumination in the confessional is attributed. The penitent will then formulate everything so carefully and will bring together so many things that it becomes clear that he is hoping this confession will bring about a major life decision and in a certain sense even a conversion and transformation. He is sick of his indifferent life, and he somehow senses that things have to change completely. He poses the question, expressly or parenthetically, with such intensity that the confessor is able to penetrate into the living element, and the grace of God, through him, stills the yearning for rebirth. In this form of conversion confession it is even more advisable than in the first form for the priest to concern himself with the penitent later; more has been anticipated and prepared in advance, and it is possible that the penitent may be tempted unsuspectingly to view this grace that apparently has seized him as a product of his own imagination or of an earthly hope, a hope so intense that it has extraordinary expectations and has difficulty adapting when only small changes are demanded.

In a conversion confession the behavior of the confessor and penitent is strikingly different than in normal confessions. For a while, at least, it will seem providential that precisely this penitent met this confessor. The latter should not let this situation pass without making a few essential decisions concerning the future, and, if possible, making an appointment to see the penitent again, whether for another confession or a meeting outside the confessional. The conversion confession may well be the only one which merits being a point of reference later. Although exceptions are possible, one need not in that case refer to the confession of sin itself, but rather to the grace of confession, particularly if the penitent has an insufficient experience of grace and if the result might thus appear improbable in the light of daily life and the demands of grace appear impossible. He becomes suspicious, and that moment of grace may appear to him to have been mere false enthusiasm. Often, however, grace causes mundane circumstances to recede into the background precisely so that it may be accepted. It alone is essential; everything else is oriented toward it and must appear secondary the moment grace shows itself. From the perspective of the one receiving the grace, who is totally immersed in it, this grace may seem so overwhelming that he believes himself to be capable of overcoming all hindrances. This is why it is absolutely essential that the experience of a good confessor be brought into play to provide guidance. In addition, because the confessor was the witness and participant in that decisive hour of grace, the penitent quite naturally will usually continue to see him in connection with it and in a subsequent confession or discussion will encounter no difficulty in letting himself be advised and guided by him.

The penitent leaves the conversion confession as a transformed person. Since this transformation, like every other less noticeable one, belongs to the Church and is to be administered or guided by it, just as are all effects of grace, the confessor needs to exchange a word or two with the penitent about it. The latter may be as one intoxicated by grace and beside himself, so that he no longer knows how to behave. This new thing may appear so overwhelming that he does not believe himself capable of assimilating it. He is then liable to take this experience to the wrong place, where someone will try to talk him out of it by every means possible, or where there is some other threat to which he is not equal, and in that case, instead of the gain, only a correspondingly greater loss would be left behind: the experience of a great, unheeded grace, a discarded treasure.

The grace of confession has an indivisibility which the penitent must learn to see, although to a certain extent he must handle it prudently. He must not waste it in unimportant, small actions and must try to accommodate himself to grace rather than it to himself. Neither should he try to attain everything at once, by dismembering the grace so that at least something will take place. He should steadfastly let himself be initiated into the wholeness of the gospel and know that conversion continues to be a daily challenge, whereas much of what was part of that conversion experience will not repeat itself. He should know that he does not have the right to expect this same tangible level of grace from subsequent confessions; this does not, however, allow him to become more distant from one confession to another or from one conference to another, as if he possessed a kind of security that things will be filled out again, as if the conversion experience has given him a kind of right to repetition. This is probably where it is most necessary that the one confessing learn complete humility; this humility should immediately be transformed into obedience to the confessor—an obedience that for the moment is not to be reinforced by a vow but rather taken for granted as a matter of tact, of reverence, of something independent of the persons involved.

The one confessing experiences the grace of conversion as "his own", and yet it is meant for the Church; her official representative is its witness who then takes it into the Church's jurisdiction. The one who receives the grace is put into a position from which he can better serve, and yet he is actually one who has been freshly bound and given into the service of God and the Church. The experience did not happen to him personally so that he could go through the world proclaiming it and acting ostentatiously like someone who has been "converted". The fruit of this "private" experience belongs completely to the Church; rather than lifting the one blessed with this grace out of the "communion of saints", it actually places him directly in it for the first time. Of course, "you will recognize them by their fruits"—not recognize the person, but rather the Church that becomes visible in him. What others want to see is not the experience but its result. This result will no doubt always be less than what is demanded, but this "beneath" should nonetheless always be a "within." The one converted remains the "poor devil" encountered by grace who all his life will run after its excessive demands; and the more he does this, the less the real standard will remain in his own hands. His confessor should not discourage him, of course, but he should nonetheless recognize the demands of grace from the very beginning; as long as they are illuminated by the radiance of the experience, they will perhaps be more easily accepted and fulfilled.

Since the grace came with confession, it will to a certain extent maintain a reference to confession in one's subsequent life. An inner bond leads from one confession to another, just as confession itself comes from the Church and returns to her. This can mean various things. Whoever has been converted during confession must in any case be particularly careful with his own confessions; he must know that he has encountered the God of the grace of conversion, and that if indeed God has acquired this particular character for him, he must respond to God within this revealed character. This may manifest itself fully by his confessing with particular attentiveness, or it may be that he has an apostolic mission to smooth out the path to confession for others, perhaps even to speak about it or to come up with decisive formulations concerning it. The question arises of whether many ought not first to seek and strive for this kind of confessional mission. Even if it is indeed a confessional mission, one must under certain circumstances struggle to discover what it is in detail. If the former has become clear, the latter will definitely clarify itself in prayer.

General Confession

Three motivating factors can prompt a general confession. The first, the personal factor, lies within the person who confesses. He wishes to conclude his entire past and effectively summarize all the conclusions that should have lain in his previous confessions; he wishes to draw a line, to open himself to the confessor in such a way that the latter can see his whole life and in turn offer guidance for that whole life. The second motivating factor can reside in the confessor. He has a penitent whom he feels he should guide differently or further (such a wish is always associated with a certain guidance), but until now he has only seen excerpts from the penitent's life; he needs greater clarity and deeper insight. The third motivating factor is entry into a religious order. The new state of life demands a comprehensive act of conclusion, and the new obedience a complete opening-up.

During a general confession one must pay particular attention to one element, even more than in normal confessions: namely, that one let the sins one wishes to confess keep the same character they had for the conscience at the time they were committed. Two dangers lurk here. The first is that if I have recently made an effort to lead a life according to the will of God, I may no longer want to admit in confession what once was but would rather see it in a smaller, revised and no longer really commensurate form. Or I lend too much significance to certain laudatory and encouraging evaluations of my life, evaluations that cannot adequately do justice to my past. Consciously or unconsciously, I also would like to influence the confessor by downplaying the past. The other danger is that I do just the opposite. Perhaps made insecure by an impending decision or out of resignation before my present fate, I depict the past as so burdensome and inhibiting that it becomes clear nothing good can become of me. This may be a maneuver intended to silence the inner quiet of my conscience or of the voice of God within.

An example of the first type would perhaps be a person who wishes to enter a monastery, but whose instability causes his spiritual director to have second thoughts. The penitent thus makes a general confession that is to prove to this director (and to himself) how his life has run in a straight line toward this goal. An example of the second type would be someone who has committed some terrible sins in moment of folly and wants to show either himself or the confessor that it is impossible that he really is called, and that one must be content that he simply is the way he is. "You will be appalled when you see how I really am; be content with what you have been able to accomplish!"

If every confession should be objective, this is particularly true for a general confession. Otherwise the temptation would be too great to justify oneself in one direction or the other, to seek some ad hoc reassurance no longer based on the truth. On the other hand, a general confession should not give rise to the appearance, from the perspective of the one confessing, of a final, irrevocable reckoning. Otherwise a new danger arises: Pharisaism. One comes to terms with one's fate and can enumerate and survey one's sins. During every preparation for confession one must spend some time examining one's sins; in the midst of the Church one sinks into a kind of loneliness that might end up being prolonged in an unhealthy way in the case of general confession. One might misuse the period of self-examination by prolonging it inordinately and thereby withdrawing from the life of the Church, trying to create a kind of personal security that in reality can only be found within the Church's life. In any case, this period must be accompanied by increased prayer, eliminating any suggestion of Pharisaic self-importance.

The essential part of the general confession is really the confession itself, not an ad hoc formulated "self-demonstration". Perhaps an earlier serious sin has acquired the character of a "story" or extended anecdote in the course of time. Now, however, it must not be a "story", but rather a sin one admits. The general confession is a means of grace which seeks to let a person experience—in all three cases mentioned—the grace of confession in a deepened, comprehensive form.

If the penitent feels the need for a general confession, it is because he has the impression of having gotten out-of-joint in some way and cannot shake the feeling that somewhere in his past he has taken a wrong turn; he does not want to delude himself into thinking that he alone can put things back in their proper order. He seeks this reordering from the grace of God, and would like to unfold and present his entire life so that he can come naked before God and the Church and accept in complete humility and childlike confidence what is said and demanded. An immense Christian hope can reside in this desire for a general confession.

If it is the confessor who expresses this wish for a general confession, it will be prompted by similar motives but from the opposite direction. The penitent is like a question God has posed for him, one he is unable to answer completely because certain reference points are missing. It may also be that he knows something about the penitent's previous life, but before he can get any further he would like to know what the penitent's own position is concerning it, how the penitent confesses it. Or he would like to examine the spirit in which the penitent accepts the new humiliation which a general confession involves. A confessor who asks for a general confession, however, obligates himself to the penitent to a larger extent than to the ordinary penitent. He will likewise deal somewhat differently with both the exhortation and the required penance and adapt both to the singularity of this event of grace. In a general confession he has requested he will act as he would during a conversion confession. He is more deeply involved, accepts more responsibility before God and must be more aware of what he is doing. He will usually ask more questions during a general confession than at other times since he must examine the effects of the humiliation, of the love of truth and of the penitent's care in making the confession. In doing so he will always have to take into consideration the remoteness of the sins confessed and feel his way back to the point of the original true contrition and confession. The truth must shine through at every point. A general confession looks directly at the Lord's Cross and presupposes the willingness to encounter it in all its fullness—with more willingness, more nakedness, more submission than at any other time.

Whenever the general confession is required by the novice master before someone's entrance into an order, as is usually the case, it must be adapted to this entry and to the character of the order concerned. Both the penitent and the confessor must attempt to come closer together. The former must remain aware that in this position within an order he will encounter a new objectivity that is probably quite different from the objective self-consciousness he previously possessed. In addition, this general confession of the novitiate must be performed in the spirit of obedience that conceals nothing and reveals everything without allowing itself to imbue things with its own accent or significance. The confessor will listen in the spirit of the order; his exhortation and subsequent guidance should point out the areas where the order requires changes to be made, and he should not hesitate to humiliate the novice and, as it were, to bring him down to point zero. "*This* fault has no place in the order!" At this point the penitent will still be full of willingness and not yet be "rusted shut" within the "security of the order". It is essential to use this moment in order to penetrate as deeply and as decisively as possible. The penitent should not get the impression that he is being humiliated intentionally but should perceive the whole process as simple truth and necessity. The general confession is not an "exercise for the novitiate" or an "experiment" but is rather the expression of his own intention to begin a new life for God.

Once the general confession has been made—in whatever form—the penitent should not have the feeling that he should have said things differently and will indeed do so at the next opportunity. It must have a certain character of finality, as regards both the confession itself and the new disclosure of grace. This general confession really was grace, and the penitent has received it as such. If he should repeatedly come back to his confession, this would block the path of grace. To want to confess again immediately after a decisive confession would be a misuse of the sacrament; it would place the emphasis on the act of confessing and on what the human person has accomplished, instead of on God's grace.

Finally, there is the general confession within the context of the Spiritual Exercises. Here confession functions within the overall process of such Spiritual Exercises, and these receive the emphasis. The Exercises are intended to help a person attain a Christian form of life in the light of a deepened recognition of God's ways, within which the Christian should let God determine his individual path. This all takes place in a kind of expansion of the loneliness experienced and needed by every person who confesses, apart from daily life and removed from its obligations and involvements, in an environment attuned to the significance of these few days, a sphere of prayer. Nonetheless, the exercitant is not left alone. He is accompanied and instructed by an experienced priest who knows how to give the Spiritual Exercises and is familiar with their effect; this priest is also accessible as a confessor and advisor and is ready for any dialogue. One thus confesses and finishes with one's old life, though not while still in it. Instead, this takes place in an atmosphere of quiet, of listening to the word of God, of the daily holy Mass, in the middle of the sacramental life to which confession also belongs. Not only does the exercitant prepare for this confession by examining himself, the confessor also contributes by presenting in a new, penetrating objectivity the true nature of sin, its seriousness and its frequency. This objectivity is so powerful and untouchable that no other choice remains than to come to terms with it. This acquaintance with the reality of sin should shape the subsequent confession. That is the main reason why it is advisable to make a general confession during this period so that one no longer judges and evaluates according to one's own, necessarily limited, perspective, but from the perspective of the limitless realities of sin and grace as they both stand before God's gaze.

The common understanding of "mortal sin" is destroyed. One reads about theft and murder in the newspaper but never imagines that one might ever have anything to do with them. One sees one's own sins as biographical facts within one's own existence, facts resulting like everything else from sufficient causes and about which psychological or other kinds of theories might be developed. At the beginning of the Exercises, however, one becomes acquainted with sin completely independent of one's own evaluation, with complete objectivity and yet completely in reference to one's own responsibility. The sinner must recognize that Christ bore his sins on the Cross and that they were terrible enough to kill him, the purest man of all, the God-man. Christ's relationship to sin makes his relationship to the sinner visible in a completely new fashion, and this fundamentally influences the latter's view of his own existence. My relationship to Christ is renewed; it reveals what he as the Redeemer has done for me and what he signifies, and reveals further the relationship that he, as the world's Redeemer, has to the Father. The first leads to the second, and the second to a third, namely, entrance into a discipleship of the Cross-laden Lord as the practical result of the confession associated with these Exercises. This discipleship, however, will remain fundamentally determined by the first and second elements, by the way I am represented in the dialogue between the Redeemer and the Father. The confession during the Exercises is vertically open and is extended into the trinitarian sphere; the intimacy of the mystery of confession between sinner and Redeemer is as if ripped open—in the "triple colloquy"—into an open realm that on the one hand includes Mary–Church and on the other Father–Spirit. The exercitant stands in this realm initially as a sinner, and what emerges in the Second, Third and Fourth Weeks of the Exercises will be decisively influenced by this initial situation.

The judgment and superior knowledge one has of one's own sin is taken away. One stands face to face with a reality one can no longer subdivide for the sake of controlling it and coming to terms with it. If the miracle of a vocation is still possible in spite of everything, it will have to be just that: miraculous. All that is said means much more precisely because the words between the Father and the Son, words in which sin is spoken of, themselves mean fundamentally more than we understand or even suspect. Nothing hollows a person out more than does this confession, so that, having been "disposed of", one can begin to realize the meaning of the meditations on the life of Christ. Even though I as a sinner am inconsiderable, the miracle has occurred that God considers me in spite of everything. The normal confession extracts from the melon only water and seeds; the confession during the Spiritual Exercises extracts all the flesh as well, so that only the husk is left, into which one later places a candle in order to make a lantern. The grace of initiation into the life of the Lord is essentially the grace of absolution. It lives completely from the double event of confession: joy from fear, fear which changes to joy. The darkness of my own self-recognition in the light of the Lord becomes the light in which I view the darkness of the Redeemer's existence unto the Cross. From within confession there thus emerges a new connection between one's own life and the gospel, a connection generating a new sensibility for the decisive Christian experiences one encounters upon returning to normal life. In its effect the confession during the Exercises resembles the conversion confession, since it, too, creates new postulates for one's whole existence. In a conversion confession it is above all the experience of the grace of conversion itself that generates these postulates; in the confession during the Spiritual Exercises it is the opportunity to let this confessional experience echo and soar in the experience of the life of Christ. Although the result is in the latter case perhaps less radiant than in the former, under certain conditions it may prove to be more lasting.

After the Cross the Lord's first gift to the assembled Church was confession. Then he spent forty days initiating the disciples into the meaning of the Scriptures and of the order of salvation before finally sending them out into all the world. The Spiritual Exercises are patterned after this activity of the risen Lord.

The Devotional Confession

The confession during the Spiritual Exercises occupies a special position within Christian life because the meditations and conferences during these Exercises influence it so strongly. The devotional confession also involves guidance. The sinner does not seek it out as much for the sake of cleaning house and putting things in order as for maintaining himself within a particular sphere, one that always demands a certain degree of purity, in order to pray and sacrifice according to the intentions of the Church. This confession has less the intention of releasing the sinner from the communion of unpardoned sinners than of making him better able to live among these sinners and to participate in their lives. Anyone who wanted to make a devotional confession only to be absolved *for himself* in order to feel more pure would already be a Pharisee, one who cannot stand to see himself burdened with sins and errors or—especially—to be considered a sinner like others. Such a person repeatedly calls attention to the special nature of his own path and creates distance between himself and sinners. The Christian devotional confession must include the desire to participate in a more intimate fashion in the lot of sinners, even to allow the grace of absolution to come to those who either do not know confession or do not practice it and likewise to obtain as much grace as possible for others by means of frequent, even daily, communion. One's own ego must be so objectified that it no longer offers a hindrance to the grace flowing through it.

A person who rises early every day in order to go to Mass and receive the Lord and who perhaps makes a daily meditation or spiritual reading will probably feel the need to keep himself as pure as possible so that he can assume the responsibility that such actions involve. To be sure, whoever did this only for himself would probably consider that his condition was good enough for him and that God could be satisfied with him, since he would have been included in the category of the pious and zealous. But as soon as he recognizes the apostolic responsibility inherent in such actions he knows for certain that the way he is will not be sufficient for his actions, that the actions unconditionally demand a higher purity and that it is simply his obligation to purify himself. If he does it only for himself, in his own eyes his inattentiveness, or lack of reverence and so forth, will be balanced out simply by the fact that he does it at all. But someone who is there for the sake of others, the Church and the world, will be expected precisely by the world and the Church—who have a claim on him—to do something considerable and effective, something that does not end in ineffectiveness because lack of reverence or the force of indifferent habit outweighs the "merit".

The devotional confession must be an especially humble confession precisely because it claims to be an act of *devotio*. Precisely here the power of binding and loosing must be considered with greater seriousness. And because absolution is viewed here so much in its function as regards the larger whole, one must be sure that one has no claim to it as such; the sword of Damocles—the possibility of being "bound"—must hover above the one confessing.

The devotional confession also demands a special attitude on the part of the confessor not only insofar as he must take it extremely seriously but also because he must assure that the penitent always perceives it as humiliation. If this confession is supposed to have the character of a sacrifice, then it should be given that form. It could be that a large percentage of those practicing devotional confession are reasonably satisfied with themselves and would cease the practice if it were made a bit more strict. These penitents must also be advised to practice a particular kind of discretion; because they are easily convinced that they are not very great sinners, they like to boast a bit about the frequency of their confessions. They are not among those who are able to go on for years without a confession, who wait until they have a store of coarse sins gathered together! And then in the confessional they act as if they could not bear it any longer that they were irreverent two days ago!

It is difficult and almost a work of art to make a devotional confession faultlessly: actually an art for saints, to make it through the straits between the Pharisaism of a consciousness of purity and that of the scrupulous consciousness of sin. The frequency of confession almost of necessity brings with it a certain psychological dulling, whereas the nature of confession ought to effect just the opposite, namely, a deepening of one's insight into sin, a deepening which is necessary in order to maintain the vitality and freshness of the act of confession time after time. The absolute honesty demanded disappears most easily from the devotional confession; it should not be merely an "exercise of penance", but rather a humiliation experienced in a fresh and more profound way each time. To avoid slipping into a distorted condition, one needs the proper preparation in which one convinces oneself of the seriousness of one's own situation. A person cannot confess if from the very beginning he sees a chasm between himself and sin. He must be completely and truly convinced that he belongs to the realm of sin.

The confessor must view everything from the perspective of the Son and the Holy Spirit and bring this perspective to expression in his own words without letting his own mediocrity, indifference and weary forbearance manifest themselves in the slightest. Although among normal penitents there are a great many who no longer expect anything from confession, anyone who decides to make a devotional confession does so with great hope and expectation. He perceives it as a service intended for the Lord and his Church, and the confessor must keep this consciousness of service alert in the name of the Son and the Holy Spirit and concern himself with the manner of service.

The Confession of Priests

The priest occupies a special position in the Church, situated at a rationally indeterminable point between the institutional element and the living event of the sacraments that are dispensed and received. He is at the same time the concentration of the community to a unity that is bestowed and shaped from above and that emerges from below. This also defines his confession as a sinner, as a sinning priest. He stands as a sinner like every other before the ecclesiastical authority and owes it confession and responsibility. On the other hand, that authority has been entrusted to him personally, and as such it is up to him as a person to show himself worthy of this office. This situation characterizes him fully; he does not have in addition, as religious do, a Rule and a spirit of the order to shape and support him and give him a sense for exactly what the religious community, in the name of the Church, expects of him. On the basis of this mediating Rule the religious is able to see the discrepancy between the ideal and reality much more concretely and emphatically. The Rule is almost an adequate confessional mirror for him. The realm in which the secular priest is able to move according to his own judgment is broader; he can form his own opinion about many things (whether it is justified or not) and can lend this opinion official weight; and, if he becomes neglectful, he can obscure his own sins with views he has formed himself. Depending on the circumstances his sin can be either the collapse or the successful maintenance of such opinions.

Like many religious, the priest is accustomed to hearing confessions himself and to giving absolution. Whereas all sins can be interpreted as transgressions against the one commandment of love, generally a priest's sins will not be similar to those of ordinary penitents, and to the extent they are determined by his milieu they may even be extremely different.

Sins within the community result to a large extent from an inadequate defense of faith: one misses Mass and the sacraments, forgets to pray, develops a fear of others, misses the opportunity for apostolic activity, pursues forbidden pleasures. Because of his office, his official obligations and his outward clerical dress, the priest is to a large extent protected from this kind of thing. His sins arise when he puts too much trust in collar and cassock; he thinks he has already accomplished something simply because he wears them. He also may have turned away from his fellow men; the rectory and his association with his colleagues seem like a kind of protective wall to him, and not much can happen to him behind it. His official functions are so organized that in time they may cloud his vision of God's ever-present preeminence that addresses and concerns him in an extremely personal fashion. He may completely lose his sense for what priestly sanctity should be and completely barricade himself behind his external vocational activity.

His position as confessor gives him access to an incredible source of grace, precisely for his own confession. If he hears confessions with genuine alertness, he will be sharpening his own understanding of what sin really is; for he must not merely listen to the confession itself but also evaluate and answer the questions of that confession. He needs only to keep his eyes open to perceive in his penitents both that which is worthy of imitation and that which should be avoided. His penitents are God's gifts of grace to him. Even if the faults in their state of life are different from his own, both of them— priest and penitent—must coincide in their Christian attitude. He thus really does not need to imitate the confession of those entrusted to him, but he should always encounter something for himself in their attitude, not a jumble of wildly different attitudes, but rather the unity of his own confessional attitude, just as Christ had his own unified attitude before the Father. Here the effect of the communion of saints on its official representatives and pastors is particularly noticeable, more so than during the administration of the other sacraments. It is this communion of saints that prevents the priest from imitating the attitude of each individual; he can and must understand the attitude of each from the perspective of the communion of saints and refer it to this communion.

He may encounter a situation in which a penitent confesses quite properly, and yet something is not right with the person. He is confessing in some way only for himself, not within the communion of saints. In this case the priest must return the penitent to this communion. Yet the priest, too, should act correspondingly when he himself confesses by giving his preparation, confession, contrition and resolution the perspective of this communion of saints.

The Son, while on earth, maintains a confessional attitude before the Father and draws his fellow men—his emerging Church—closer and closer to this attitude. He does this most clearly in the prayer on the Mount of Olives when he asks the disciples to stay awake and be there with him. Although one usually sees only that the disciples failed, one should notice above all that the Lord wanted to see them participate in his suffering. It is a matter of redemption, the imminent institution of confession! The Son invites the representatives of the Church to pray and suffer with him, to be active at his side in instituting the sacrament of redemption in a way that transforms them into initiates already and, when his suffering begins, enables them to experience it more profoundly, more personally and at the same time more officially. He does not require them to confess their sins with him now, before the sacrament has been instituted, but he would like to take them along and be accompanied by their wakeful prayer. This is an extremely tender binding of the office to the Lord's Passion. At this moment the Lord is the official priest and the disciples, as it were, the Church, the communion of saints. Whenever a priest asks his congregation to pray for him, he is unconsciously doing something similar to what the Lord did before his suffering. Priests very often do not take this request for prayer before the Holy Mass and at other occasions (*commendo me*) literally. This request, however, is repeatedly expressed in conjunction with the Lord, who would not have wanted to abandon, but rather to endure, his suffering among his own, something that would have been an infinite enrichment of Christian life for those who experienced it with him. When a priest prepares himself for confession and afterwards carries out the penance, he is in a similar situation. He should put into practice what it means both to give and to receive something genuinely alive by means of his confession, to lend to his personal confession features of the confession of community and Church so that he can simultaneously give to the confession of community and Church something of the grace of his own act of confession.

This is perhaps above all a matter of prayer. The priest can entreat his people to pray for him, but it would be indiscreet to ask them to pray for his confession. The Lord, too, only made a general request, "Watch and pray!" and announced to them that the hour was coming. He did not consider asking them "to make up for what was still lacking in his own suffering". There is a sphere of tender silence, but since this sphere is disclosed before God, the confessing priest should ask God and his heavenly court to view his confession in connection with the community entrusted to him; this, he hopes, will enable him to confess in some way with his flock in a representative fashion and will enable them to participate in his confession. If he considers the tender relationship between the Lord and his disciples on the Mount of Olives, much could become more tender, true and loving, in the sense of the communion of saints, in his relationship to his own community.

The community should know something of this mystery and should be present, concealed by the veil of the mystery; as the shepherd, so also the flock. They should take seriously the "Priest's Saturday" on which one prays for good priests, not just for the coming ones but for the ones now in office and in particular for their confession. Saturday is the day of confession and of the priest, and in this way one is able to unite one's own confession with the prayer for the priest in a living fashion.

The confessions the priest hears are much more numerous than his own. While listening to confessions he hears the most varied and at times most serious sins, ones that startle him and perhaps have an enduring influence on him. There is, of course, the grace of office that protects him in this respect, but he must deal properly with it. On the one hand he should not employ its objectifying power as a kind of trick by which he pushes away everything he has heard so that he need know nothing more of it, simply locking the office door in order to be left alone. On the other hand he should not immerse himself dangerously in what he has heard. In order to strike the proper balance here he must look at the Son and his relationship to the Father. The unique Son has become the Son of Man and has been depersonalized in the generality of human existence; but this individual man, looking up to the Father, is at the same time personalized as the unique Son of God. He has become flesh and has to defend this flesh against the world, but he does so as one who perpetually offers this same flesh to the Father in his service of redemption. He is continually gathering himself together in order to give perpetually of himself, of his flesh and blood. He defends himself against the world so that he may be collected for the Father and let himself be scattered into all the world by the Father and in the Father's will. The Father desires that the Son be this individual flesh that remains intact in the face of the world no matter how intensely it gives itself to the world. In giving his own flesh he must have the experience of incarnate existence, not in such a way that he succumbs within it and becomes tainted, nor in such a way that he feels elevated above it and closes himself off. The real priestly situation of the Son is found where the Son is both a body surrendered in suffering and in the sacrament and the unique Son of the Father in human form. And that is also the position of the priest who must administer the confession of those entrusted to him, yet must himself confess and embody before the Father in a single totality both the complete authority and the complete submission to confession. He gathers confessions, but he scatters them as well by confessing along with his penitents, by intervening in their confessions as penitent and by rounding out the confessional sacrifice of his penitents through his own sacrifice. Wherever it may appear that he stands above confession, there he as a genuine priest must stand under it; he washes the feet of the Lord's disciples.

The penitent comes as a person and experiences the official authority within the confessional; the priest comes as the representative of the office and must enter into the personal realm. As a priest he can do this only if he is intact in his own existence as a person; only thus can he infuse the official aspect with a personal element. At Cana the Lord offered the best wine; it would have sufficed for the miracle if it had been any wine at all or if the water had taken on that taste of wine. What the Lord offers beyond that is an expression of his own personal standard; he knows what good wine is, and this is the wine he wants to give. The priest should administer confession similarly so that the very best emerges from within it, and thus he must become ever more personal according to God's intentions so that he may fructify the office in a more enduring fashion.

In this way he will avoid treating all his penitents alike and thereby too perfunctorily, will avoid forcing upon them his own manner of confession and instead will allow each his own personality, freedom and uniqueness. In each one he should concentrate, collect and strengthen the personal element so that each may give more fruitfully of himself in love. The confessor will encounter no greater danger than that of becoming too perfunctory both in hearing confession and in his own confessing. In the course of time one runs the risk of viewing a sin which one once clearly recognized as such only as an old, familiar, recurring error and, finally, only as formula that one presents in every confession, but without seeing and feeling any longer the concrete relationship between the fact and the word used to describe it.

In a word, the priest has authority as a confessor and is under authority as a penitent, and he runs the risk of overlooking his own subjection to authority because of his authoritative function. He escapes this danger by keeping in mind the Son's attitude; the Son defends his own personal element over against humanity in order to keep it accessible to the Father for the world. For the priest this "self-defense" of the personal element means staying alive; he must be *this* man and not an admixture of functions and things he has heard. And if necessary he must be *this* sinner before God and not a compromise composed of all the absolutions of his penitents' sins.

The Confession of Religious

The confessional situation of religious is characterized by two things that one can discover from the Lord's encounter with the rich young man. The first is that the Lord defines perfection, and this ideal of perfection hovers before every order. The second is that the rich young man does not follow and thus fails in his relationship to the Lord. All confessions in the religious state are situated somewhere in this tension between the ideal that is established and the reality that falls short. One knows what would be required and knows equally—not just theoretically or philosophically—that reality always falls short of the ideal. Finally, one knows quite concretely that the first person who came to the Lord in the Gospel with the desire for perfection refused to travel the path shown to him. The memory of this refusal should accompany all religious into confession. Confession demonstrates to them ever anew what the Lord requires of them and how they must admit that they have not done justice to it. This unconditional and sober knowledge casts them into humility from the very beginning, a humility proper to the order, which surrounds them during their entire lives and in which they must live and above all confess.

The confession of the individual should accommodate itself to the structure of this humility within the spirit of the order in question and be personal within that spirit. This generates a new tension between the personal sin the religious sees and has committed and the sinfulness of the order which as a whole falls short of Christ's demands. Similarly, the religious state itself from the beginning carries onward through the ages the burden of the rich young man's failure; and this second failing does not diminish but makes even more grievous the sin of the individual who participates in it. Thus a third failure emerges, the failure of the individual to the extent that he is a member of the order, his personal failure in matters concerning the ideal of the order, a failure more or less coinciding with his personal sin.

The founding of an order always embodies a particular aspect of the imitation of Christ, yet even the highest idealism during its foundation cannot get beyond the rich man's failure. From the very first day the order is burdened with the weight of those who have not obeyed the call of the Lord and of those who, although they have come and know him, do not really follow him. This is quite unnerving. The Lord shows what Christian perfection is, and already the first candidate has said No. Every person who founds a way of discipleship and imitation is already burdened with the original situation we see in the Gospel itself. It is a proto-Christian situation: the Lord discloses an unprecedented opportunity, and the gift is rejected. What unnerves one even further is that, even after the order is founded, it can never free itself completely from the ballast that pulls down the rich young man; the challenge is such that every individual and every generation discovers the rich young man again in itself and in addition knows that an indeterminably large number of people who have received a call have not come.

Hence one confesses in recognizing that one is carrying

those who do not confess at all, and that the line of demarcation between the two cannot be sharply drawn. For the one not confessing is the religious himself, since he never gives all that is required and never keeps the Rule as it is meant to be kept, and because his vows give him an appearance contradicting his real existence. Here, too, one cannot sharply distinguish what is the order's inadequacy and what is one's own inadequacy. For the order has also made concessions; it has not maintained the original fire. Yet every member shares the guilt of this demise—so that finally the life of the order consists of this impossible, contradictory synthesis between the Lord's own word and the non-word or refusal of the rich young man. This refusal, of course, came after the young man had inquired, for he could not find peace until he knew the word of the Lord had been spoken!

One sees how much the religious life exists to bear a particular burden. One can explain both the contemplative and the active religious life from the perspective of this confessional attitude of bearing such a burden. The contemplatives are those who bear this situation by means of their lives, and the actives are those who try to change it by demonstrating the urgency of the call of the Lord.

Whoever speaks of religious life by definition refers to a life that chooses the confessional attitude as the attitude of life, a life that follows the call to discipleship though it will experience more and more intensely the continual increase of the challenge and thus also the continual increase of its own failure. The rich young man wanted to follow in discipleship, and only then did it seem too difficult to him; because he wanted to, the Lord opened the way for him. To those religious who remain willing, the Lord will not cease—in all their failure—to show them the way. The religious state offers an amazingly close contact between the man who has the will but is not able, and the Lord who is resolved to open all to him. Even if one's own failure becomes ever clearer, at the same time one's offer to the Lord and his question and answer also become ever clearer. This is the consolation in the midst of disconsolateness. The one who fails and happens to be a religious also shows the Lord by his very presence that he is willing to bear this neglected and yet continuing opportunity. In spite of all failure he remains in the situation of love, an incomplete love that nonetheless remains before the Lord's word of perfect love; it is a love that in this enduring contact knows the concrete personal love of the Lord.

The confession of a religious should make clear his failure before this love and should make it clear specifically as the failure of one called to the religious life, the basic characteristics of which must appear in this confession. Yet even in the face of his profound failure he must not forget that he is called to console the Lord for the loss of the rich young man (and of all like him). He must remember that, seeking to keep him from becoming the one who ultimately flees, the Lord offers him surpassing graces from day to day so that he may try again, endure, repeat his offer to the Lord every day and keep the Lord's ideal before him. Confessing in bitterness, he will simultaneously try to console the Lord for the bitter loss of the rich young man.

The difficult part of the religious life is that one should not console oneself by looking past the present situation, but rather have the courage to look at it directly in order to bear it with the Lord. Even though the Lord bears so much because of me, I bear it with him. The religious life claims to be a life of sacrifice, and where should sacrifice begin if not here? The religious must walk through the fire of confession, in which his failure appears, burning. Though he may receive consolation from the Lord elsewhere, for example holy communion, there is no pardon there.

If the Lord has borne his Cross in order to redeem all, and yet invites his own to bear his Cross with him, it is self-evident that this bearing takes place within a Christian insight, an insight that cannot see the failure of others without one's own sinfulness being given its precise, visible place. If in the confession of religious the representative aspect plays such an essential role (representative of the rich young man and of all to whom the Lord's demands seem too hard), it does so only because the one confessing takes his own sin seriously. Real Christian substitution makes no distinction between what is mine and what is yours; it is rather the acceptance of yours into mine so that in the essentials yours can no longer be distinguished from mine. This does not exclude the fact that the religious stands at the point from which the rich young man has gone away and that he thus can make some distinction between himself and that young man; but in the next instant he can still recognize himself in the person who has failed.

From this same perspective, the religious who is also a priest and hears confessions will be challenged with particular intensity to share the burden of his penitents, to lift up their uncomprehending sacrifice in his own sacrifice and to include them emphatically within his own confession. It is no accident that Vianney felt himself so strongly drawn to religious life.

The Confession of contemplatives. A person chooses the contemplative life with two things in mind. First, that the Lord needs contemplatives, ones who contemplate *him*, who spend their lives in contemplation, not in leisure, but rather in the most severe work of the spirit. This work seeks and wants nothing but him; in contemplation it finds the means to approach him more closely so that the Church as a whole may be brought closer to him and the sacrifice of one person may include that of all. The second factor prompting such a life is the desire to bear burdens anonymously, a desire that rather surrounds and accompanies the contemplative act than coincides with it. It encompasses the entire life of sacrifice in a contemplative monastery and sees this sacrifice and its fruits in the anonymity of the entire community that bears these burdens. The first reason is more the Lord's own need, the second more the need of the sinful world. The unity of the two takes place within the contemplative life. The contemplative tries to be what both the Lord and the world need: what the

Lord needs in order to save the world and what the world needs in order to be saved by the Lord, even if the world does not itself know it.

Confession here will repeatedly seek to reestablish the original order; the contemplation chosen as the content of one's life allows a particular intimacy with the Lord presupposing a devotion and surrender so intense that the Lord really can reveal himself. The confession of the contemplative will approach and touch a great many things that never come into question for the active religious or the Christian in the world, since the contemplative must persevere in inner purity with no loss of vitality—a task often extremely difficult to achieve. Confession must offer the possibility of bringing new life in this perseverance, a new fullness in the stillness of contemplation, a new yearning in the weary and new spiritual organs with which to grasp what the Lord chooses to reveal.

In ordinary confession outside religious life, someone usually seeks reorganization for the sake of somehow being presentable again. He thinks of himself when confessing. The religious, particularly the contemplative, should think primarily of the Lord. He should confess for the sake of the man whom the Lord needs pure and who happens to be himself. This again has to do with his desire to share anonymously the burden of the anonymous world guilt. His confessional attitude thus to a large extent becomes a test for the seriousness of his contemplation. Just as the incarnate Son lingers with the Father and beholds the Father so that he may disclose this vision to his brothers, so the contemplative gazes at the Son, not in order to please him because he is being observed, but rather in order to help disclose to the world the access to the Lord, and through him to the Father. From this contemplative vision emerges the vision in confession, the vision that confesses to the Lord and that joins itself to the vision of sin through the bearing and suffering Lord. Confessional attitude and contemplative attitude mutually generate each other and flow into one another.

The power of contemplation to realize things both in vision

and in the vision's effectiveness, both as capacity for comprehension and as work performed, is so great that only the
best confessors are able to do justice to it. One cannot recall too
often how highly God values the sacrifice of contemplatives
and with what amplitude and power of dissemination it can be
equipped if it is performed properly. The confessor must be
familiar with this scope not only in theory but also from
within an inner participation that must be accompanied by
the necessary theological and practical insight. The ordinary
sinner's knowledge revolves around the insight into his own
sin; that of the contemplative penitent and his confessor
revolves around the Lord's own need, recognized only through
genuine contemplation. The contemplative's prayer must be
such that it nourishes his confession, and his confession such
that it nourishes the contemplation.

The Confession of active religious. The distinguishing feature of
the active religious is that he is to offer himself to his brothers
through the power and mission of the Lord. He always has a
criterion and corrective for this activity. When he finds himself
confronted with the people entrusted to him or the task he is to
master, he can ask himself: am I really the one God wishes to
see in this position? From his own effect, and in part from the
reaction of others, he can tell to a certain extent what he is
lacking: for example, prayer, collectedness, sacrificial spirit or
zeal. The contemplative sees in the Lord what the Lord misses
in him, and the active religious sees in others what they miss in
him. His contemplation is there certainly in part to enrich his
inner life so that he can give of himself more fruitfully. Of
course, it is not external success that serves as a standard for his
inner condition, and yet the confrontation with his mission—
if he is honest—is a reflection of his shortcomings. He will
not pay attention to people's gossip, disfavor or superficial
admiration, nor to the way his contemporaries receive his
sermons or books. He will, however, pay attention to the
shortcomings he himself feels whenever he goes about his task

and gives of himself, shortcomings reflected in a certain disappointment, often unspoken, in others. He should also look into this mirror when he examines before confession. Does a "power" really "radiate from him" whenever he preaches, hears confession or instructs and strengthens souls? He descries his shortcomings not in himself but rather in what he has given, in what already lies outside of him, what already has been accomplished. This is by no means the external, visible "accomplishment", the completed work, but rather the relationship between what can be expected of him apostolically and what he actually brings about. The one confessing will be able to sense this relationship without too much difficulty, but he may not find it equally easy to make it clear to the confessor. The latter, however, if he makes a genuine loving effort, will know how to sense what is meant and will not talk around it with superficial consolations. Indeed, he will best be able to understand the penitent's insufficiency by considering his own insufficiency, which issues from the same sphere.

Hence whenever the religious confesses, there is something that cannot be expressed adequately, but which nonetheless makes itself clearly felt in an uneasiness corresponding to an uneasiness in the confessor and issuing finally from an uneasiness within the nature of religious life in itself. It resides in the place from which the rich young man fled. One seat always remains empty during the feasts in religious life, and yet one celebrates even though the hole is gaping. Even if the chairs are spread apart in order to conceal the empty spot, everybody knows that someone is absent. It is fine to speak of "substitution", but one must understand it in a very real sense and from the very beginning expect there to be excessive demands so the Lord's expectations may be met.

The Confession of Married Persons

The confessions previously mentioned were those of individuals standing in the communion of saints. The confession of religious also indirectly included the shortcomings of the order itself. With married persons, however, the spouse is much more closely included in everything that has to do with the wide field of married life. Transgressions no doubt occur which concern only one partner, instances when one egoistically holds back while the other gives of himself. But one first would have to ask whether the desire or surrender of the other were not also egoistic or, if some misuse of marriage occurs, to what extent there is an expressed or concealed consent from the partner. In these cases the confession of one spouse already announces that of the other, and the confessor's exhortation to the one takes into account the influence upon the other. On the one hand, one spouse accuses the other in confession, and, on the other, the one confessing gives the priest the opportunity to examine the confession of the other which perhaps will be given later. If this really is the case, that is, if both partners confess properly, then from the spirit of confession they will acquire an understanding of their mutual situation. The person "co-accused" will not consider himself betrayed but will understand that out of Christian love the spouse's confession could not have been any different, even if the spouses do not speak about it together either before or afterward. Each knows that in the other's confession the indivisible common element may come to expression, that he in any case is borne by that confession, that the absolution of the one already prefigures that of the other, and that in this shared bearing of sin there lies a very special way in which one can participate in the Lord's own act of bearing sin.

Everyone knows, of course, that God knows and sees all, but it is something altogether different when someone bound to me points out to God my sins with his own in confession. This involves a certain humiliation, since I do not know whether he does it or how he expresses it. Yet he can show it to God in a new, Christian fashion. In this way, the marriage confession is for both partners an emphatic representation of their presence before God and of God's own gaze penetrating into their most intimate sphere. Every sacrament tends to express more clearly God's omnipresence in human life, and this is true even of sacraments that we ourselves do not receive, ones we participate in only through the communion of sinners and saints. This is particularly the case in the confession of married persons, just as this confession also constitutes a special way of understanding the *communio sanctorum* and the responsibility of the one for all. If you show God our sin as one we have committed together, it becomes almost impossible to distinguish sharply between what is yours and what is mine. One understands that if evil is capable of this kind of communion, this will be even more true of good—and this also holds true for the good of absolution. The sacraments have an overflowing effect; they transcend the very sphere they externally appear to delimit.

The confession of married persons thus has a retroactive effect on the sacrament of marriage. The spouses now recognize more profoundly to what extent they are indissolubly united in Christ by the sacrament, in the good as well as in the bad. They are able to understand one part of their mutual love; another, larger part lies hidden in God's mysteries. It also must emerge from confession that they love one another. Confession does not constitute, as it were, a limiting of this love by the unbridgeable chasm of the private sphere. When one spouse includes the other in confession, God ties the bond of love even more tightly through the Church and makes the relationship deeper and richer. When the confession of one partner gives new order to his own relationship to God, it also makes the other partner aware of a new obligation to God and, in God, to his spouse.

8. THE ACT OF CONFESSION

The Legacy of the Lord

The institution of confession on Easter shows that it is the fruit of the Cross. It is the perfect fruit eternally bound to the tree of the Redeemer: confession is his commmandment and his discipleship, and absolution is his authority. He bestows confession as a gift of redemption on his Church; she herself is to bind and loose and administer his redemption. He bequeaths it to her as a whole by fixing the essential points through the words of institution and their interpretation in his own life and in the prehistory of that institution. He then leaves it to the Church to understand the individual elements lying within that gift; he also leaves it to her to carry out the concrete and practical development of the sacrament.

In the institutions he founded he often showed only the preliminary features, the outlines, and for the rest knew that he would send his Holy Spirit into the Church. "He who is able to receive, let him receive it"; and the Church will be able to receive. She will give an enduring form to what he has bequeathed to her in a preliminary form. The Church, however, will never develop the bequest arbitrarily but rather in obedience to the seed she has received, and she will always take care that what belongs to her continues to belong completely to him.

He gives us the sacrament as the fruit of his life, something itself alive that should also become alive in us. It is a fruit that remains bound to sin, and he knows that there will never be any lack of sin in our lives and that we will always be confronted with our own sinfulness. But he builds a path leading to him from sin. It should no longer be an outright hindrance separating us from the Father; when we sinners recognize that he bore this sin for us, that is, when we believe, the path of reconciliation simultaneously discloses itself before our very eyes. Sin is by no means necessary, and the Cross by no means makes it into something good. Yet if we have faith, we as sinners will repeatedly encounter "God with us".

The Church is to fashion a suitable means of grace out of those few words of institution that give the authority and the command to carry out. It is suitable because it is the Lord's word and his fruit, a divine fruit that he as a man brought to ripeness and gave to us like a seed that is to grow and bear fruit in us: as the fruit of the Church and of the institution, and thereby as a fruit in every contrite sinner. Because he bore this fruit in suffering as God and man and paid for it with his death, it contains mysteries of his Incarnation, his sojourn among us, his Passion and Resurrection, but also mysteries of his divinity, his unity with the Father and the Spirit. This fruit thus contains two elements: first, divine grace, and for us that means the Ever-More beyond both our comprehension and our practical capacity, an Ever-More that in addition always remains richer—even in its flowing forth—than we can accommodate. Second, this fruit contains human usefulness, something adapted to the weakness of fallen humanity. The truth of the one element establishes the truth of the other: the more profoundly we become aware of our weakness and sinfulness, the more closely we resemble the humiliated Son of Man, and the more radiantly do resurrection and absolution reveal themselves.

Divinity and humanity are not separate spheres within the Son. Everywhere we try to penetrate into his humanity we encounter the mystery of his being more than a man, that is, his divine sonship. He is not beyond all understanding, and yet precisely in our understanding, the incomprehensible over-whelms us; rather than being able to see him in his entirety, it is we who find ourselves seen by him and drawn into his ever-greater dimensions. Because we are incorporated in this way, we lose any overview of our own situation. It is he who contains us in his perfect openness both to the Father and to the world.

Whenever we confess according to his will, we must consider his double attitude so that we, too, may learn the correct attitude. He shows us who he is by opening himself to us: he is the one open to the Father who, in disclosing himself to us, also shows us the Father. He is the one who, in opening himself and showing the Father, also glorifies the Father. Only from the perspective of this attitude does the fruit, the work he bequeaths, become comprehensible. Suppose a poet lies dying. He bequeaths to his friend a volume of poems and says to him, "I am giving you these verses, but I don't want you merely to spend a few pleasant hours reading them. You yourself should live from within the source of inspiration I was allowed to experience. It was my most sublime possession. Although you will find it reflected in these poems, they are only a brief indication and testimony of something much greater that happened to me. You would obscure my memory if you went back no further than these constructed verses." The friend would revere these poems and yet, while reading them, would always remain aware of the larger framework that he cannot really see all at once, yet which alone lends the finished work that infinite quality inherent in genuine beauty. He would look everywhere for the larger aspect, seek everywhere in the result the testimony of the original inspiration and experience the falling rain as evidence of the heavenly clouds. In this search and in this effort the deceased would remain living.

In a similar fashion, confession is the fruit of the divine-human life. The Lord's turning to us, the form bequeathed to the Church, would be the poetic legacy that in some way is comprehensible in itself, and the turning to the Father would be the unsurveyable sphere of inspiration. We can understand a great deal about confession, just as we could about miracles. We know, for example, that before the woman was hemorrhaging and now she is healthy. Only the nexus between these two facts remains incomprehensible. Or we understand that the Lord was dead and now lives, but we do not understand how that is possible. We do understand, however, that the things extending into the sphere of understanding are related in the sphere of the incomprehensible and are its manifestation. We understand a great deal about confession in the same way: for example, that there must be penance, that it is advisable for a person to admit his errors and that there also must be an authority and a judgment upon good and evil on earth. We also more or less understand many things about faith: that the God-man did penance for our sins on the Cross and that for this reason the penance that we accept for our guilt acquires a somehow symbolic character. Yet all the comprehensible elements are integrated into a whole which as such remains beyond our vision. In the course of centuries the Church may acquire an increased understanding both of many individual elements and of the incomprehensibility of the whole, and with both of these an understanding of the mystery of Christ, the way in which he wishes to remain alive for us in the vitality of the Father.

There is a certain withering of this in Protestantism, since there one clings only to the word and attributes to that word only a limited significance: this is what the Lord said, and there is nothing more to it! One tries to guard against the "introduction of mysteries" but does not see how much the word is an expression of mystery and is itself a mystery. The word of the Lord is like a coin; whoever is hungry must convert the coin into something edible, and it is left to the hungry person's faculties of reason to carry out this conversion. The tradition of the Church issues from the word and its conversions, and any contemporary conversions must recall and consider the transmitted word and its historical interpretations. Many of these interpretations and forms of application are determined by their age, but the relationship at any given time between the enduring word and its temporal interpretation is not; it is rather the expression of the Church's understanding of faith. Nevertheless, this understanding of faith, the Church's meditation on the mystery of the Lord, can become more profound and more central. Thus the interpretation of confession in earlier ages may have paid less attention to the Son's central *attitude* than we do; they may have tried to see and imitate more the Son's individual deeds, acts and words than the one consistent attitude. There have been epochs—such as that of the Crusade—in which being a Christian was taken for granted, epochs, however, in which Christianity sought to express itself apostolically in great external activity. Interest was centered more on an external fruit to be acquired than on the fruit of an enduring attitude. The problematical issue of Christian existence as an ultimate attitude was less urgent and conscious than it is today. We of today are so threatened in our own existence that we can find no other answer than to lend this entire threatened existence the same meaning that Christ gave to his existence as a whole. By doing so we go beyond both the interpretation of Christian existence from the perspective of individual acts in Christian life and the interpretation from the perspective of the mere word (as text) of the Holy Scriptures.

We must certainly always interpret confession from the perspective of the *word* of the Lord, but precisely from the word of the *Lord*, who always infinitely exceeds his human word because he, as the living one, is himself the Word. Hence we confess not only at the command of the Lord and according to the word of the Lord but *in the Lord* who is the divine-human Word and Life. We place our own deed inside his all-encompassing existence as the ever-greater one. Just as his deeds stand within his own all-encompassing attitude, so also our deed, in the end, stands within his attitude, a deed that is necessarily also an expression of our own attitude insofar as it has integrated itself into the attitude of the Lord.

Human attitudes and conditions are transitory, just as are all human acts. Two lovers within their mutual love thus may perceive all the acts, words and feelings of love as something totally new, unique and virtually created by them, even though before them, with them, and after them there are innumerable lovers, and even though they may smile at their former behavior after they have stepped out of this particular condition of love or even out of genuine human love itself. The love of the incarnate Son for the Father and, for the sake of the Father, for us, knows nothing of such transitoriness. It is grounded in the eternal triune love itself, and there is no position from which one may observe and evaluate it as if from a point external to it. It is the true condition, the true attitude, indeed truth itself, and all words and deeds are true only to the extent that they are expressions and manifestations of this attitude. Every Christian who loves participates in the Son's attitude and is one whom the Son leads to the Father. The acts of his love are the steps he takes into this ever-greater triune love. And the Holy Spirit sees to it that whenever a Christian really loves the Son, he invariably sees this triune mystery radiating within him. If this were not so, he would run the risk of judging the Lord as a man and of submitting his acts and condition to normal human psychology (something one can know and examine). In that case, the unique person that the Lord is would be submerged in the masses and with him the Christian religion.

Preparation

One may start from the assumption that the Son did not come to earth unprepared. He decided in heaven to come into the world in order to show himself to the Father from the earthly perspective, and to show not only himself but sinners as well in an association that he intends to shape as intimately as possible. Nothing would be more welcome to him than for the Father to see the world's sin upon him and in him—indeed, for the Father no longer to see him at all because of that vision of sin. He needs the entire immeasurable period between his eternal decision and his temporal Incarnation in order to prepare himself for that Incarnation, and on earth he needs the long period of his hidden, contemplative life in order to prepare himself for his Cross. His ability to come before the Father so naked and so engaged in the act of revealing is in no small way the fruit of his prayerful preparation.

The confessing sinner needs a preparation all the more. He is in the first place a sinner, and as such his ability to see the truth has been clouded or entirely obscured by sin. Secondly, however, he is perpetually invited by the Son to be rid of his sin by means of confession, something that is possible only if the Lord mediates to us something of his own true version of sin. Thus the sinner's preparation will consist in measuring against the Lord the disparity and lost ground and in considering the distance between himself and the will and nature of God. The penitent will thereby refer to his condition after the last confession and absolution and will recall where he stood then and how much he has alienated himself from that condition. He must consider what has caused that alienation—his sins—until they have become clear and unambiguous, both the sins themselves and their concrete circumstances, both their pre- and post-history. Within this examining gaze we know that God himself is observing us in a vision of mercy, for he does want to forgive, and yet in a vision demanding unconditional truthfulness. Hence we must see our sins as sharply as possible and place them under the harsh light of truth. We must be relentless with ourselves, not so that God may be "touched" and be more generous with his mercy, but in order to be better equipped for his subsequent service. We should not view absolution only as a boundless gift of grace of which we are in no way worthy, but as a gift meant to be integrated into the recognition of the seriousness of our guilt so that we may accept it in a fitting manner. This gift conceals a profound humiliation, but it is a humiliation that is meant to be fruitful and instruct us for better service.

It is not enough for us merely to see our sins before us in the harsh light of truth; we must expressly recognize them as ours and be permeated by the fact that they are unpardonable and that God has given us sufficient faith and love to avoid them. We must recognize the malevolence of our sin and our intention to commit it and persist in it. If we try to excuse it, we ourselves become hindrances to grace and rob ourselves of the best part of its effect.

One cannot prepare oneself properly for the confession without a living relationship to the Holy Scriptures, inasmuch as they contain the life of the Lord or interpret his intentions. One can use any single earthly event in his life as a point of departure and gain an insight into one's own perversity. Everywhere it becomes evident that the Son lives from his relationship to the Father. He is always the pure child of the Father. No matter what age or in what situation we imagine him, he is always surrounded by an unutterable innocence. Then can we go further and compare ourselves to him, and we immediately see where we are unable to move freely because our sin is hindering us. He remains in the Father; his whole existence is love for the Father, prayer to the Father, service of the Father. In his light we immediately see how things stand with our own existence, our own prayer, our own service, what we have not done correctly and what we have missed. Everywhere we find signs of death instead of life, of coldness and indifference and lukewarm interest. It will not be difficult for us to discover our failings in all three spheres determining our relationship to God, namely, existence in love, prayer and service.

The same holds true for the relationship between the incarnate Lord and his fellow men. He has not bequeathed to us his commandment of love for one's fellow man as a dry prescription, but rather as a summary of what his life among us was. He loves us as he loves himself, and in this love he cares for us, reveals himself to us, shares our material and spiritual life, lets us participate in his life, takes our guilt upon himself and dies for us. He gives everything he has and can, yet in his love he also wants to receive. We can view our own relationship to our fellow men from this perspective, and we

will discover how paltry our love was, how selfish, how
ambitious, how much we have disdained, undervalued, harmed
and perhaps even hated our fellow men. The treasures God
entrusted to us so that we might pass them on we have let
decay inside us. And we must recognize that all our sins
against brotherly love have alienated us from the Son.

Finally, we can consider the Son's life in itself, his attitude
toward himself. This attitude has but one goal, namely, his
relationship to the Father and to us. He is never an end in
himself, but rather only a means to the Father and us. The
things he grants himself—rest, relaxation, participation in a
festival—the things determined by his own existence as a
human being, are all bathed completely in the grace of giving.
He rests in order to be capable of new work. He rejoices in
order that he may give of his joy. In this light we can see where
we have granted ourselves too little or too much and how it
has had a negative effect on our own mission.

Although we should examine ourselves as truthfully as
possible, we should not do so in fear; for it is a grace that God
requires this examination of us. As soon as we enter upon the
process of confession, even if we are just beginning to prepare
for it, we are already invited by grace and are thus not without
some contact with it. That should remove a good deal of our
fear. We should examine ourselves until the contours of guilt
emerge clearly, but we should stop as soon as further examination no longer promises to yield fruit, when we begin to
lose ourselves in brooding and to examine not only sin and its
immediate circumstances but the circumstances of the circumstances as well. Otherwise we are in danger of falling into
new guilt altogether, namely, the overestimation of our own
importance, in the face of guilt wanting to play the all-too-
clever one and perhaps bring the "merit" of not having sinned
into consideration instead of simply grace. But grace always
has for us a completely spontaneous, almost primitive and
always childlike character, not least because God always shows
us the way of grace from him to us in a kind of shortened

perspective. If we were to follow our sins back at length to their origins and circumstances, the circumstances would soon become more important to us than the sins themselves: everything would become more and more complicated and interesting in precisely the wrong way, and we would merely end up dulling our Christian awareness of sin and becoming ourselves dulled to the direct effects of grace. Our relationship to God, to absolution and to the Son who offers this confessional grace would then only be accessible by means of long detours. Most important to God, however, is that our relationship to him be direct and childlike, for only thus is it a relationship of love; hence all false science, psychology and philosophy of sin must yield before this demand. We should remain simple and straightforward even toward our sin and be satisfied with the essential things—the really essential things—that become immediately visible when we view ourselves in the light of the gospel. This simplicity and straightforwardness of what is true will also help us attain genuine contrition and the proper resolution, whereas boundless self-observation only cripples us, makes us distrustful and robs us of our faith in the power of grace. It also fragments us so that we no longer see the simple main road which the Lord marks out for us.

Of course, there is also the other extreme in which we only examine ourselves superficially, only skim the cream from the top, as it were. Reflection upon the Lord also protects us from this. For the superficial examination is usually a characteristic of our failure to ask about the Lord's fundamental precepts; instead, we evaluate and orient ourselves according to our own precepts—which in their turn have long adapted themselves to our sinful condition—according to precepts enmeshed in the world around us ("everyone does it that way"), according to an aid to examination of conscience that is formalistically understood and not interpreted in the light of the gospel, or according to a schema that has become mere habit, one we employ for all our confessions and whose sharpness or dullness we no longer question. On the other hand, an unhesitating push forward into the essentials results whenever we look the Lord straight in the eye, submit ourselves to his truth and take him, his message and his life as our aid to examination of conscience.

If we have committed a sin that we normally do not commit, we must look with particularly sharp intensity at its factual character. We should not first examine the psychological causes (that will come too, only later) but rather should see ourselves burdened with this sin. We should recall the security we had beforehand, perhaps a thoughtless or sacrilegious one, when we thought we could not commit that sin, and should feel the terrible humiliation of nonetheless having committed it. If, on the other hand, we fall into sins we commit repeatedly and habitually, our first concern should be to consider the circumstances and causes, the false attitudes of laxity and yielding that again have led us astray, the temptations and occasions of sin we need to avoid, and then from this perspective our relationship to God. In the first case, our overall attitude is decisive and will explain how this thing could happen. In the second, the quality of this particular sin plays a role, and we must dig down and get to the bottom of it.

Our preparation for confession demands that we be strict with ourselves in two respects: we must recognize what *is*, and what is not must not be considered. One should not play up trivialities that are not really sins at all for the sake of a more profound humility before God, things one's everyday consciousness does not normally recognize as sins and which one perhaps discovers in the aid to examination of conscience and immediately applies to oneself. If one insists on taking all sorts of trivialities seriously and on referring them to oneself, one robs oneself of the capacity to evaluate one's own sins properly and to share the burden of the sin of others. Taking imagined sins upon oneself for the sake of being humiliated in one's own eyes only leads one into a certain pride and makes one awkward when one really does have to bear the burden. One is as if blinded by what is not genuine and loses the ability to see clearly what *is*.

If for the sake of confessing properly a person were to try to reconstruct each past day, and within each of those days every hour and situation inasmuch as they may have been an occasion for sin, he would again put sin at a distance from himself and lay it at the feet of time—which, of course, is not capable of sin. Christian perfection is something completely different from the avoidance of myriad possible imperfections. It is first of all a totality and something positive, and we are invited to become perfect by means of a complete, undivided Yes to the Lord and through participation in his perfect attitude before the Father. We are not permitted to let ourselves splinter away from this totality by confession so that we are no longer capable of any synthesis; neither are we permitted to imagine ourselves caught in every crevice of our existence to the point that not even God himself, so to speak, would know how to glue our fragments back together. Let your Yes be a Yes, and your No a No! That is an expression of Christian confession. At the base of God's infinitely flowing mercy with us sinners lies one divine deed: the Incarnation. If the sinner loses himself in every possible and impossible possibility, he will no longer find his way back to this One and will not be the creature that God created in order to redeem it in himself. He will become instead a person broken into a thousand pieces, incurably fragmented. Confession is there so that a person may collect himself; what is already done should receive a name and place and should not collapse into irrevocable confusion, in sin-schizophrenia. There exists a certain discretion toward both God and the confessor. The confessing Christian is confirmed, and how should the Spirit dwelling within him not give him a mature, valiant confessional attitude? Whoever presents nothing but trivialities will find that the power of absolution of necessity shatters on these very trivialities; he is totally unable to receive the great, healing impact of absolution. Whoever moves in the direction of psychological dissection is moving in a direction diametrically opposed to Christian confession.

Whoever wishes to accommodate himself to a new, living relationship to the Lord should consider that the Lord always spent a great deal of time reflecting upon the Father, but none in reflecting upon himself. The object of contemplation is always God, never oneself. By examining one's own conscience in a falsely concerned fashion, one steals time from God and claims it for oneself. It is good to see that sins have kept one from going to God, but this only means that one should find the right path again as soon as possible. True, the confession of sin normally will be more summmarily accomplished than the examination of conscience, but even in the latter case the most essential element is still one's attention to God and to the grace of the Lord in which alone one's own ingratitude may become visible.

Suppose that a holy man really had done nothing bad since his last confession. In confessing he would nevertheless participate just as fully in the grace of the confession, even if he had to confess only a single word. Hence the confessional grace cannot depend on the length of the confession. The grace of confession also has a eucharistic, outflowing character, and one should not try to exhaust that grace for oneself, so to speak, by means of an "exhaustive" confession. On the contrary, it is somehow a part of the punishment of sin that the sinner really must bind part of this grace to himself personally so that it may redeem his sin, instead of simply letting that grace overflow into the world.

One's entire preparation must take place in the Holy Spirit. It is this Spirit whom one will call on at the start so that he may act and reveal. Let him be the true light, while we as humbly as possible make ourselves transparent; let him judge and let us participate in his manner of reason. The same Spirit that later will bring about absolution should now illuminate me so that spirit may encounter Spirit, and spirit may attain the proper analogy to Spirit. This should not take place apart from me; I should make my own contribution through prayer and effort, through faith and my own reason.

There are confessions which one senses are not based on true preparation. A few things are said somewhat schematically, and this shows that the person concerned is not confessing in love. The totality of attitude in which the Father and Son stand before one another in the Spirit is an expression of love and can be imitated only in love. Everything the incarnate Son shows to the Father—even the apparently most insignificant things— he shows in the totality of love; everything is integrated into this totality and receives its significance through it. Whoever confesses in a formula no longer participates in the Son's love. He is confessing sins as if they were self-contained, abstract entities with no real existential connection to him. That is Pharasaic. One would almost rather hear the sinner hesitate about the seriousness of his guilt ("I'm not really sure . . .") than such an apodictic, self-assured recitation of sins.

The decisive element in all this is humility, and humility is the missing factor in each of the shortcomings discussed here.

A person preparing for confession generally has no particular problem finding his sins. He knows where a bad conscience is oppressing him. He can discover his sins as though by so many signposts in his circumstances and conditions, in the inner discomfort or even revulsion he felt when he committed them, in the anxiety that befell him before or afterward, in the temptations with which he is familiar and to which he fell prey. Yet there is often the danger that in proceeding in this fashion he may view sin too one-sidedly as being imbedded in his life and determined by his particular situation and as a result no longer perceive its objective, independent character. As long as he does not perceive that character, he will not really attain Christian contrition; he will regret that *he* failed, but not so intensely that he affronted *God*. He must learn to see the sinfulness of sin as such; only then will the necessary connection become clear: on the one hand that of sinners to one another, on the other hand that of various sins to one another. This dramatically increases the weight of the sins he has committed, since his own sin can no longer be isolated, but instead becomes a part of a totality into which the sinner has integrated himself. The relative, usually mitigating personal circumstances lose significance; sin can no longer be subdivided but is rather a block. Its absolute character becomes visible; it is that to which God speaks an unconditional No, and I, the sinner, stand within this No. I have so accommodated sin to myself that I now dwell and live in its sphere. Hence any separation from it cannot be effected by a mere act of will; it needs God's pardoning grace, his absolution. No matter how intensely the sinner recognizes, regrets and admits his sin, to be rid of it he needs absolution. The terrible insight issuing from the preparation for confession is the discovery of how intimately sinner and sin are fused together. He aches to be separated from it, to be pure, but before the words of absolution are spoken he cannot be certain of having become someone other than the sinner he had been until now. Nor can he foresee what kind of person he will be after he really has received absolution.

The sinner who goes to confession is homesick for God: he is living in banishment and loneliness. Although he is a sinner among sinners, he senses no communion. Only absolution will give him a feeling of communion again, of the communion of saints and of being at home with God. And this new feeling awakens in him an understanding for those who are still banished, distant, searching and without communion. Before confession he was an I tied to sin, one that could only understand itself as bound with this fetter. After confession he is an I that has been freed by the most inward binding to a Thou, the Thou of God, and thereby to the Thou of every person belonging to the communion of saints. The person himself cannot undertake this most inward transformation of self; it requires the power and miracle of God.

The penitent will fall into sin again, but in the new preparation for confession the experience of the earlier absolution can help him to heighten his yearning to enter again into purity, into proximity to God and into the kingdom of love. He knows that this kingdom is something indivisible, unique and incomparable, not to be approached by any sort of preliminary steps. It is like marital love; a person either knows it through experience or does not know it at all. It is something that cannot be reduced to individual concepts; the blinding light irradiates all details, and the great flood is so torrential that no one wave can be singled out. So it is with the kingdom of grace and love into which the penitent is reintegrated; the experience corresponding to it is so interior that the objective element implied in it infinitely transcends every other experience and every subjective decision and attempt.

Contrition

The spirit of the examination of conscience first collects facts and produces a dry insight. The highest possible objectivity must emerge. One must not perceive the sins merely as a general burden but should rather examine and recognize their number, seriousness and circumstances.

As soon as this result is in, contrition is in order—not before. For the entire preparation for confession is a process with clearly defined stages. If one were to mix the stages together too much, if one were to repent each sin as soon as one became aware of it and feel it to be so unbearable that one could think only of absolution, then one would rob oneself of the possibility of properly recognizing the rest of one's sins. The clarity required as the first essential issues from the clarity that the Lord maintains in all his behavior and actions toward the Father. He came in order to suffer, but as long as the hour has not come he does not anticipate it; he does not want to be distracted in his present mission by a foretaste of the Passion.

From him we should learn to organize and separate the different phases in our examination of conscience. That does not mean that we find our recognized errors so interesting and fascinating in the mere insight that there is scarcely room for the subsequent act of contrition. The whole sequence from insight to contrition and resolution, from confession to absolution, is as such logical and clear. We should always know where we are within it.

Contrition means that we are horrified at the degree of alienation between God and ourselves resulting from our guilt. Contrition has no place for excuses and benevolent consideration of circumstances and motives. Neither is there initially any place for good intentions; we must view our guilt as guilt, stand up to it, measure its scope. We measure it not only against the negative things we ourselves have brought about but equally against the positive things the Son on earth continually performs before the Father, his uninterrupted attitude of love which human sin is incapable of destroying or even of changing. He carries the sinners to the Father in a love so purifying that the Father sees only the love and reconciliatory spirit of the Son. Nothing in the Son's life, no difficulty, no exhaustion, no sojourn, no sermon, no miracle, can distract him from this attitude of love. He inclines everything toward the Father so that everything in his vision of the Father is transformed into something positive for the Father, be it the labors of his mission or the fruit of these labors. If we view the Son's deeds and days from our human perspective in faith, we see that his unshakeable proximity to the Father is growing continually, since the Son is ever nearer to the Father; this nearness should make us sensitive to our own distance. Only against this proximity can we measure in a Christian way how far removed we are. We do not have a standard even remotely this precise for measuring the proximity we possessed in the days of grace and have now lost. If we measure our own nearness and distance against the enduring nearness of the Son to the Father, our contrition will be

oriented toward God from the very beginning and will be a
searching, Christian contrition. We will not merely be sorry
because we are not better than we are. We get to know our
own lack of love not by staring at our failure, but rather by
viewing the positive aspects of the Son.

This contrition should be painful. As soon as it is Christian,
it can no longer be merely an affair of the intellect. We *are* the
lost sheep. The pain should be in our heart, in the place where
our heart should have loved and did not. Hence a person
cannot pray or meditate if he has just seriously insulted
another. His meditation will be totally unfruitful, and the
Spirit will reveal nothing to him; at most it will send him away
to be reconciled with his brother. A person cannot pray and
meditate with understanding alone; the entire person must
participate. Equally the entire person must be contrite. Admittedly, whoever is in sin will sense the difficulty of not even
being able to evaluate the Lord's purity; he has forfeited his eye
and his sensitivity for such things. Yet by wanting to confess
he has already begun the return to God and to his renewed
vision of God. He has at least a glimmer of hope that he can
change himself, even if he does not yet know that he is
converted or saved. He is not simply despairing or resigned; he
does not want to take his life. A person's intention to confess
already places him in the hands of grace, though perhaps an
imperceptible grace. But it is at work. Perhaps a person does
not believe he is capable, on his own, of becoming reconciled
to God or of finding any access to him at all. But no matter
how terrible the situation may be, he always knows that God is
greater and that God can find a way that the sinner does not
know. Insofar as the possibility of confession stands open to
us, God has not made the final break with us. Even if a sinner
has not confessed and to that extent cannot be sure of God's
whole love, he nonetheless knows in the very depths of his
faith that this love is there, that he cannot lose it and that it is
what first makes his contrition possible. Only within this love
can he feel contrition, even if at the moment he does not yet

have access to it. This love, unfelt but unforgettable in faith, lends a special quality to his contrition. Only in the light of this love will his sin become sin for him, more than mere human, innerworldly guilt. If he had sinned "behind God's back" things would not be half as bad, but he sinned "before him", in the face of his unforgettable love!

Precisely this "before him" must become as concrete as possible in the awakened contrition. Precisely "before him" I have taken a position against him. One must imagine this situation with as much animation as possible. In contrition one should not seek to heighten things to some abstract, ethereal level but should rather realize how exposed one stands before God—as exposed as the Son before the Father. Even Adam, when he hides himself, is no less exposed before God. One should realize what it means to have insulted God to his face, to have insulted God in man, Jesus Christ, who stood before sin as a human being and who stands as a human being before me when I sin. One must see that as a man he is at the same time God and that his earthly life was supported by his heavenly life. An encounter must take place within my contrition not only with the man Jesus but also with the eternal God mediated by Jesus' humanity. God supplies the grace, and this is a reality I cannot doubt. My will to contrition is already an effect of grace, and as soon as that grace lays hold of me at any one point, it is able and desires to expand and to leaven everything. I am the lost sheep. But as soon as I recognize that, I also know that I am not completely lost—forlorn, but not lost; sought as one gone astray. I am like a child that let go of its mother's hand in the street and is hiding until she comes back; when she passes by him without noticing him, he is suddenly terrified. She *might* go on without turning around and looking for him. In the same instant, however, he also knows that is impossible, and in this knowledge and this fear he runs after her. The sinner runs to God in this same fear and certainty. The fear: could he perhaps forsake me? The certainty: he will never leave me! After the child has found his mother again he cries perhaps for a while longer because it is so wonderful to be consoled by her. It is not easy to say when contrition begins. This feeling of consolation elicits less a feeling of I than one of Thou; the consciousness of ultimate security reveals more the greatness and strength of God than one's own weakness and vulnerability. The negative element in contrition develops within the positive element on the side of God; his love is the overwhelming element pushing contrition to the fore. Yet contrition does not lose itself in a kind of excess of feeling; it grows instead as genuine contrition within the realm of the ever-greater God, and to that extent it, too, is grounded in insight. Before contrition stands the insight into one's own guilt; at the end of contrition stands the insight into the ever-greater God.

This brings the sinner onto the path of "perfect" contrition. He stands on that path as soon as the perspective of God is chosen; he sees God's absolute greatness—the greatness of all his traits, above all his love—and is shocked that he could have forgotten himself so completely, shocked not so much because of what is awaiting *him* or what is *his* as because of God. Only the view from the perspective of God—the view that is grace—enables him to measure his own remoteness and thereby acquire that particular conclusive insight into God's identity, the insight supporting contrition itself.

Fear of God's punishment may very well play a role here, but it is not the presence or absence of such fear that determines the perfection or imperfection of contrition. In an enormous fear prompted by the absence of any priestly aid, Joan of Arc renounced what she believed. Many a saint has been led through fear without imperfection. The vision of God's qualities can strengthen him; if God will, it can also crush him so that he and all that is his appears as if annihilated before the greatness of God. And perhaps he dates his own true insight into God from this experience. Contrition is imperfect as long as it remains bound to one's own ego and is not viewed from the perspective of God. If a young boy steals an apple and in the process falls from the tree, he may very well be sorry he has broken his leg. It may also occur to him that he could have died, and who knows what God would have done with him then? The first motive is purely natural, the second contains a supernatural element, and yet the step from the one to the other is not really very large. He may fear the police on earth, Purgatory in the beyond. The actual conversion comes about only when God becomes the motive. That "supernatural" element that relates God only to one's own self is still a form of egoism even if one believes in God. What is essential is that one is moving toward viewing things from the perspective of God. Even if the sinner were moving toward contrition only in this way, he would still—through the grace of confession, the pure, infused gift of the Lord—attain in confession to full love and thereby full contrition, and be overwhelmed by God's greater love.

Two people who love one another want to console one another; each expects of this consolation an enrichment and fulfillment, not so much of their mutual relationship as of themselves. In this expected enrichment lies the element of that which is new; things will not be the same as yesterday, and it will not be merely a quantitative heightening, but rather a qualitative increase. Supposing they were at odds and have been reconciled, they do not expect this new togetherness to be the same state as that before the rift. If one was the cause of their alienation, he will have to make up the most. He must not merely announce that he was wrong, not merely excuse himself and demonstrate that he has recognized his wrong; he must also present signs of his contrition. He knows he is not worthy of being considered a friend again. He will try to behave better than before. For he also knows that the alienation did not just begin at the moment he behaved unsuitably; for a long time he had been half-hearted and indifferent and had taken the friendship too much for granted. But when the other person sees the new signs of a generous love, when he clearly recognizes that the erring one is sorry and that he is grateful if his friend is solicitous for him again, the relationship will not simply begin again where it left off but will commence on a higher, more intimate level.

It is also possible that the one who offends is not particularly distressed by his error. He excuses himself only to himself or makes a brief apology enabling him to carry on as before. In that case the effect of the other person's overflowing, forgiving love is naturally absent; at least it does not become visible, even though the one who offended somehow presupposes it in spite of everything. But it cannot take effect. The relationship cannot begin again at the same point, but only on a lower level.

Or he does not excuse himself at all and merely watches to see what happens next. He has a somewhat bad conscience, but he does not avoid his friend. He thinks things will smooth themselves out in time. Why should allowances not be made for him now and then? When his friend sees him again, he will naturally understand that things were not meant as seriously as they seemed.

The last two examples, in contrast to the first, show how the sinner can close himself off from God. He does not capitulate; he stays in control, and he feels no obligation to demonstrate any contrition before God (only perhaps a bit of disappointment with himself). In this way the relationship of living love between God and man must die out sooner or later.

Living contrition, in contrast, can bring about a vitality in the face of which everything previous appears lifeless. Everything else pales and becomes dull beside the unprecedented formative power with which the pardoning God stands before the soul as if for the first time. Thus it can happen that a person who has had many visions of heavenly things may have a vision of heaven at the end of his life, a vision of such power and immediacy that everything previous seems like a dream to him. Or perhaps he sees how his mission will be carried out in heaven, and what he sees had no connection whatever to his earthly mission. Thus he no longer clings to that mission, though not because of virtuous indifference; he is so attracted by the new one that he releases the other quite naturally. Or the word for which he has lived, the message of the Son, now finally becomes the living Son himself and the eternal Word for him, and everything previous appears to him to be mere paper. He loses interest in what was, he may even deny it; he may go so far as to say it was a mistake. That is how powerfully the new truth overshadows everything. Similarly, a person totally seized by contrition may not only see specific sins behind him which he despises; he may perceive his entire life as having been alienated from God. He wants to hear nothing more of it. This entire life can be condemned because it did not prevent those sins but produced them. The new encounter with God has caused him to view his whole life in this light. This whole life must now give way, be extinguished, and must make way for what has just been experienced and demanded, for the new assent to God, for today and for tomorrow.

The Lord instituted confession in his new life after death. In conjunction with this the contrite sinner sees himself as a dead person lying in a grave, a finished person to whom the resurrected Lord gives the opportunity to be no longer of this world—similar to the way in which the Lord was no longer of this world between Easter and the Ascension. The same holds true for the mystical life previously discussed. When God gives someone visions, they form a kind of chain through his life, which from link to link may very well permit new beginnings, may be expanded. But a really different, new beginning, a new mission in that vision—if it is not a matter of conversion—is usually only possible in death. Here the Lord gives us a share in his eternal life. Contrition in confession is like an anticipatory sign of this new and eternal life in death. In the contrition within confession something of eternity shines into our own temporality. We do not merely receive objective new graces: in contrition we may have a genuine encounter with eternity, and within a sacramental experience we may acquire new certainty of eternal life.

A person who does not attain real contrition while confessing because he is thinking of tomorrow and how it will be exactly like yesterday has a finite faith. He is looking at himself and at his own impossibilities instead of at God and his possibilities. A man has a garden and has planted six trees in it, a bed of flowers and a few other things. One evening when he gets into bed he tells himself how boring life has become. Every day the same thing! Admittedly, the days are longer in summer than in winter, but what difference does that make? In the morning he looks out his window and sees his garden where cheerful tulips are now standing, but all he can say is, "How boring; tulips again just as before." A few months later he looks out the same window, and everything is lying under a blanket of white snow. But he has already seen this, too. And still later he sees that it has rained hard and all the garden paths are flooded, but the trees already have begun to bud. After a couple of years he looks out again, and behold! Only four trees are still there. One was struck by lightning; another froze because he had neglected it. Two are not doing well because he did not fertilize them properly when he planted them. Only two are still healthy. . . . This man must learn from the trees what he refused to learn from the seasons: God is continually changing man's world so that it confronts us with an incredible fullness and multiplicity; no two springs are just alike. But the human being is able massively to damage both himself and his environment by his lack of faith and love, his peevish indifference toward life and its richness, whereas he can profoundly ennoble both the world and himself through participation and work.

Confession, even the monthly or weekly one, always brings something new. It is our own fault if we get little or nothing from it, because we are such utter bores, bores with bad will who confront God with our boring sins and our bored existence and play all this as a trump card.

Resolution

Our resolution should arise at the point where the Son resolves to save the world for the Father, to become man so that the Father has a friend on earth in him, the Incarnate One, at the point where in the course of his life the Son strictly carries out this friendship, does the will of the Father without ever falling away from him and is always able to meet the Father as a friend meets a friend. We sinners, however, should resolve to improve ourselves so that the Father and the Son may take pleasure in us. We also know that it is the Spirit that brings us back to the Son and to the Father; the Spirit seeks to make this resolution with us and simultaneously shows us where our own lack prevents this friendship from coming about and which path we must take in order to grow into this friendship once again. We know further that God has offered this friendship and is waiting only for our agreement, waiting to see whether or not we intend to reciprocate his own will to friendship. Hence before the Father we must consider our own future; all those circumstances upon which it was suggested earlier that one should not brood excessively now come into question again, for they can now serve as signposts for our future. One should reflect upon them as long as they are fruitful for a good resolution and should view them as quite concrete and personal as long as they offer concrete possibilities for improvement. One should not, of course, begin a new examination of conscience; we are a step beyond that now. But this series of resolutions should grow out of contrition; similarly, they will be confirmed and strengthened in the actual confession later on. It is these resolutions also which, out of the entire sacrament, must accompany us most effectively into the life we return to; after all, they should be carried out. We can evaluate our progress from confession to confession by the extent to which we have realized them.

Hence a consideration of progress and retrogression is both possible and permissible while making these resolutions.

It would, of course, be pharisaical to mention this progress in confession. "I lied *only* three times this week, whereas it was five times two weeks ago." It could be that these three times are more grievous before God than the previous five. But in making resolutions one must see to it that progress is made. If contrition has been genuine, the seriousness and will to effective improvement will be there in one's resolution; it should by no means express itself merely in the general mood: "Things can't go on like this! Things absolutely have to get better!" the question remains of just what must get better and how.

Meditation upon the Lord's perfection necessarily contains the negative antithesis which I am myself. A conclusion emerging with equal necessity from this meditation upon how things stand with the Lord is that things cannot go on with me as they have. This is initially only a general observation. After the sin has become recognized and repented and the sinner completely humiliated by the discoveries he has made, he comes necessarily to the conclusion that this resolution must be made concrete. That which contrition has broken up is lying there like a fallow field, neglected, uncultivated and yet ready to be planted again. The inner significance of contrition seeks resolution, seeks to flow into it. The resolution issuing from it is not intended to put the penitent at ease. It is the initial step toward a real act required by contrition, an act no less real than the sins to be confessed, sins which are certainly not imaginary. I myself have committed them in this or that particular situation. Because I remain myself, because the situation certainly will return in one way or another, and because I by no means wish to fall into sin again, I must take concrete measures. Within the resolution there must reside a moment in which everything is to become concrete, as concrete as the Son's resolution to die on the Cross; otherwise that resolution is not genuine.

An encounter between two worlds is involved in this resolution, just as the Lord's resolution to become incarnate coerces heaven and earth—two worlds separated by sin—into a perfect encounter. I must now bring my own world, a world that has also been one of sin, into accord with the world of the Lord in heaven, the eternal resolution of the Son. A plan extends from God's eternal decree all the way to its execution, a decision extending into every detail and determining that things should happen thus and only thus. The Son abides by this plan. He views the various situations with which he will be confronted; he has not yet experienced them as a man, but he is God who knows everything in advance. The sinner also knows in part the situations into which he will come, though less as external than as internal ones, since he knows himself and knows how he normally reacts. He knows his own weaknesses, but he also knows that improvement is a very real possibility. His improvement and choice of the proper behavior have been preordained as genuine possibilities in the Lord's plan of salvation, just as real as the Son's own preordained path of life. In faith this possibility in Christ—our possibility—should be just as real as Christ himself, the content of our faith. In all his own resolutions, Christ knows one thing without fail: he wants to do the will of the Father. We sinners, however, can integrate ourselves into his activity, for there is our real place.

Hence we must concretize our own circumstances and remain faithful to the resolutions we make in light of them, remain faithful within a true fidelity issuing from true contrition. In the process, however, we must carve out steps and footholds, handles to which we can hold fast. It is good to strive for perfection, and no doubt the Lord wants us to be perfect. But if we had only this ideal in view, we would become resigned after the brief initial enthusiasm and perhaps even fall into despair. We must keep to details: how can I avoid this or that in the future, or avoid this if I already know my own inclinations and danger? Concretization, then, also means choosing the places where we will direct our efforts. They should not be too numerous if we expect success. In all this we should remain clearly aware that the carrying out of these resolutions is grace, and that we may therefore pray to succeed in keeping them. The resolution to pray better will thus never be absent, and we can begin with it right away.

Since the resolutions are to be carried out in one's present situation, their actual execution lives from the perpetual "now" of eternal life. Even the things that will not concern us until tomorrow or next week are to be carried out now, to the extent that the attitude toward them should be practiced now. Here, too, one should reflect upon the Lord, upon how he realizes everything in his life ahead of time with such assurance that he can anticipate the actual accomplishment in its fruits: "Drink the blood that is poured out for you."

The attitude out of which the Son speaks his "I am thirsty" and "My God, why have you forsaken me?" on the Cross is not only an expression of his unique suffering; it is simultaneously the essence of every correct confessional attitude. The penitent who receives the sacrament of the fruit of the Cross, who stands naked and exposed before the Father, must thirst for absolution and for the nearness to God that he has lost through sin. If he confesses openly and with humility, God will grant him this thirst and this yearning to be stilled—not as something the penitent imagines or presses out of himself, as it were, but as an objective gift of grace. This gift will perhaps take effect less when the sinner begins his examination of conscience, and for a time is completely concerned with himself, than when he begins to consider the result of this scrutiny, namely, how he really stands in his relationship to God. His intention to cleanse himself then is transformed into a yearning to be cleansed, a yearning only God can satisfy. Only when he receives absolution does sin become an objective quantity for him, something that no longer clings to his person, yet something from which he still must separate himself and take leave of in a highly conscious act. This leave-taking from sin is not simply identical with contrition and resolution. The confessed and absolved sin will remain in his memory as something of which he was once capable. It should not, however, be the object of continued subjective reflection upon his own possibilities and probabilities, but rather should have become a separated, objective quantity withdrawn from self-reflection and brought by God to the place that is fitting for it according to his will. Within the subjective realm it has made way for the yearning and love for God, the yearning of someone who was once a sinner, someone aware of his own unworthiness, someone who also knows about the weight of all sin, be it his own or someone else's. The sinner's burning, thirsting desire for absolution should generate something enduring, namely, that perpetual search for God that characterizes love here below, a searching which is the discipleship of the suffering and "confessing" Son on the Cross who thirsts more and more until finally "it is finished".

The sacrament of confession is not a psychological affair in which the essential elements are self-reflection and self-recognition. It is rather a matter of God's nearness, a nearness attained by the effective will to show oneself to God as one is in a condition brought by the grace of the triune God to resemble that of the Son on the Cross.

Confession

When a person goes to confession he should ask himself: what is this act I am about to undertake? He should remember how the Lord dispensed confession and what it cost him. It is his gift to every sinner, but first of all his gift to the Church as a whole. That is why a person confesses as a member of the Church, the community; he is to take the community along and include it in his confession.

A person comes to a confessional where perhaps several people are already waiting, where "the business of confession" is going on. He should come in an attitude in which he is willing to share the burden of all these other confessions and commend them to God, an attitude in which he also knows that his burden is shared by the others. Perhaps the person is nervous and touchy now because this humbling act of confession is about to become serious. Nevertheless, he should accept everything encountered on the way to the confessional—things that under certain circumstances might go against the grain—in a spirit that deepens his understanding of the confessional community in the Church.

Finally it is his turn. He enters the peculiar atmosphere of the confessional. We have been created much more supernatural than we think; we should notice something. This darkened place is a locus of grace, a place of the solitary person and of the community, the Church and I, I and the Church. Anyone who enters a church instinctively becomes silent and is seized by the present moment. This is all the more true in the place of confession, which is a locus of the Holy Spirit. It is also a place of fear, for one is rarely more endangered than before confession; a feeling of false pride can so easily arise, a pride that does not want to be humbled or challenged. In children it may seem charming; in adults it is intolerable. With children it is a feeling of being an adult, because they are allowed to confess; it is something spontaneous and unreflective. With adults it has lost its spontaneity and has frozen into a sclerotic "church consciousness". Confession is taken care of hastily between two errands on Saturday evening, and the person presses forward a bit as if he were in a store and wanted to be served sooner. He is, after all, in a hurry. But if someone tried to overcome this false haste, he would probably affect the others who are waiting and help relax the tense atmosphere of nervousness and prayerless impatience. When someone says, "Go ahead of me, I'm not really in a hurry", in a store where many people are waiting impatiently, this relaxes everyone's tension; the atmosphere becomes more human and seemly because everyone accepts part of the blame. All who are waiting before the confessional should sense something like this. They should know that every time a person is present in the church he is in the presence of the eucharistic Lord. We have been permitted to enter as honored guests. He is the host who is there completely for us, who listens to us, accommodates us and does everything to make us happy. He would like for us, too, to show him that we have been invited, even by the mere service of our presence. Almost incidentally, we should also be there to create an atmosphere, an atmosphere of love. We should be there in a way that implies we are willing to offer help and not just come into church with the purely individualistic intention of putting our own personal affairs into order while the others who are there do not concern us at all or at most disturb us. . . . Even if one must wait for a long while, one should not let the time be lost; for here is both a place and a time of grace. The penance of waiting is also a penance rising out of grace. Perhaps I will get home a bit later, but how many times have I come home much later merely because I stayed and chatted with someone on the street? Perhaps this confession that is taking so long and holding everyone up is an extremely essential one. Should not my own confession, the one for which I am waiting, also become something just as essential, something next to which everything else I have to do is really trivial?

It is now my turn to confess what I have prepared. The confession should not be made in the exultation of my resolution and the expected absolution, but in humility. It really is true; I did these things, and I am this kind of person. In a confession the priest should really recognize the sinner, not someone who is above sin. In the light of one's resolution it is easy to see one's past as something distant and no longer to want to admit to it.

One should confess in the stillness of truth, in completeness, in unfeigned humility. In a way one should go back once more and feel the entire pressing weight of one's sin. Yet one should confess in a faith that expects everything. Of course, I already have repented, made my resolutions and thereby somehow have gotten out of the deepest regions of sin; none-theless it is not up to me to pardon, but to God. I must take a step back. Or perhaps I should have become more humble through my contrition and resolution and should remember that at first my resolution was just a human one; it still must proceed through the grace of absolution, through the exhortation and through penance in order to find its full validity through the sacrament. I have nothing to hope from myself and everything from the grace of the Lord—including the keeping of my own resolutions. In faith I will hear the exhortation of the Spirit, in faith receive absolution, and also in faith now offer my confession.

One should confess with as little fuss as possible—only the naked sins, those one really has committed. Only occasionally should one say, "I don't know whether this or that was a sin." If one thought long enough one could no doubt find an excuse for almost everything. Instead, a person should depend on his own straightforward insight and conscience and quietly confess. So much the better if something was laid beneath the absolution that did not burden the Cross of the Lord any further. What is unbearable in confession is when a penitent continually absolves himself. He certainly should not accuse himself pharisaically of things he does not even consider to be sin; but he should own up openly to things and not exchange roles with the confessor. So many people confess as if they knew nothing of grace. The grace of confession is a special, unique, singular grace that wants nothing more from a person than that he absolutely own up to his sin and that he do so in truth (that includes contrition) and in faith. Only in faith can the penitent hear the voice of the Spirit and respond to it in the right way, in the personal way expected precisely of him. For the grace of confession is not meant for just any sinner, but rather for me. It personalizes itself somehow to the same degree that the sinner personalizes himself. When a wife asks her husband, "Can I help you?" she is showing him where she stands and that at the same time she is prepared to accept any response. With her question she puts him into a certain frame of mind, but in doing this she simultaneously wants to accommodate herself to his mood. In confession it is the person confessing who is asking; God's mood, however, is an objective one that he must recognize as he confesses, namely, what God is to answer him. Objective does not, however, mean colorless and impersonal. The person confessing within the New Covenant too easily forgets that God is legitimately angry with the sinner, and for this reason he often does not understand what God's infinite mercy means and how very much God, whose gracious mercy comes before all conversion, nevertheless expects with his pardon that the sinner convert and turn to him. This should be a turning to God that expresses itself in a contrite confession that as such is something far different than a mere ecclesiastical and disciplinary requirement. It is the New Testament compliance with God, which follows the Crucified One in discipleship. It is a great grace that a sinner may comply through his confession; we forget that. When a person loves someone, he tries to be the kind of person he is expected to be so that the other can also adapt himself to what is expected. With God, however, we no longer attempt anything; we do not comply in the relationship that grace both presupposes and brings about. When someone invites a friend to go on an outing of some sort, he asks whether it suits him, whether he has time and is not too tired. He expects an answer that is reliable so that he may act accordingly. God, too, is always planning something for us, and he would like to know how things stand with us—not just on the basis of his own omniscience, but rather through our own disclosure. The person thus disclosing himself should show himself capable of understanding what God has planned. He can comprehend the Spirit of God only if that Spirit is responding to the truth of confession. If someone confesses, "During the past two weeks I was offensive to my domestic servants, but that's all", the confessor knows something is not right with this confession; but he has no handle with which to

set it aright. He will no doubt say a few words concerning the
confessed fault, but he will feel as if he is actually missing the
mark. The Spirit seeking to speak through him cannot reach
the penitent's heart through his confession.

God has given man a sense for sin. It can become dulled; a
person no longer concerns himself with what sin is, commits
sins in a kind of good conscience and does not wish to be
pursued by sin. Nonetheless, when others do wrong, he
perceives it as wrong; he only flees from his own guilt. Most
people are left with a thorn inside that reminds them of that
guilt, and for this reason they feel the need for purification. If
they do not know about the sacrament, they try to confess
their guilt to someone. Yet they never get to the end of their
confession. They turn around in a circle and often get so lost
that they no longer are capable of distinguishing the essential
from the nonessential, their own from what is alien. The
definitive leap is not made.

Confession is definitive. For the sinner it is exhilarating
clarity: the turning about in a circle comes to an end. Yet this
clarity does not lie in the hands of the sinner who confesses but
is rather the clarity that the Lord bestows upon his Church.

Three times the Lord asks the disciple who has denied him:
"Simon, do you love me?" He asks him as the one who stands
before the triple sin. He might also ask in the name of the
triune God whose essential unity expresses itself in him before
this unique sinner. There is nothing chaotic about his unity
with the Father and Spirit; it is the communion of three
Persons in the unity of essence. The same Son can present
himself sometimes as the only-begotten Son, sometimes as the
one who reveals the triune life.

Peter, the sinner, thereby comes to stand before an infinitely
mysterious clarity that he can never fully grasp. He is questioned, and he must be content to be questioned in whatever
fashion the one triune God wants to question him. All of us
who sin and confess are in Peter. The sacrament does not

lie in our hands, and the confession itself does not come about
only according to our preferences—it is a response, and we cannot know in advance the question to which we must respond.
Every scene between Jesus and a sinner—man or woman—is
structured differently. The Lord is the one who guides. He
puts his finger on this and that, he handles the situation with
flexibility, but he is always the representative of the living
triune God. He can insist on the letter or let it fall and insist on
the spirit. He deals with the sinful woman in the Temple
differently than he does with the Samaritan woman or the
unbelieving Thomas.

The Lord also imbues sacramental confession with something of this free character; within its own official framework
it becomes an encounter between two persons. The priest
hears the confession, but he can nonetheless interrupt it with
questions and, as it were, change the course of the flow. He
does this in the Holy Spirit, who lends every confession that
mysterious, ultimately trinitarian unity between the official
and the personal. The sinner comes with a prepared confession.
He may find that his structure is toppled, that the grace that
questions him takes on different features than he expected and
draws him onto a different path than he imagined. As long as
absolution has not been dispensed, he still confesses as one
who not only must speak but also must face up to questioning.
He is not the one doing the directing. It even may happen that
during the dialogue he loses track of himself and no longer
knows where he stands—all the better! What he originally
wanted to serve up on a platter now looks alien to him; the
center of gravity has shifted, things have to be expressed
differently or they seem wholly inexpressible.

The person absolved who now leaves the confessional has
had an entirely new experience of his sin. What he planned
and intended to present has also been integrated into this
experience, but it has been transformed by the experience
itself, which transcends it. This experience also encompasses
a living experience of the Church, of her subjectivity and

objectivity, the unity given in her foundations of official and personal elements, and a new experience of the nature of the sacramental in which fixed elements encounter elements incapable of ever being fixed. It is exhilarating for the sinner when he is permitted to immerse himself in this mysterious gift of God, since he could no more express himself and explain himself in words than he could comprehend and explain God.

Exhortation

The correct attitude in which to receive the exhortation is that of trusting faith. If I have confessed truthfully and have prepared myself ahead of time in the light of the Spirit, I then know with absolute certainty that through the exhortation I am receiving the message of God meant precisely for me. As far as content is concerned, this message can contain either a general truth or, if the confessor will, an extremely personal truth; it makes no difference. However it may be structured, a person should accept it with a childlike faith that from the very beginning recognizes it as correct and useful precisely for him and in an openness enabling it to abide in his memory. The word given me is addressed to me and is a word that binds me; it simultaneously joins me to all other penitents and issues from within the indivisible treasure of the divine word. It is addressed to me, but it is to go through and beyond me to affect the others and to manifest its effects in the Church herself. I should be recognizable by the word I have received. It is like a seal impressed upon me, a stamp of authenticity that ought to be visible in me to others, a word in which both election and obligation express themselves. And finally it is a word that God has chosen especially for me from the infinite breadth of his eternal word in order to speak it to me; yet this does not separate it from the totality of the divine word. God's whole word is like a circle and the Church like another circle; the point of contact between the two is the word that I hear, a word descending like lightning out of the totality that is God, through me, into the totality that is the Church. I the sinner, at the moment I am to be cleansed, am made worthy to represent the Church before the redeeming God. God is always the whole one who always has in view the totality of the world in need of redemption. And I, as the Church, am to hear his message for the world in need of redemption. I am "worthy" of this word within the framework of the burden of the sacrament and the responsibility for it which I bear. This approaches the mystery of the Incarnation. The Son who becomes man also becomes God's representative on earth. He is wholly man and remains wholly God; as a whole man and as the New Adam he carries in himself the Bride, the Church, to whom he gives birth through his suffering and whom he imbues with the Holy Spirit.

The penitent is always in danger of subjectively narrowing the entire process. He somehow thinks he has offered his personal confession and the priest is now giving him a personal response. Through all the subjective elements, however— be they ever so subjective—he must still keep sight of the objective elements. The sacrament itself should so expand the penitent that he becomes aware of the singular essence of the Spirit of God. Hence in confession he must try to hear as much as possible of what really lies in the exhortation, and should do this within the mandate inherent in confession, the mandate given by God to encounter his Holy Spirit as a sinner and to receive it. This is a totally objective mandate which the sinner is always inclined to make subjective, perhaps most often precisely during the exhortation. Perhaps the penitent thinks, "He's already told me that ten times, and he has probably said it to all the others today as well." Instead, one should listen to the objective correctness of what has been said. That can be extremely difficult.

When the priest says, "We want to consider everything together in the way God sees it", this is not just an easy way to avoid having to evaluate specifics. For the penitent it is the unprecedented opportunity to submit his entire self and his entire subjectivity to God's omniscient objectivity and to live from then on within this submission. Even if a person receives a seemingly empty exhortation to a confession that he has offered in all seriousness, he nonetheless should tell himself that in these words, too, there dwells a certain relationship to the Holy Spirit. He should believe in this relationship, since the sacrament belongs to the Spirit. Of course, human stupidity and neglect miss a great deal and very often rob the word of God of its power; nonetheless we should allow this seemingly empty word to return to the power and fullness of God, to issue from within God and to express his truth. Our knowledge that it is an official word also should console us, and we should seek the source of dullness within ourselves and assume that the word is meaningful.

We should keep this message we receive inside ourselves so that we can then be guided by it. During the time of coming temptation, for example, when we no longer hear the incisive demands of confession as clearly, this word should be clearly audible. It should not seem as if we are being guided merely by a distant God, but by the Holy Spirit who was audible to us in the confessional and concerned himself with us personally. This existential aspect living on from our past confession can give us the strength to withstand temptation. If we had heard the same exhortation merely as a general, long-familiar truth, its power would not remain in us.

At the conclusion of the exhortation the penance is given. It teaches us two things. The first is that the same benevolent God who consoled, admonished and encouraged us in the word of the Spirit now also punishes. The same person who is to be accepted in grace is one who has done penance before God and through God. Second, one learns from the slightness of the penance, from its disproportion to the seriousness of the sin, that the God who bears all sin—the redeemer God—gives us this kind of penance. It is like a sudden insight into all that

God himself so disproportionately took upon himself for my sake and is something much more startling, indeed shaming, than the mere fact that I receive a punishment. Yet a person also should accept this penance in a Christian spirit, with a willingness to carry out all that is asked without measuring and weighing. A heavier penance might sometime be imposed, but even then it would be infinitely slight compared to the transgression.

If one receives a prayer as penance, as is usually the case, one should remember that this prayer is a part of worshipping God—just as, for example, the Son speaks and offers the Lord's prayer as a glorification of the Father—and that when we utter this prayer as those who have been absolved, we are joined to the almighty God in a new way. The consideration of the Son's suffering inherent in our penance immediately issues in the insistent impulse to worship. As penitents we have not been left alone, but, quite the contrary, have been invited anew and reunited. This activity of ours can be called penance only in an analogous sense; it could just as well be called thanksgiving. It is called penance because the Lord did penance for us and we thereby receive the spirit of penance as a gift through reference to the Cross. People reflect too little upon the extent to which this penance is only a symbol. God, however, is hoping that we will understand; here, too, he treats us as mature Christians.

It is part of the Father's joy to shape the person confessing so that the Son can recognize himself in that person. The opposite also appears (as in John); the Son shapes men so that the Father can recognize himself in them. But the Father's love also shapes us. The Son demands that we imitate him in his confessional attitude, in his nakedness before the Father. If a Christian approximates this attitude in reality, then it is the Father who is doing the shaping. Confession means being naked before God, and the shaping is the Father's exhortation through the Holy Spirit. In demanding confession the confessor represents the Son; giving the exhortation he represents the Father and the Spirit. By eliciting the positive willingness on the part of the penitent to live a Christian life of discipleship, the confessor reveals the participation of the Father in the sacrament of confession. The whole path leads from the confession, in which the sinner shows himself as he is, to perfect Christian readiness. It is a great thing that the Son brings a person to confession. The Father helps, however, by revealing to the penitent the Son in the Holy Spirit and thus preventing him from returning to the same point where he stood earlier. God's representative cannot be satisfied with simply taking cognizance of what is said to him. Precisely as God's representative he must intervene in an active and structuring way in the penitent's life. He must awaken a new predisposition for purity—not just for the purity of absolution but for a purity that arises new out of confession and the act of self-disclosure. That is a creative act that makes something out of nothing, an act of the Father executed and inspired by the Creator Spirit. It is the Spirit that creates a living unity and totality out of our many weak attempts.

The confessor does not shape merely good will and willingness in the penitent; rather, he expressly forms an eternal willingness, something the penitent really cannot control. A lump of clay—no one knows yet what will be formed from it. The soul has been swept up and stands within the collision of time and eternity filled with indistinct but joyous expectation. Although it may sink back or succumb to exhaustion, during the next exhortation it realizes anew that it is being infused with something that cannot be exhausted, something resembling the suspension of time in God, something potential that slumbers within the soul unless grace keeps it awake. The devil can misuse this potential so that the soul closes itself off in unwillingness. But the Spirit, through the confessor, brings the power of the act and unfolds the soul's entire blind self-opening toward eternal life. The soul undoes the buttons, the Spirit undresses it; the soul tries to say Yes, the Spirit brings about that Yes.

From the perspective of baptism the Son maintains the right to supervise the soul. Every soul that has once said Yes (and it does this through baptism) is the Lord's bride, and the Bridegroom has the right to see her as she is. The souls that have not said Yes, the heathen souls, are only potentially brides, and the Lord cannot carry out his right of supervision with them. He cannot demand confession, and the Father cannot shape them through confession. The Son entrusts his supervisory right to his Church, his complete Bride. The Church demands confession in the name of the Son. The Lord supervises the Church, and the Church supervises the individual believer, exercising an almost androgynous function.

The Son gives us the garment of grace of the children of God. Though he gives it to us open, we can close it. He does, however, require that we open it from time to time and show ourselves to him as we are, thereby also submitting ourselves to the Father to be shaped further in the image of the Son. When we do close it, we should do so in the true mystery of the Son and not in the false mystery of sin, so that we can open ourselves to the Son again at any time. And in every confession we should rejoice that we belong to the Son and are formed by the hand of the Father in the Holy Spirit.

Absolution

Absolution follows directly upon the penance. At the end of the exhortation, when the penitent is brought to a spirit of penance, to a rending of the heart, he suddenly is engulfed by grace, as if unexpectedly. One realized at the time of penance that it is infinitely slight, and that God has compensated; this realization was shaming and sobering and corresponded to the sobering phase of the examination of conscience, which itself was just the right preparation for being struck by the disproportionate power of grace.

The sinner is absolved from his sins. They are gone, are no longer there. Hence from now on any further consideration of them is eclipsed; they have been extinguished, have disappeared and have been submerged totally in the Passion of the Lord—but not so that we now search for them within that Passion or try to recognize or measure the extent to which we share the guilt in the Lord's death. They are now like a memory for which we no longer have room because all our space is needed to accept the fullness of grace, a grace of totality, of the indivisible God, a grace that not only fills us but expands us as well. It penetrates us, lays claim to the space already there and creates new space. The content is larger than the vessel. We are nothing but a relationship to this grace. It is truth, so that now Christ really does live in us, and his ever-greater grace demands ever more room. It shares with no one; it demands everything. It is as if until now we had tried to give ourselves in a small way, and now we are being taken forcibly. Even if we have been expecting absolution, have counted on it and have known it inevitably must come, we must now be surprised by it, because every grace of absolution transcends every expectation and is such a challenge that only the Lord can do justice to it. And he brings himself along in order to do a certain amount of justice to his own grace, knowing that our dwelling would be too small for him.

In the light of absolution it becomes clear why we were not allowed to do any grumbling beforehand, why a concluding line of demarcation, a separation from sin, was demanded and why we are not permitted to analyze the circumstances of our guilt and follow them all the way back to their origins. We were not allowed to acquire any sort of comprehensive overview from a distance, since we would only have contracted into our own ego. On the contrary, through recognition of our sin and through confession, exhortation and penance we had to objectify ourselves more and more, and in a certain sense even become depersonalized, even in—one might say, precisely in—our most personal sphere, in order to make room for the all-fulfilling personality of Christ. This clearing-out and separation had to come about at a certain pace so that all our time will be at the disposal of the Lord when he comes.

The grumbler or overly scrupulous person must stop before he really wants to. He must keep to the pace God sets for the sacrament; he cannot catch up at his present pace because he is too concerned with himself, whereas grace itself moves decisively forward. He will half ignore absolution. Indeed, he may not even have been listening very closely to the exhortation, thinking perhaps that he knew better than the confessor how things stand with him. Yet he must be brought to adapt his own time to that of God. One also encounters the opposite type: those who have finished long ago and, before God's absolution has even reached them, have already absolved themselves. They must slow down their pace. A sure sign is present in the entire sacramental sequence that God recognizes and considers our time and its pace but expects us to consider his time as well. Two standards of time collide which should exist for each other, just as husband and wife have to accommodate their time to one another in order to find one another. The person confessing cannot tell God, "Go faster, I'm already through", or, "Wait a moment, I'm not ready yet." The one confessing must integrate himself into the objective sacramental pace of the Church, similar to the way a woman must accommodate herself to labor pains and birth at the time they occur. In the "now" of the Church lies a compelling necessity.

Absolution comes in the name of the Father, the Son and the Holy Spirit. The entire sequence of redemption from the Father to the Son to the Spirit and from the Spirit back to the Son and to the Father becomes visible in this formula. In order that he may exercise his office, the priest possesses the Holy Spirit sent by the Son to be at the service of the sacrament to be administered, and the Son institutes this sacrament after his own suffering in order to complete the Father's mission. Hence both at the beginning and at the end everything leads back to the fulfillment of the Father's desire to save the world, and in every stage of redemption the triune will actively demonstrates and manifests itself. The power of the Father, the Son and the Spirit—the most comprehensive and absolute power—is given over to the priest in his office so that the power of absolution is not open to challenge or interpretation. It is an expression of the Trinity in the Church of sinners and saints. But the penitent knows that he has received a share in this unity of the Trinity within the Church of confession. It is as if the Church that both confesses and hears confession is lifted up into the Trinity, into the field of its divine grace, the grace given over to the Church for the sake of saving the sinful world. This space stands in the triune God ready to receive, a space of the perpetually bestowed reconciliation into the unity of God.

The penitent perceives absolution as a humbling experience: he can do nothing, God can do everything. This is the crowning of the humbling experience of confession as a whole, which never gives one occasion to glorify oneself, but at every turn gives one occasion to glorify the triune God who came down to us in the Son.

At the conclusion of the priestly prayer the penitent receives a concluding word: "Praised be Jesus Christ." This releases him. Yet in his response he has the last word, a word he clings to: that Jesus Christ be praised "forever"—praised in what has been because Christ has freed him from his sins, and praised in what will be, serving to remind him that the future is to be one of praise. It is like a promise the departing person makes to the priest, like provisions that he takes along in order to maintain himself. He demonstrates that he has understood and has grasped the sublimity of the gift, that through confession he has become capable of remaining within the praise of God, not through his own power, but rather through grace. In his perseverance he must always remind himself of the grace he has received, particularly in the temptations he must withstand. This final word left to him is one that has its beginning in the Spirit—the priest speaks it officially—but its continuation and end in the person who has confessed. It is the word in which he gets up and goes and begins his new life.

The Performance of Penance

Penance, too, is like the last word; it is both end and beginning. It is imposed as punishment for what has been, but it is spoken from within the new attitude. Here the character of penance reveals itself in a new light. Since it is so slight and is only a symbol, it must at least be taken for what it is: prayer. The Lord has had us confess so that we may be redeemed, but being redeemed is meaningful only if we seek the path to God anew and assume a new attitude of prayer toward him. Penance should bring this about in us. It is not only a deed performed externally but is also something that should shape us and bring us closer to God, the seed of a new fruit. It is like a deception: we think we are performing penance, but at the same time new seeds are being planted in our field, and we only notice it when we have begun to pray. We notice how infinitely slight the actual penitential character of this prayer is, and we are joined to what the Lord did by himself. Nonetheless, it is imposed penance which we must seek to accept as fully as possible in the spirit of penance. Then, without our knowledge, this penance becomes grace, a grace that guides us without interruption from the grace of absolution into the grace of daily life.

This penance acquires a free and manifold character because we can extend and expand it at will and may view what has been imposed as a minimum instead of as a maximum. We can do more and pray that God may accept this excess graciously and do with it as he pleases. Our doing more would show that we are beginning to understand what the Ever-More of grace means and that we are willing to put ourselves at the disposal of the new measure of grace that God has placed in us through confession.

In summary, a few practical hints for confession.

Above all we should seek God in confession more than

ourselves; we should realize that God is listening to us and thus should speak in a way we know he would want to hear, not in a slavish service of love, but by making a serious effort to direct all honor to God. Let us think back to our earlier confessions and consider where we have deviated from what were certainly correct insights and resolutions. Or perhaps our latest confessions were no longer quite right; perhaps they were only perfunctory recitations of sins. Let us listen to them with our interior ear, with a sense for the indifference and tepidity with which we confessed then. Let us try through the present confession to become ourselves again, approximately as God planned us in his love. In this way let us try to lay the foundation for our new life already in our preparation for confession.

How was our last preparation for confession? Did we lack at that time—and even earlier—the desire or enough time to get at the root of the problem? Did we simply pull together hastily a couple of things that more or less looked like a confession and then not sincerely repent of them? Sincere contrition does not permit haste; it may not be truncated before it has a chance to develop fully. If we know beforehand that we will not have much time on the day of confession, we ought to put things in some sort of order at an earlier time, perhaps the night before.

In examining one's conscience one should ask what was an isolated act and what a constant attitude. If we confess that we have sinned against truth, the question arises of what this really means. Did we consciously tell two or three lies, or perhaps many more? Or have we lived in an ongoing attitude of falsity such that at virtually every turn in our dealings with God and men we instinctively seek a suitable excuse or lie? Could we catch ourselves in a lie again at this very moment during the formulation of our confession, because we clothe things in words that only express them inadequately or even conceal them?

A person should ask himself further whether he really is confessing his sins as sins, and that means as things that must disappear, or more or less as mere facts and events that he recognizes and regrets. Do we confess our sins in an attitude that, within the perspective of our resolutions, has already concerned itself seriously with getting rid of these faults? The act of resolution should not consist merely in the acquaintance with certain recipes according to which we hope to overcome our faults but should arise rather from the entire openness to God and to the Church that constitutes our confessional attitude; we must see to it that something of this attitude of openness accompanies us afterward while we carry out those resolutions.

Now and then, at least, it is advisable to draw on the New Testament as an aid for the examination of conscience, since here the true encounter becomes so much more concrete than in the schematic "aids" in which only potential sins are treated. How do we appear within the real expectations of the incarnate God? It is easier to understand that we have insulted the crucified Lord than one who is "good and deserving of all my love". We ought to recall some of the Lord's own words or reread a couple of the Apostles' challenges to their communities. We should try to imagine how the Lord takes the Apostles to one side and explains his teaching to them, or how he reprimands them and, as it were, takes over their confession in so doing. Where does he find the most fault? Where does he place the most emphasis? Instead of confessing as a lonely individual, one ought to confess in community with the Apostles, whom the Lord himself admonished and heard "confess". Perhaps one might select a parable. The king wants to settle up with his servants. That is the kingdom of God: the purifying encounter between the king and his servants. Or, "How difficult is it for a rich man to get into heaven!" And we cling to our sins and are as little willing to be separated from them as the rich man is from his sacks of money. . . . The Holy Scriptures everywhere extend to us the suitable standard and demonstrate the correct relationship between God and man. Everywhere we are addressed personally and placed thereby in the original Christian situation, that of truth.

Everywhere we are invited to, prepared for and drawn to confession. We are told continually these days that we ought to read the Holy Scriptures more. To what purpose? With what disposition? Why, certainly in order to become the persons God's revelation wants us to become.

If we have the feeling we are not making progress with our confessions and always are standing in the same place, we should make the effort to find out where the personal, fundamental difficulty really lies. We should not let the matter go with a general sort of regret or a vague sense of defeat, a feeling that, after all, we cannot be helped. In the spirit of faith we should know that we can be helped. Again and again I catch myself in smaller or larger untruths. But why? Out of convenience? Ambition? Because I cannot tolerate exposing myself? Out of the need to count for something? Out of the joy I get from deceiving others? One must make an effort to examine one's fundamental attitudes and motives and to look them squarely in the face.

Perhaps we have made a decent confession but then are no longer listening carefully to the exhortation. We have already immersed ourselves again in our habitual perplexity and one-upmanship, in both simultaneously. What the confessor says to us he has said already weeks and even years ago; if it did not help then, neither will it help now. We do not hear the message for what it is in truth, namely, the ever-present admonition of the Holy Spirit. We already know about the teaching and its uselessness for us. It is now time to admit that we really have never yet heard the message correctly. We think we have fulfilled our obligation by confessing our sins before God, and we do not understand that in this exchange God's words to us are infinitely more important and effective than our own. If the confessor ever happens to say something different, we even become suspicious. "Why is he speaking differently than the others?" we ask.

Of course, confessors also should be inspired by a living faith. If they no longer hope and expect that something decisive may happen in confession, it would be better if they ceased hearing confessions altogether. Then those who do not go to confession could legitimately believe that a change might indeed come about if they would confess. . . . This holds particularly true for confessors in certain privileged times and places, for example, those at places of pilgrimage who have to hear a great many confessions, but who should be especially alert, present and personal. From them the pilgrims should always sense the ever-new, ever-relevant grace of this holy place. Just as the Scriptures helped us before, this holy place can help us now. If it is a shrine of Mary we ought to let ourselves be influenced by the attitude of the Mother; if it is the church of a saint we ought to give ourselves over to his attitude and guidance and go to confession in his spirit. If here, too, we are disappointed by a confessor, we should remember the objective grace of the shrine and, even more, that of the ecclesiastical office. Through the mediation of this office we continually and in an unobstructed fashion are encountering the Lord, who instituted it for our sake. This office is his way of letting his grace flow to us, and we should be in a position to return to him even through the rigid exterior of this office.

9. LIVING FROM THE GRACE OF CONFESSION

The New Man

After absolution the encounter with God looks very different than before. God helps the sinner in absolution; so that the sinner may become aware of this help, he is permitted to hear the words of absolution. He is liberated from his chains and as a free man he now stands before God quite differently than he did when in the state of sin. The distance between him and God has changed totally because at this moment he is determined by love alone, by loving reverence.

God in his one and triune life is eternal. The human being is mortal. Yet in absolution God breathes on man with a breath of his own eternity. The freedom man receives comes from the eternal love. From within this love he can now live anew, not just more freely but also more unconditionally, from within the totality of his condition that belongs to God, has been created by God, is maintained in purity by God and, if necessary, is cleansed again by God. In this condition everything acquires a clarity issuing from eternal life.

If a person falls back into sin, the distance is again characterized by anxiety, and a thousand things now come between the sinner and God. In this interim between two absolutions the sinner can have a great many experiences that separate him from God, diminish his freedom, burden his faith and conceal eternal life as if behind a curtain. Absolution opens this curtain for whomever is prepared to kneel before God in contrition and confession. Both happen simultaneously: absolution opens the curtain while the person stands ready and expects its opening, and experiences something of that eternity that he knows in depth only at this moment. God's eternal goodness, mercy and love are freed again for the sinner; it is as if God has sent them out anew to meet man and bring him home.

From here the person returns to daily life. If he has tried to confess properly, then for a moment he has seen his life and surroundings in a new light. He goes to work with new hope, and this hope carries the imprint of the absolution he has received. He will not think back on the purity of absolution as if on a fairyland that has been closed off again, for God has placed at his disposal through it an effective obedience in purity, a treasure that the person should now make his own. If he is confronted with new problems regarding his life, all these questions generated by confession find their solution in God, a solution God is ready to offer to us. That solution is always more love! Love that does not stagnate, the love of the triune God in that exchange in which man has acquired an effective share through absolution. The only question remaining is how a person uses this received love. His use is what confirms the presence of this purity and love. If he jealously guarded that love, thinking it were meant for him alone, it would quickly atrophy. But if he recognizes its mystery, which is its desire to be used and given, it will stay alive in him. Only if it is squandered does the treasure remain intact and the love maintain the original miraculous power it possessed in ab-solution, the power of a continuing, accumulating miracle. Once the chains of sin are broken, the chains and series of graces begin. If the possibilities of sin are numerous, and if these sins beget one another in a chain reaction, the possibilities of grace are much more numerous and open a glimpse of eternity itself.

During his life among us the Son sees how much effort is necessary for something of the word of God to acquire longevity. He shows in the parable of the sower how many conditions must be met for the seed to sprout. It remains a parable, and he knows what his followers who heard it have made of it: very little. His words have not led his listeners to become the good soil or forced them to create the conditions for this.

From the perspective of this parable, then, he instituted the sacraments. All of them have an absolute character, and they all effect something absolute, an immeasurable totality that comes from God and remains unsurpassable because of its own divine character. Perhaps the Lord could have instituted confession so that through it only the unendurable aspect of sin was removed, the part that goes beyond what we find tolerable. A person then would be left with a certain portion of his past life and past sin remaining and would be illumined concerning what was still to come. Instead, the Lord gives us in the sacrament a completely new beginning, a divine pardon that takes everything away. Someone who sins again after confession is not adding to what is already there but rather is starting over again with sin. But—and this is the essential point—he begins beforehand with a sinless life. If he considers what this moment of absolution has given him for his coming life, he will understand that he has become the good soil, that every burden has been taken away from him and that his soul has become innocent. Only his torpor and lukewarmness and perhaps his love of sin have made a sinner of him again.

If one considers the whole potential of the grace of absolution, one sees what one can make of it. If only one would truly contemplate the love of God, the grace, the word of the Lord, one would have everything one needed to respond as one should. The worry and toil of daily life have not been removed, but sin and our slavery to it have been. Liberated in this way one could take the decisive step toward the Lord every time, not just offer a prayer of penance and let that suffice, but rather give oneself over to the Lord in a completely fresh way, with a pure soul, and at this moment of weightlessness give him the chance to break through. A few days or weeks later, after daily life has "sobered" one again, one will perhaps look back at this surrender as if it were a moment of intoxication and surprise; one may have the feeling that one was not "normal". One might also become aware, however, that this condition of being liberated from sin was actually the most normal of all, and that the decision made in haste at the time was nonetheless the truest; it should be the magnetic point to which all other moments should converge. By genuinely making it the center, it is possible to orient the rest of one's life toward it. One simply must destroy the image of what is "permissible" that hovered before one, and without replacing it with another simply hold fast to one's assent and one's offer to the Lord, at the same time asking that he accept us fully and shape us. Then if necessary one should confess again soon in order to strengthen this condition of post-confessional purity. One should be convinced that one can be the good earth upon which God's seed falls and sprouts, soil that is simply open and stands at his disposal instead of complacently reflecting upon itself. This is a work of the sacrament, not of "good will". The sower himself has prepared the ground in which he can sow successfully.

The post-confessional condition is also the best for gaining indulgences. The person is cleansed and inwardly joined to the Lord and can easily fulfill the suggestions and prescriptions of the Church.

Sin with its origin and effect can be the subject of a worldly conversation; if one's own sin is under discussion, the facts are usually embellished. Perhaps it is discussed to pass the time, to make something else clear, to make oneself feel important or even occasionally just to give it expression. In a more or less conscious fashion one is always concerned with the listener's reaction: whether what is depicted gains or loses in significance, or so that one may acquire a point of comparison—*he* sees it that way, whereas *I* see it this way. The conversation with another person also may come about in order to put an end to an inner conversation between oneself and one's guilt,

an exchange one really could not identify as either a monologue or a dialogue.

In Christian confession, because of the objectivity of the
sacrament, everything is eliminated from the very beginning
that embellishes, compares or is geared to elicit reaction. The
penitent can prepare himself for his confession, can know
exactly how he will formulate it, can even know the tone of
voice in which he will present it and where he will insert a
meaningful pause. He can learn it by heart; yet, when he
presents it, it will sound much different. For now it is carried
by the listening confessor to God as an answer to God's
demand. It is integrated into the framework of unchangeable
laws, laws that long have been a part of ecclesiastical tradition
and practice and give sin its objective character. His sin stands
there like that of the first human couple in the garden,
unmercifully clear, this way and no other, incapable of being
glossed over, imponderable to man and indeterminable in
its ultimate effects. This creates a new relationship between
penitent and confessor; but the relationship also is incomprehensible, for it is like the residue of a certain relationship
between God and the sinner. In relation to the confessor God
stands in precisely the position he wishes to occupy and which
has been characterized once and for all by the Cross. The sinner
stands in a focal point which lies in himself yet is not generated
by him alone, and which itself radiates out to a great many
things that cannot be calculated. It is a focal point at which the
rays of all his past situations and deeds converge, his motives,
his life circumstances; yet the focal point never can be determined from these psychological factors because everywhere
grace is working and revaluing in an incomprehensible way.
Hence the sinner cannot know where he really stands. This
illumination of grace, which already has fallen upon his entire
past and now becomes visible to the sinner in confession, has
removed his last standard of measurement. On the one hand,
his entire past appears in this light in all its leaden weight. Yet

precisely where conclusions would have to be drawn from this, the light of grace itself appears that seeks to absolve him and that nonetheless appears almost terrifying during the preparation of the confession because it makes confession appear as a compelling inevitable necessity. It appears as an inexorable demand because I, the sinner, now *must* traverse the path of grace. I cannot lose myself in my past; it now lives in no other form than as a demand to be confessed.

The sinner encounters truth in this demand. To him who has lived with a certain past and who previously thought he knew who he was, a new face is given, a face that is not new only to him, a face from which has been withdrawn every guarantee of recognition by the world surrounding the sinner or of a recovery of his earlier relationships and concerns— indeed of everything that should have made up his future. What is now mine is in any case not what was mine before. I can accept that I will no longer recognize myself; but the most difficult part of confession is that others will not recognize me. They will have to see that until now I have lived among them behind a mask, one behind which they will continue to seek me because it seemed a part of me; now, however, I may show them my true face, that of a redeemed Christian. After the unravelling of my guilt I now fall into the confusing state of being someone other than everyone expects. How should I, a sinner, live in the future as a child of grace? If only things around me would change! If only I could go to a foreign country with foreign people! But this concession is not granted me. I must stay where I am. Only now the words, "No longer is it I who live, but Christ lives in me", must apply to me, words that have waited two thousand years for me. Does my confession not constitute an enormous lack of foresight? Now everything will be a surprise. But this surprise does not begin with me at all; it commences with the word of the Lord which the priest authoritatively speaks and which then extends to me and to the entire confessing Church, who says the *confiteor* in the prayers at the foot of the altar. From me and the Church the word goes out to our surrounding world, a world that shakes its head in disbelief or perhaps quietly begins to believe.

Confession and Daily Life

Human life throws us from one extreme to another. If we are successful, our mood reflects it. We enjoy celebrations, even though they may not concern us personally except because they are, after all, celebrations. Then suddenly something sad happens; our mood does a turnabout, and we are depressed. The sacraments of the Church, however, give us the opportunity to avoid being exposed so helplessly to such oscillations, to acquire an attitude instead of a mood. A good confession, of course, itself results in extreme moods ranging from a shuddering before the seriousness of our sin to a rejoicing in absolution. These moods, however, are connected centrally to one another and can all be integrated at a central Christian locus, in the confessional attitude given to us and infused in us by the Lord, an attitude which at the same time is his claim on us. This attitude means being open before him; it means trying to realize that he sees everything we do, but as one who helps, intervenes and dispenses grace. We do not experience this in aggravating changes of mood, but rather within a stable and stabilizing attitude supported by his work of redemption. If in spite of all changes of mood we have accommodated ourselves to this one attitude in confession, the opportunity then arises for us to keep ourselves fresh and alert within it, to integrate all our circumstances and feelings into this enduring confessional attitude and to remain a penitent before God, always open to his grace.

In daily life everything happens differently than in the fixed form of confession, and yet every occurrence in daily life can be ordered toward confession. It would be highly inappropriate to leave the confessional with a feeling of liberation, relief and purity, and then to move quite unconcerned toward all the new opportunities for sin as if we had a right to be supported by the grace we have received, audaciously assuming that God surely will bring us back again, at best before we sin again, at worst afterward.

We are not permitted to reduce our own idea of confession to absolution, so that, in consequence, confessing would weaken our inner attitude rather than strengthen it; the sacrament should not effect in us a kind of indifference toward sin so that we employ the *ama et fac quod vis* in a distorted, perverse way by reserving the *fac quod vis* for ourselves and leaving the *ama* for God, the God who will pardon us again no matter what we do. Confession obligates us in the direction of the Cross; because it comes from the Cross, it leads back to it as well. That is why it generates an attitude that seeks to imitate the attitude of the Lord.

The Lord, too, comes from the Cross and returns to it. He comes with the intention of going to the Cross. In the beginning of the world the Creator separated the elements above and below, right and left; the Son already saw in this an omen of the coming Cross. The Father separated and created order; human beings, through sin, have separated themselves from God, distinguished good from evil and put the disorder of chaos in the place of his order; on the Cross the Son separates anew according to the will of the Father. He judges by elevating and orienting. He introduces the new separation as a decision for the Father. He brings good and evil back into unity by doing good and suffering evil. His dividing is directed into the unity of redemption. And because he carried everything into his own death, he descends at the locus of the Father's own righteousness, sees the Father's work and at the same time his own work of separating sin from sinner. In a final condition of composure and acquittal he leaves certain things behind him here with which he as the Resurrected One intends to have nothing more to do and with which we, too, have nothing more to do. A parallel to this is found in confession. According to the logic inherent in confession, the things the Son left behind during his descent into hell also should have become inaccessible to us. Indeed, they are inaccessible if we persevere in our confessional attitude. What is settled in confession is settled once and for all. But that, again, means that we live toward the Cross.

After each confession we should live toward another confession that will be ever more spacious and comprehensive and include ever more of the world and the world's guilt, a confession that increasingly acquires the dimensions of the Church. We should be aware that we have always confessed too much as isolated individuals—supported, to be sure, by the confessions of others, but not contributing our full share of support. The Church that carries all confessions and meditates upon the Cross of the Lord should shape our confession more and more.

If confession has come alive in the life of a Christian, if rather than remaining a mere formality it becomes a significant part of the sinner's conversation with God in which the sinner is pardoned and receives a portion of the one great grace of pardon (for this pardon does not merely extinguish, it also gives new substance for one's life, indeed, substance of its own kind), then something of confession must enter into daily life. It must not be something that is merely suitable for meditation or something one pulls out when things go badly, either when one has sinned again or has successfully withstood a serious temptation; it must be something so strong that consciously or unconsciously it accompanies one at each moment. The course of confession with its various contrasting situations shows the Christian within the unity of the sacrament the many paths of encounter that the Lord wishes to walk with him in his sacrament of redemption. Everywhere he shows himself as the living Lord by pointing out, demanding, listening, admonishing and lifting up; he binds to himself and simultaneously releases to freedom; one thing he takes upon himself, another, which is his, he gives. All these forms of encounter should remain efficacious by developing individually, being experienced individually and yet always remaining oriented toward the unity instituted and formed in the sacrament. Again and again the sacrament reveals an unprecedented expansion of all the possibilities of Christian existence in the Lord.

If one confesses properly, however, this multiplicity itself will have an aftereffect on the sacrament; it will lose all trace of monotony and will reveal ever-new aspects within its greatness, aspects which have grown familiar to the penitent in his daily life and have strengthened his attitude and given it a wider scope. He sees everywhere what confession has made possible and also what it has done away with once and for all, what now no longer even comes into question. If reflection and the reading of Scripture have found their place in one's preparation for confession, this place should also be reserved for them in daily life so that the more narrowly understood preparation for confession does not have to reach too far back or too far forward. The living, well-tended relationship to the Lord and to his revelation in Scripture should offer the natural preconditions for carrying out the examination of conscience easily and fruitfully. Whoever looks daily into the mirror of the Christian (the mirror that is Jesus Christ himself) will, when he examines himself, quickly recognize his own features in it.

The grace of confession also allows us to encounter our fellow men more magnanimously. A person who has experienced grace himself will sooner grant it to his neighbor. He knows that grace seeks to be mediated further, and he will look everywhere for opportunities to do so. Each person will find new solutions he can use, none of which have anything to do with overzealousness or indiscretion. A person with no external apostolic mission will consider that every one of us has an inner mission to prayer that has an apostolic effect. This he must nurture, and at the same time his own behavior must make the Christian faith palatable for others. For each Christian there exists the possibility of an effect that extends across all his action and passion, even if it does not express itself in audible words. His neighbor will not appear to him merely as a lost sinner, but as one who, if he is Catholic, has a share in the grace of absolution and should be seen in its light. If he is not Catholic it is more difficult for him because he does not know the grace of confession. We meet so many people who are tied up completely in their own egoism and inconsequential daily business. But how do we know that they will not soon be immersed in the great grace of absolution? And what can we do so that they may begin to see this light?

To many an individual, going to confession appears insurmountably difficult; and then once he has confessed it turns out not to have been so very hard. A mysterious grace carries him through, and suddenly he understands something of the Church's own prayers; he feels supported by the spirit of so many nameless people and perhaps also by the prayer of a particular person. Now he himself feels obligated to pray. Nothing is more private than the confession of the individual, and yet there is enormous space in it for the prayers of all the others who are participating without really knowing what is happening and who make their prayer available without any curiosity or need to know. This supporting power of prayer shows us quite well the discretion with which the Lord treats our sins. Confession takes place at the center of the Church; all participate and are able to know that they do, but they neither know nor want to know what is discussed between the sinner and the Lord. In many cases aid to one's neighbor is given by a word; yet precisely here, not wanting to know constitutes intimate, helpful service. Two people who love one another very much and are very close will not know, when they go to confession together, what the heaviest burden for each of them was. In spite of the secrecy of confession, however, they will be joined more closely to each other precisely through confession, because they each have received the same grace and have walked the same path. One of them knows perhaps that the other was impatient with him yesterday and that he probably will confess that impatience; but the person suspecting this not only will not dwell on the knowledge, he will push it away immediately as something that does not concern him. Nonetheless, as much as he can, he will pray for the other's confession. The knowledge of individual sins neither advances nor hinders the relationship between two people who love one another, and a lover will not even ask for a confirmation that his own prayer benefited the confession of the beloved. Everything surrounding confession is concealed in the mystery of the communion of saints.

Confession and Mission

Anyone who has recognized, in confession and in the prayer belonging to it, the possibility not only of ridding himself of his own sins through the grace of the Lord but also of helping others at the same time will suddenly realize that there is a place where confession and mission encounter and permeate one another to the point of coincidence. The Son's mission is a completely divine one, and even as a man he carries it out in a divine fashion. In order to carry it out he remains all his life in the attitude of complete openness before the Father and the Spirit, and that means the attitude of confession; this always allows him to do the will of the Father in the Holy Spirit and to carry out his mission as personally and at the same time as obediently as possible. His attitude of openness and his actions comprise a single unity. Even on the Cross, where he no longer feels the Father and yet suffers under the burden of our sins, where he effects not only general, abstract redemption for everyone but also concrete confession, he stands at the zenith both of confession and of mission. He carries out the most difficult part of his mission, death on the Cross, from within the most open confessional attitude. And since all differentiated missions take their point of departure from the Cross, they also take it from the confessional attitude and from the act of confession.

If a saintly person had never sinned, or at least not in a long while, he might, as regards himself, acquire a relationship to sin in which it lost relevance. He would see and understand it only from the perspective of the Lord's Cross. He himself would be excluded from the realm of sin by means of a special grace. He would perceive the sins of those he encounters as an aggravation in his dialogue with God but not as serious hindrance. But this is not the way it is. By reflecting upon the Cross he measures the burden of sin against it and experiences that burden in its entire weight from the perspective of its effect. He also will see how sin devastates his fellow men and will understand his entire mission as one of aiding sinners.

It also may be, however, that the saint was himself a sinner and thus will always see himself as one; he then experiences his encounter with the Lord as the perfect grace of confession. It may be that he, like the Magdalene, is permitted to encounter the Lord himself, or it may be that he meets him in a conversion confession in the Church. Here, too, the experience of confession will appear inseparable from his mission. If his confessional experience constitutes a high point in his life, he will try to keep it present in a changed form—not in order to prolong a sensation, but in order to imitate the Lord on the Cross in his own way, to let himself be sent out for the sake of the sinners among whom he was once included and still includes himself in his own heart. For others seeking to carry out their own mission, confession can be an experience that hurls them back into the center of that mission in a fresh way each time, a compass that points out the right direction and outlines the path exactly. They always complete this mountain climb under the auspices of confession. Although the danger of falling is always present, confession shows them the narrow path again and again.

If a person so perceives his own mission that he knows himself to be merely a channel and mediator within it, he also comprehends that he will have much the same experience with every sacrament. The sacrament is of significance for him to the extent that it frees him from everything not belonging to his mission, expands him and makes him more receptive. If he loves his mission and wants to live for it, if his life appears to him as his service, he will yearn for nothing so much as to carry it out according to God's will. He will seek to carry out, as thoroughly as possible, the two articulations that come to expression in the sacrament: to receive his own portion so that that which is meant for others can be given all the more purely. He will confess in order to be pure again for his task, in order to view with fresh eyes what is essential to his own mission and to be able to pass on, in as unbroken a fashion as possible, that which he has received in confession.

There is no mission that is not determined decisively by one's confessional attitude. And no sacrament makes the required receptivity of a person to his mission as clear as does confession. The slag obstructing the free flow is dissolved and swept away so that the mission can move freely again. On the other hand, the person with a mission should not become so excessively eager for confession that he makes virtually everything dependent upon it; it would be wrong to seek to confess every day in order to do justice to one's mission. God has not placed his power of grace in the sacraments alone: he also bestows it in prayer, and through membership in the Church a person perpetually receives purification and help. If the communion of saints lives to a certain extent from him, he also lives from it and is sustained and benefited to a certain extent by its needs. We should not forget that a received sacrament also has an aftereffect, an abiding in what has been received. The sacraments should not be compared exclusively with physical nourishment that strengthens a person only for a certain limited period. A person should seek to partake not only of the sacraments but to partake in a straightforward way of the grace of mission as well, the grace of office. A person may confess before a difficult undertaking in order to be purified completely for it, but he cannot seek to confess again on the occasion of the very next task. He would be forgetting the aftereffect and God's free grace. Confession does not seek to make us immature and dependent; on the contrary, we should become mature and in an increasingly sensitive obedience develop an increasingly refined sense of what is required of us.

Lesser missions are also possible, and they often become visible during confession, which itself then becomes a kind of preliminary preparation. The confessor notices that something is there that needs nurturing and amplification, and he accordingly allows it to stand out more clearly in confession. The penitent in turn senses how confession is transforming him.

Confession and Prayer

Since the Son always stood before the Father in the attitude of confession, every encounter the believer has with the Lord will teach him something of this confessional attitude. Perhaps what he receives will be very close to sacramental confession, but may appear distant from it and will prove to be a part of the atmosphere of confession only when examined more closely. Every encounter with the Lord in faith involves prayer. It is impossible for the believer to approach the Lord in a spiritual attitude that is alien to prayer, one, for example, so scientific or historical that it would contradict prayer. This spiritual attitude is rather a kind of expansion of prayer augmenting its freshness, sometimes more peripherally, sometimes more centrally. Pure prayer would be participation in the Lord's conversation with the Father in the Holy Spirit and in the triune God's conversation with the world and with us. The triune conversation is all-encompassing. The most we can experience of it is what we are able to grasp in some way, such as the Lord's words on earth, his relationship with the Church, the institution of the sacraments, the commandments, his counsels. Prayer and confession need not always be sharply differentiated; a person might pray regarding his confession as preparation or penance, in which case the connection is clear.

On the other hand, he may choose confession itself as the subject of his prayer and pray that he may better conform to both the act and the state of confession, and so on. One can also simply pray and worship without consciously having confession in mind; yet even this prayer will not be without some connection with confession, since every properly offered prayer brings us closer to the Lord's own attitude and imbues us with something of it. The Lord's attitude—quite uncomplicated in itself—is full of multiplicity and complexity for our understanding, because it is accessible from every side. Everywhere we find access to its center: openness before the Father in the service of the world's redemption. Hence every prayer we offer, every one that enriches the Church's treasury of prayer, trains us in his attitude and stands within the context of the world's redemption. That is why prayer stands in such close proximity to confession. This ever-central character of prayer also explains why the Church allows so many different forms of prayer and devotion so that each person can seek out the form commensurate with his needs. If it were not so, we would have to pray according to a precise system out of which the poor souls, the penitents, the communicants, the apostolic work of the Church and so on would then receive portions according to a very precise allotment. Since that is not the case, we are permitted—so it appears externally—to pray one-sidedly. Of course, it is always good if at the same time we clearly recognize the essential aspects of prayer, so that no matter how or what we pray, no matter what devotion we undertake or what intentions we bring to it, we offer our prayer to God so that it is at his free disposal. For every Christian prayer is ultimately an assimilation of the one praying to the will of the Father which the Son does. Just as the Son does the entire will of the Father in every one of his acts, so each of our Christian prayers has full participation in the will of the Father.

God is omniscient; what we confess to the priest God already knows. We tell him familiar things, we try to tell him what is true, and yet in doing so we become newly aware of God's omniscience. Even when we pray we should remember that God knows what we need (if it is a matter of a prayer of petition), or how we would like to adore him (if we are offering a prayer of adoration). This knowledge should not remain purely theoretical; it should spur us on and help us to come naked before God, to pray in the complete openness that knows no reservation and seeks to disclose precisely what we might want to withhold. This kind of openness is a part of the attitude of confession; over and above this, however, the latter includes readiness, an expectant, accepting movement toward God. Mere confession would be insufficient if a person felt that he had done enough and could now crawl back into his shell. Confessing is movement toward God and surrender to what he gives. The same is true of prayer: it is not just words addressed to God but at the same time—and even more intensely—a listening to his word and the willingness to follow it. Prayer is not a monologue; it is a dialogue. It is not just the expression of human needs and beliefs but also a condition of openness for everything God says and needs.

Furthermore, the penitent should allow his confession to extend beyond the act of confession itself, according to the will of the Lord: his confession should stay alive and effective afterwards as well. Similarly, the person praying should be able to live from the times of prayer even during the time he is not expressly praying. Prayer should summarize and express everything that is true and that happens during one's entire life, and should announce that one is remaining in God. Just as changes occur from one confession to the next of which perhaps the confessor is more aware than the penitent, so also a development takes place from one prayer to the next, since the believer no more lives in a static condition than the Son— who came from the Father and returned to him—ever came to a standstill during his own sojourn. The person who prays and the one who confesses (who is actually both at once) stands within the discipleship of the Son and is taken up in the Son's movement toward the Father—while the Son always has the movement from the Father in himself. Our entire life, in its unity of prayer and confessional attitude, is characterized by the unity of the attitude chosen by the Son.

Confession and prayer are also similar in that particular questions, problems and difficulties of life find expression in them. Both demonstrate clearly that the Christian alone cannot deal adequately with his situation, and that he needs the help of God and the Church. This becomes clear, in confession more after his fall, in prayer more before, in confession in a more concluding fashion, in prayer in a more preventive one. Nonetheless, the conditions of having fallen, on the one hand, and of standing before a potential fall, on the other, are not mutually exclusive. The two situations are connected so intimately within the believer that both belong to prayer as well as to confession. Hence someone who is confronted by a serious temptation can confess, and everyone who has fallen can pray.

10. THE OFFICE OF CONFESSOR

Preparation

All the right motives for becoming a priest lie with God; fundamentally they lie in the same realm in which the Son decides to become man. This decision already is reflected in the priesthood of the Old Covenant; after the realization of the Incarnation it presents itself in the New Covenant in a completely new way. Jesus Christ is the priest of priests, the pastor of souls who seeks all souls and brings them home to the Father. When young Christians decide to become priests their motives can be as different as people are different; yet they are all one in Christ, whose own priesthood is a unity of the most varied aspects and motives, all of which the Father has placed into his priestly office. Each person who chooses this office in the Son's discipleship can make a certain choice from within this fullness, and his choice, his preference, is always legitimate if in that choice he simultaneously seeks the whole.

The sacraments and their dispensation by the priest play a special role in this choice. Many view precisely the dispensing of the sacrament of penance as the most direct way to come closer to the sinner and free him again for God. A certain need to help one's neighbor in Christian love can manifest itself nowhere as strongly as here, and candidates for the priesthood will see in the dispensing of this particular sacrament the richest and most varied manner of pastoral activity. From the very beginning the seminarian is thinking about everything he will be able to accomplish in the confessional. He views confession more in its sacramental and official character and for a time remains in a state of expectation regarding people and their actual situations, an expectation fulfilled only by priestly ordination. But he studies and prays with an eye toward what is to come. He lays the foundations and imagines how the future house will look, even to the details. Only the occupants are missing.

A priest's training naturally includes not only a precise knowledge of the sacrament and its ecclesiastical administration and of the norms and rules the Church establishes but also, and above all, a personal view and position that is more than intellectual and already requires total involvement. He must learn to live in the midst of the sacramental life and to realize that he stands in precisely the position where the Son is sent by the Father. The Son's entire heavenly life beginning with his resolution and his entire earthly life all the way to the Cross can be viewed as a preparation for instituting confession. If the seminarian considers this, he will understand that the demands made on the confessor by the Church—indeed, by the Son— are infinitely broad, so broad in fact that they must encompass his entire life as a priest. At the same time they are so precise that the one sacrament's claim on his life as a priest by no means excludes the simultaneous demands of the other sacraments. From the perspective of the one, however, the entire structure can be supported and comprehended in its growth.

In heaven the Son prepared himself to institute the sacrament of confession as a man. He did so not only in his all-encompassing acceptance of the Father's will, so that he could carry out that will with all his heart and all his strength, but also in his direction of everything toward his own divine-human priesthood and the redemption and absolution of sinners. The same holds true for the priest of the New Covenant, and the confessional will offer him a similar mediating position between heaven and earth. If he sees this similarity of the discipleship of his office, everything he comprehends about the Son—obedience, love, glorification of the Father, total service—will acquire a plasticity that must manifest itself everywhere in his priestly existence. Because the Son sacrificed everything to his priesthood, the priest cannot withhold any part of his own life from his service. Since the Son was without fault, the priest is allowed no special consideration regarding his own faults. He must strive for a perfection that lies grounded in the center of the sacrament, and he will have to bear continual responsibility and thereby have to answer for himself before both the Father and men. To do this he must learn to see both divine purity and human sin in a new light, the light of the Son of God who gives himself for sinners. He will not be able to separate his vision of the Son, for example, during meditation and prayer, from his reflection upon human sins, and he should view both in the light of the office of mediator. Even when he reflects upon the triune divine life, some sort of fruit for sinners should emerge and become visible; but upon encountering sin, he should not stop at the thought of penance and absolution but should consider how he can show to the returning sinner (whose condition he himself always shares) the image of the self-sacrificing mediator.

Whenever a lay person sins, his sin—which should not be diminished in seriousness—is still in a certain way "his own affair" with which he himself must come to terms. But if a person later intends to hear confessions, this changes things dramatically inasmuch as he will be dispensing a sacrament and thus come into a different relationship to his fellow men. If he confesses today, he must do so with an eye already fixed on his future position as one who hears confessions, on the purity, submission and priestly form of brotherly love that he will need and now is obligated to acquire. Whenever the candidate for the priesthood confesses, he is standing within the communion of sinners, and this, too, must be a comprehensible reality for him as a Christian and as a priest. He should view his fellow sinners and penitents not only with the eyes of a theologian but also as one who shares with them the communion of salvation and damnation. He is not to view them with the eyes of purely human tolerance, but rather with the eyes of Jesus Christ himself in whose place he, the sinner and fellow sinner, will be carrying out the office and practicing its forgiving love. In his encounter with the most varied persons at home, in church, on the street, let him show a form of Christian love and a willingness to give of himself which already anticipates the future confessor, though without false unction and obtrusiveness. This sows seeds that must be sown long before ordination and the conferring of jurisdiction, even though for the time being they cannot really sprout. A medical student sees potential patients in all people, patients he would very much like to help if they were sick. The same is the case with the seminarian. He would like to offer help to every person because he knows that each will have to confess.

What applies to the confession of every Christian applies to his own as well—indeed, to an even higher degree, since in his own confession he also seeks to be a priest. The confession of a candidate for the priesthood already takes place with an eye to his future position as one who will hear confessions. His confession must be void of gaps; he should be severe regarding his own sins and should pay particular attention to the perspective of mercy and aid to one's neighbor. He should also see that the grace which he himself claims comes from the same store of grace from which he will later distribute. In every part of confession he should view himself in communion with his future penitents. This requires that he assume a conscious confessional attitude. Regarding his future penitents he should become increasingly more transparent, just as a woman who wants children and marries already looks forward to those children and is developing her own motherly characteristics. This is no abstract demand; it definitely has a practical side in the struggle against his own errors, in the sincerity with which he sees them, in his openness before God, in his contrition, in his humility when receiving the exhortation, in his joy at absolution and in the new power he draws from the sacrament. He must surrender himself as one who is seeking to be newly formed and modelled, and the model itself hovers before him: he puts himself into the hands of his confessor and surrenders himself to the power of the sacrament in order to approximate more closely the model of the Son and to be influenced by his character as the founder of confession, so that he in turn can form new penitents. Even if he can make no noticeable progress from one confession to the next, his willingness to submit will not diminish; he will persevere in his condition of continually being under way and of setting forth toward the unattainable divine-human example. He will be under way his entire life. The Son's perfection will seize him only as an incomprehensible confusion of which only one thing is certain: it is the rhythm of the Son. The best he can attain is never to let himself be cast out of this confusion, never to secure for himself a more quiet corner where he no longer perceives very much of those powerful currents. In this way he must experience the meaning of: "No longer I live, Christ lives in me." He should never put this experience behind him but rather should realize it perpetually, particularly in his situation as penitent and confessor.

As one who will hear confessions, he should even now acquire an interior relationship to the Holy Spirit in exhortation; he should hear what is spoken to him as something spoken in the Spirit. Allowing the Spirit to speak it, he should thereby recognize the conditions that will enable his own later exhortations to be given in the Spirit. The important condition is that the pentitent submit to the confessor's exhortation in humility; the spiritual content of the exhortation itself can contribute toward bringing this about. He should also try to take this exhortation with him afterward until he has fulfilled its demands or until a new exhortation has replaced it. Here, too, he must simultaneously conduct himself as an ordinary Christian and acquire experience for his penitents; through both he will be trained in a spiritual conception of his office as a future confessor. His relationship to the confessor and to the Spirit speaking through him should become an expression of his personal life and striving.

Once again, this is the Church's imitation of the Son's triune life. The decision to become incarnate is a dialogue between

Father and Son in the Holy Spirit, and from this dialogue the sacrament emerges as an effective image through the Son's own institution of it and through its vivification by the Holy Spirit. Through the exhortation the penitent receives a share in the contact between the confessor and the Holy Spirit, who is the witness and expression of what the Father and Son say in the dialogue of redemption. This is possible only because the incarnate Son in his confessional attitude remains open for the dialogue between the Father and Spirit in heaven concerning the Son's mission. The roles appear reversed, but the Son is the one who institutes confession by infusing his filial spirit into it, and to this extent the reception of the sacrament remains simultaneously imitation of the Son, obedience in his obedience. Not even the Incarnation itself gives us an overview of this triune dialogue; but in spite of that, indeed even because of it, our participation in the sacrament remains a varied one and allows confession to emerge more clearly as a supernatural source of life. One can never participate in the triune life as a mere listener, as someone from the outside who really does not belong, but only by being placed in a situation of Christian dialogue which as such is found worthy of participation in the triune life. What situation is better suited for this than the one instituted by the Son between penitent and confessor, between the sinner and the redeeming God in the Church? If the penitent himself is a future confessor, it is doubly important that he acquire an understanding and sense for the trinitarian character of the confessional dialogue and particularly for the multilayered character and interchangeability of the various perspectives, since the same person is changing his point of view from that of the penitent to that of the confessor. Such interchangeability makes the official quality of the process more familiar; it clarifies the function of the hierarchical element because this ability to be both penitent and confessor is not illuminated simply by human relationships but rather both presupposes and reveals a higher level of being instituted from above. Analogies could also be made to the natural "hierarchy" of man and woman; the penitent would then be feminine, the officiating priest masculine. To a certain extent the absolved penitent has emerged from the confessor as Eve did from Adam's rib, though in this case it is the rib of the second Adam, Christ, who is officiating through the confessor. For Christ in his representative confessional attitude creates the Church out of sinners and offers to them, who have been created personally by God, a personal return to the Father.

Hearing Confession

Whether a new priest longingly anticipates his first confession as the fulfillment of a long-held wish to help, or whether he secretly fears he might be overwhelmed by the sheer immensity of the task, feeling he is not yet mature enough to intervene officially in other people's souls, the first time he hears confession will be a shock for him. The first time he dispenses absolution he must feel as if he is exposed helplessly to the storm of grace and to the disproportionate relationship between him, the newly ordained, and God's unprecedented gift of grace. He pronounces the words he has learned by heart and probably says them correctly; nevertheless, as regards the exhortation he will probably feel that the Spirit asked more of him, that he should have spoken differently both in what he said and how he said it. During the absolution he will feel lost and overwhelmed by the power entrusted to him.

He will gradually grow accustomed to it, however, and out of this familiarity will emerge all the real dangers. As long as he feels overwhelmed he will struggle, will give the best he has and will live from the grace of hearing confession. Familiarity dulls him; sitting in the confessional becomes merely one task among others, and a fatiguing one at that, and uncomfortable as well, since the place is often cramped and cold. The many confessions, one following upon the other, are monotonous and soporific so that he comprehends the individual confessions only incompletely, and thus they become even more similar in his mind.

The struggle against over-familiarity is nowhere more important and necessary than here. The Lord's unique death and Resurrection enter into confession, which itself is always unique. It is whole and undivided, and every sinner who comes has a right to this wholeness that leads him to the unique Cross and thereby redeems him. If the priest always remembers this, he will immediately see that he must not let hearing confession become a matter of mere habit. This would almost be the same as becoming accustomed to the Lord's Cross: the Cross then would no longer be the unique event that it is, but rather just another historical fact, and that, basically, would be unbelief. His own life would no longer be a "making up what is lacking" in the Pauline sense, a participation in the Lord's suffering; everything would have been concluded and finished with the death on the Cross and hence meaningless for us who are living today, meaningless because its entire significance would have been fulfilled in the past. At best we would be those who have been redeemed once and for all; after every sin or even a number of sins we could make use of the things at hand as we wished. Confession's entire moral power would be lost along with sacramental power, and all personal power as well which the Lord wanted to join to the official power, and finally the priest's responsibility before God, the obligation of faith. Faith would become a kind of consumer article; no one would have to get excited about it or pay particular attention to it. Confession would be merely an interpersonal dialogue with a reference to something that has long since taken place (as in the Protestant "confession"); it would no longer be a Christian event as the participation in the unique event of the Lord's Cross. Such a ceremony would contain the danger (one with which Catholic confession is often charged) that a person could sin as much as he wanted because, after all, confession is always possible. If it is not an event in the Christian sense, then it is merely the ever-present reference to a fact that has long been with us. The mere "sign" that confession then would be would thus acquire such power that the way a person

confessed or the way confession was heard would be meaningless. In reality the person would not be participating at all;
indeed, perhaps nothing at all really would have taken place. In
heaven he would be absolved, on earth he would remain a
sinner.

The routine hearing of confession is probably partially to
blame for all this distorted doctrine, this misuse and destruc-
tion of the sacrament. The essential content is lost whenever
the formality alone is seen and emphasized (including instruc-
tion about confession). There the priest no longer must
commit himself personally and participate in the Son's own
commitment before the Father, a participation the Son has
integrated into his own confession. Every confession should
be a genuine Christian accomplishment for both the confessor
and the penitent; it is genuine because it joins genuine human
beings to the genuine God, and an accomplishment because
each gives what he can within the measure of what is possible.
Just as the Lord feels power go out from him when he
performs his miracles, so must the priest give something of his
spiritual substance to the miracle of absolution and to the
entire confessional process. Or think of the sending forth of
the Apostles after the Resurrection. They are to perform
miracles and signs, not primarily miracles and signs external to
the Lord himself, but rather ones that lie in his own words and
most emphatically in the sacraments. We are accustomed to
view the Eucharist as an unprecedented miracle, the miracle of
transubstantiation. Next to it the miracle of confession can
easily pale and then seem frozen within the framework of
Church and office. Quite often the priest only does justice to
this framework without really calling himself to account for
the true content. He concerns himself above all with what is
"valid" and "invalid" but has lost his sense for the infinite
expansion of this sacramental power through the Cross.

Yet the office of hearing confession has arisen from God's
own most strenuous and personal efforts and thus justifiably
can expect the efforts of the person officiating. The "mere

office" itself is the lowest level, whereas what is required is an effort to attain the highest level—effort in the preparation for confession and while saying the prayers, which should indeed be prayed and not merely recited, effort while hearing every confession of sins that have added something to Christ's unique suffering on the Cross, effort during the exhortation, which should take place in the Spirit. Let him listen to the word of the Spirit so that he himself can find the right word with which to encounter the penitent. The proper consolation, strengthening and guidance come about only if the priest gives his own and his best in conjunction with the Spirit. The confessor must exert effort during penance by being willing to have a share in the penance of all his penitents; as far as possible he should choose the penance so that it fulfills its purpose meaningfully. Effort and participation are also required during absolution, a sense for the grace, a sense for his own un-worthiness to have this grace pass through him, a sense also for the joy. Even though this process takes place innumerable times, something living must accompany it each time.

Priests can find an example in the Curé of Ars. Of course, the usual confessor will counter that it is not for everyone to become a Curé of Ars. He does not see that the Lord gives every one of his priests, in an undivided way, the undivided grace of confession, and that thus each of them is given the opportunity to equal Vianney. For what is conspicuous about him is not his charismatic gift of seeing things that people tried to conceal from him and anticipating other matters, but rather his participation in confession. His nocturnal suffering, his weakness, all the toil of his life that he can hardly bear and from which he occasionally tries to escape—all this shows how he accompanies sinners, and all the grace he is given in the process he immediately passes on again to his penitents. His whole existence is that of a channel that receives in order to give; he lets things happen to him so that he, in his turn, can pass them on. (However, he did not always find things easy or completely transparent—occasionally he even deceived himself. That is part of it! How often did he offer the right exhortation, which was received either wrongly or not at all!)

One's participation in confession is not merely a matter of feeling. It is grounded in the Lord himself and in his own participation in all that is human, celebrating a feast with others, weeping with others at the grave of a friend, shaken by an impenitent Jerusalem, rejoicing at the understanding of the little ones. In all this he is wholly man and yet nowhere separated from the Father and nowhere denying his own divinity. The Father's will and his own decision to die for sins are what inspire him. Precisely this fundamental attitude makes possible rather than prevents his participation in everything. There is no betrayal in him. If the confessor remains aware of this, it will keep those motives alive which convinced him to become a confessor in the first place, keep them as fresh as his faith and his love of God. This awareness of Christ's attitude will determine his own fundamental attitude, and, drawing from it, he will be present wherever his office requires it. He will not have to go through any swings of the spiritual pendulum while hearing confession. With his will and his love he will be where the Son's own place is as regards this particular confession; he will try to hear it just as the Spirit hears it, and this will train him in the reception of the Spirit for the exhortation. Then it will not be just an empty phrase to say that in the exhortation, absolution and prayers he is speaking words of the Spirit. No tension need exist between the official and the spiritual, between his word and the word of the Spirit; every confession will be for him an encounter with the confessing sinner, with the gift of grace of the resurrected Lord and with the Holy Spirit so that this threefold encounter—that becomes unified in confession—is already an enrichment for him.

When the Incarnate One encounters the Father in his vision, one can never say that as a man he is growing accustomed to viewing God. Because every earthly encounter between the Son and Father is just as new as their eternal encounter in heaven, the priest's own encounter with the Son and the Spirit in confession must and can always be new itself, and from this perspective it will not be difficult to allow the encounter with the sinner to be ever new. After all, God accepts the sinner in confession in an act that is always unique. Men, to be sure, grow accustomed to everything, and perhaps we would also finally grow accustomed to God and his grace if the all-encompassing element here were not God's eternal encounter with God, in which God never grows accustomed to God but is rather eternally new to himself. This is a guarantee for us that no excessive familiarity need dull us and that we need not fear the law of familiarity. Whenever we use our temporality as a standard, our experience withers and fades away, as, for example, in infatuation compared to real love, which endures through time. One who truly loves, loves the beloved as he is now and as he will be in fifty years and in eternity. He is prepared to endure every temporal disappointment.

The Lord remains in the same fundamental attitude his entire life. It does not matter whether he enjoys a good meal in the tax collector's house or dies torturously of thirst on the Cross or prays for the passing of the chalice for which he had always yearned. Everything takes place in one and the same attitude. So too the confessor who hears a tragic confession today can be present tomorrow at a celebration. If he has modeled his own attitude after that of the Lord, no contradiction arises. The confession he has heard will not so influence him during the celebration that he finds it impossible to sit among cheerful sinners who have committed or are committing many a sin. But his present joy and participation, because they do come from confession, will also be such that at some point they lead back to confession again; all the daily trifles in a priest's life must be integrated into his priestly attitude precisely where he meets the Lord, who as the Son encounters the Father in the Holy Spirit.

From every confession he hears the priest receives a grace

that not only enables him to hear confession better but also strengthens and secures his entire priesthood. Wherever he appears, in whatever atmosphere his activity takes place, he will do it in a priestly fashion, so that openly or in a hidden way he brings people closer to God; what he radiates will cause those who confess to do so more effectively and those who do not confess to come back to the confessional. If there is no noticeable tension in him between life and function, the tensions and contradictions in others will either disappear or diminish—tensions between their sins and their joys, their good will and their hardness of heart, their own lay life and the sudden appearance of the priest, their own worldliness and the fact that God exists. Everything the priest performs as a priestly function, indeed his very existence as a priest, benefits each function and circumstance of his life. Whether under grave or happy conditions, his obligation to God can only increase; he feels responsible before God everywhere. In the same way a mother is always motherly toward her child: while she punishes him and makes him stand in the corner, she is dressing the doll she will give him at Christmas. Similarly, the Son is always both the Son and the Redeemer of the world, and every situation in his life is a potential access to confession; for he lived his entire life from the perspective of confession, a full human life with all its affairs preserved in unity.

Nothing in the course of a confession is unimportant to the confessor. He must learn to accord every part of confession its proper significance. The listening to the confession itself seems initially to be the part that will be most varied, since every person confesses differently and will confess differently each time. The confessor should pay attention to two things during this confession: the attitude assumed and the facts presented. The attitude of the penitent is more interesting than the facts. The priest must take cognizance of the facts he hears so that he acquires an overall picture of the penitent's life and is able to

separate the important from the unimportant. The preliminary
evaluation that he undertakes during the course of the confession can always be corrected or even reversed by what
follows. In that preliminary evaluation he will orient himself
more toward things that lie within himself, things he himself
has learned and things he has experienced while hearing confession. He can organize what he hears into various categories:
serious sins, mortal sins, possible sins, imperfections and so on
—more as a mnemonic aid in enabling him to acquire a kind of
picture and overview. By proceeding in this way he no doubt
will also see—in the sequence followed in the confession, for
example—how the sinner has evaluated himself and in what
order he ranks his sins. But by this procedure the confessor has
not yet grasped the more profound element, the attitude. An
entire path leads from sin to confession; after finding out what
the sin is, it is no less important to discover why the sinner has
come to confession. The connection is not self-evident. From
the manner in which the confession is presented the confessor
should be able to determine the relationship the penitent has
to confession, whether it be urgent need, force of habit or
whatever. This would be informative regarding the confessional attitude. There are other signs, such as the manner
of confessing, the choice of words and the more or less
parenthetical remarks offered.

There is the objective sin that is presented in an objective
confession and is covered by the form of the sacrament itself;
but along with this there is the person who has transgressed
and now confesses. These cannot and should not be separated
totally from one another, and above all the second should not
be slighted in favor of the first. The act of confession involves
humility, and this humility is grace, and this grace must not
go unused. It is, as it were, dual, both an objective and a
subjective grace. The priest hears confession by the power of
his objective office; but he is subjectively a man who has
chosen the path of that office. Across from him sits another
man. In order to reach him, the priest must see to it that his

own existence as a man does not disappear behind what is official. In the form instituted by the Lord he must see the content dear to the Lord's heart, namely, grace in judgment, brotherly love in the official framework.

The act of listening usually begins completely within the objective realm, and the sins the priest hears hardly differentiate themselves from other sins; they are identified and ordered beforehand—nothing new. Then suddenly something else becomes visible through the confession: the sinning and confessing person, the self, which is always something unique. Viewing things from this perspective the confessor will perhaps have to reverse his entire scale. An accent, a scarcely formulated "something" suffices to allow this second view to appear. Of course, there are countless average people in whom it is difficult to discover something truly personal; yet one must always try, all the more because the priest himself is always in danger of becoming another average confessor. If he does not make an effort, the circle of those he personally encounters and helps in confession will become ever smaller. If he makes that effort, however, this circle will become ever larger, and both in himself and in his penitents he will diminish the scope of the merely habitual. At some point there will be nothing more he can do because the penitent is too rusted and encrusted. Nevertheless, the confessor must hear as much as possible, and not just through psychological technique but rather in empathy with the Spirit and with a view toward the exhortation. A cooperation between the Spirit and the priest must take place even while he listens to the sins.

Every confession is an individual act, but none stands alone; it refers to earlier ones and anticipates those in the future. This, too, must be kept in mind by the priest: he is not listening to a confession of unconnected sins, but rather to an excerpt from a historical existence. What he hears is no doubt a summary intended for the present moment, but it represents a more or less lengthy period of time. Similarly, the grace of this confession is to nourish an entire period of life. By means of the confession the priest must be able to determine where he should sow the seed, where he can intervene and where the really fertile element lies in this person. He is someone who is on his way to Christ and to eternal life, and he should receive something that makes him abler for this journey.

In the normal life of a Christian there are only a few moments in which a priest can intervene formatively. Confession is one of the most sublimely appropriate moments. During communion the priest distributes the Body of the Lord and leaves the communicant to receive its effect; personally, he can hardly have a real effect. But if a person has become a priest in order to lead as many souls as possible to the Lord, he must remember that the confessional is a privileged place for this. Although the sacrament itself has its own fixed form, a great deal of space is left open to the priest's own humanity, to him who as a sinner is permitted to help other sinners. As a sinner he stands in communion with sinners; as a priest, however, he stands in communion with the Holy Spirit, whom he must allow to be active within him. Such an occurrence presupposes a great deal of readiness and genuine will on the part of the priest as well as effort: when he acts, the Spirit acts through him.

Insight into the penitent's attitude is important for two reasons: first, so that the proper exhortation can be given; second, so that the proper prayer for the sinner becomes possible. There is a priestly prayer that originates in the act of hearing confession and that presupposes that the priest has correctly recognized and evaluated his penitents. There is, of course, also a general prayer for all penitents that is distributed anonymously and resembles the Church's store of prayer. In addition to this, however, it is important that there be a personal prayer, and this prayer must be combined with genuine recognition.

One who decides to become a priest in the Lord's service wants both to serve the Lord and to help men reach him. But service to man also involves something twofold: service to humanity as a whole—of whom the priest has actually only heard at second-hand how seriously it sins and how deep it has fallen—and to a circle of people that he actually reaches and that consists of nothing but individuals. Even the seminarian must include "his" people in a special prayer. Every penitent is an exponent of all sinners, but he is always this individual Christian who thirsts for absolution. The priest must recognize both in every penitent, and this presupposes continual spiritual alertness both to recognize the individual as such and to see in this individual his connection to limitless, nameless humanity. The penitent thus obligates him doubly for himself and for the others. Everything is both personal and general: behind this confessor stand all other confessors, and among his penitents there are perhaps future confessors who can experience through him what genuine confessing and hearing confession means, and who have a special right to his prayer.

When dealing with people one often has the feeling that something is not quite right and that the situation is opaque. A person tells his story and one somehow lets oneself be taken in by him, and yet one knows that things really could not be as he says. One becomes involved in a lie and leaves the other person without being able to come up with the right solution. There are always excuses: it was time to go, or one was tired or sick. But perhaps a certain degree of alertness was lacking.

Here we can refer to the example of the Curé of Ars. He does not let himself be caught unaware. He stands in a truth that is much greater than he, and he stands in it continuously. He does not differentiate between his own truth and that of God. He always participates in the truth of the confessional. He tells people the truth straight to their faces, and as he does so the truth finds an opening in them. The situation he creates very often does not coincide at all with the one the penitent himself wanted to create. He gives his penitents a share in God's own way of seeing and puts them in a position to see correctly themselves, often without their even noticing. It is not as if they deceive him intentionally; they really wanted to confess their sins, but they do not see them in truth.

From this we may conclude that it can be right to confess even if a person is not aware of having committed a specific sin. His intention may be to bring his life back to the proper axis of truth, one that otherwise may become displaced without his noticing. If this person has a confessor who is as penetratingly honest as was the Curé of Ars, the idea of opening himself to him can have a clarifying effect as early as the preparation for confession. Indeed, the mere existence of the holy Curé and of all holy confessors offers to all penitents an increase in the grace of truth. They have performed a preliminary function that forces the penitents to confess in the proper orientations.

This situation of confession in the truth can and must extend itself to include the Christian's entire life. A person has the opportunity to live in what might be called a latent confessional situation. And there is the communion among all penitents that extends through the very heart of the Church herself, of the Church-Bride who stands in unconcealed truth before her Bridegroom. But one must always pray for confession in order to increase its store of truth.

In the human relationship between penitent and confessor, the spheres of their mutual insight into the truth cannot coincide completely. They are like two circles that only partially overlap. At best, the penitent confesses as he believes he must; he can only approximate the ideal of God's demands. And the confessor perceives the confession only approximately the way God does. Only in God's absolute truth might these two spheres coincide.

But the Curé of Ars, in his humility, knows so well what God expects that during confession he takes what still is unclear in the penitent's sphere over into his own sphere, which is clear because of his perfect stance before God. Now the two spheres coincide. This is the perfect way to hear confession, which is not possible without an act of taking the sinner over into one's own sphere. Vianney occasionally interrupts the confession with his own comments, corrections and additions which show the penitent that the confessor sees through him better than he sees through himself. But if the penitent is not willing to break with sin completely and stand transparent before God, he will see in these comments only the one-upmanship of the person listening and not the divine light revealed in them. What the Curé says in confession normally points to what is even more important, something he leaves unsaid by taking over the confession.

Children often draw extremely peculiar letters. In writing class the teacher draws the letters on the board; the child copies them and perhaps leaves out the parts that seem too "dangerous" or too difficult. What he writes is not wrong but incomplete. The teacher then adds what is missing so that the child can show his mother his notebook at home. There comes a point at which the Curé of Ars takes the notebook and pen out of the pupil's hand in order to make additions. We are not really able to say how he does this; it is a secret between him and the penitent that not even the "mother" need learn.

Every confessor should put the confession he has just heard in another light, since God himself hears it differently, illuminates it differently and understands it more fully. Holiness in the Church knows this. A saint knows that when he confesses he always writes only part of the letter and that God, together with the confessor, adds the decisive, missing part. In his confession he must contribute as much as possible so that God and the confessor can form a totality from it. He gives over and takes over simultaneously; he surrenders what is his own and declares himself in agreement with its completion. It is a passive occurrence within the saint, an interplay of action and contemplation. The saint knows that his own confession is nothing more than an attempt. He attempts, and then he lets it be. As soon as it is a matter of someone else's confession, however, he throws himself into it and surrenders himself in order to take over. Every confessor, who is always a penitent too, should know both aspects well: both passive and active participation.

The Exhortation

The confessor should remember that he speaks the name of the Holy Spirit, and that the Spirit, because of the death on the Cross, has a right to insist that the priest make room within himself for the Spirit, the place that is his due. The Spirit descends to the act of confession from eternal life. He is God, and the confessor is God's representative and must utter his own words with reverence in the Holy Spirit. He receives them from the Spirit and must do so in humility and an attitude of service. He is permitted, as it were, to clothe these words with his voice and with the form of his sentences, but the content itself is the Spirit. Even if the priest speaks unaffectedly and naturally, he must speak so that the Spirit receives its due in his speech. The penitent must encounter the Spirit through him.

Since the Son was fully man and maintained his full human personality in spite of his divinity, the priest in turn may and should preserve his own personality in the confessional. His words, which do justice to the Spirit, must at the same time bear witness to his entire human effort, his insight and his intentions. He himself must appear together with the Spirit in his undertaking; sacramental words are not to be careless or indifferent words. The sinner's relationship to God must be mediated through a relationship between two human beings. Thus it is essential that the officiating priest somehow break through the sphere of intimacy that the individual has with God, involve himself in it and penetrate it; the sinner's confession has given him the right to do this. But he must undertake it in highest reverence, since the penitent is momentarily involved in an encounter with God. The priest takes part in a process that makes the sinner into a saint, and his words must serve to accompany this transformation, indeed to transport the sinner into this very transformation. Hence they must be so gentle, and yet so decisive and insightful, that this transformation virtually takes place with the words themselves. They must have the power to heighten the penitent's readiness to allow this sanctity to come about as far as possible. Although absolution comes as a turning point bestowed from above, it is not magic. The penitent also must be present; he must proceed as if accompanied by the confessor through a tunnel at whose end absolution awaits him. It is a path which only God can prepare, but which a person can traverse with a human companion who represents God.

The exhortation in turn has a dual countenance, according to whether the sinner is viewed as one of the mass of sinners or as this specific penitent. Absolution will also have both faces. In the exhortation one must also keep in mind that the penitent is someone who has already taken the humiliation of confession upon himself and thereby demonstrated his willingness to separate himself from his sin and to go the way of God. This specific sinner must thus be shown his specific path, and it must be shown to be feasible. Because this sinner is one of countless many, the path itself will remain the general Catholic path.

It is often good to present the exhortation so that its first part refers to the confession of sins preceding it and under certain circumstances to point out angles of vision to which the sinner has paid too little or no attention at all, motives that are hidden to him, reasons for his failings—yet always so that the penitent is able to do something with it in a practical sense. Even if one cannot simply moralize, if the individual's own situation is to be placed as far as possible into the great truth that descends from the Trinity through Christ to the Church and to the Christian himself, this whole process should reveal approaches to new life. On the other hand, not only should the personal path be pointed out, but this personal element also should be expanded expressly into the Catholic sphere. The penitent should become not only a better person but a better member of Christ and the communion of saints, and his sense for both must be expanded and deepened.

The exhortation must come from the confessor's own world of prayer, and this must be tangible. The penitent's confession has permitted the confessor to enter the former's intimate sphere. In the exhortation the penitent himself, in a different way, now receives a portion of the confessor's intimate sphere by gaining insight of some sort into the latter's life of prayer. The exchange between the Holy Spirit and the confessor is possible only in the world of prayer. Within the sacrament there arises a living communion between penitent and confessor which even in its highest discretion still maintains something infinitely close. It is part of the priest's instrumentality that he does not cloak himself in his official capacity but instead reveals himself and surrenders something of his most inward sphere—though this disclosure may under no circumstances be misused. It is an act of trust which is, for each in his own way, mutual. For a penitent who is not alert—and alertness is a function of faith—will not perceive this intimacy of prayer at all. It does not lie on a naturally comprehensible level, but rather in a zone disclosed only by prayer. The main point, however, is that the Spirit speaks and becomes transparent; this is why the confessor will never make an example of himself but rather will remain totally objective in what he says. In the case of important exhortations the penitent usually can scarcely remember the specific words, but he knows exactly what was demanded and where the path he was shown ought to lead. During confession the penitent is not disposed to hear the words of exhortation other than as words in the Holy Spirit.

Every intimacy in faith is like this. That the Lord becomes present among us during the Consecration of the Mass is an experience about which the person who really prays will not speak; at most he might speak about it with another who prays, though it is precisely with this person that he will prefer to be silent. Together they share a secret in God and deal with this secret in the greatest discretion. A similar relation exists between the penitent and confessor. What is between them they do not consider important; rather, the important thing is that, in this mutual openness to God and to one another, the activity of God and of the Holy Spirit can take place unhindered. A great deal in the sacrament is official, prescribed, ordered, impersonal and structured. But in order to hold all this together and so that both confessor and penitent know that they are open and exposed before God, there is suddenly this human contact from both sides, a contact that actually is nowhere more intensely alive than precisely in the official character of the sacrament.

For the exhortation the confessor should choose words that come from the world of the gospel. This, too, makes the penitent conscious of being taken back into the sphere of the Church and, beyond that, of being brought into a new closeness to the life of the Lord. The exhortation should, of course, be practical and personal, but in such a way that one can sense the living presence of the Lord in his divine word throughout. Just as the gospel—through the Gospel!—should be proclaimed in the sermon, so also the exhortation, which is not to be a sermon, should nonetheless be evangelical proclamation.

The conclusion should be a kind of concise summary and synthesis, allowing the listener to remember better what was said and to impress "his" exhortation upon his memory.

Spiritual Direction

In germ, the exhortation contains what is called spiritual direction, something that can be described more specifically. The Church guides the believer in the sacraments, each of which signifies and brings about a particular kind of encounter with the Lord. The believer is both an individual and a member of the communion of saints and can be guided variously from both perspectives. He can be guided, on the one hand, through the Church and through the sacraments in general, of which confession is one. He can also be guided as an individual by the individual spiritual director under special circumstances. The circumstances exist when the confessor sees the necessity of direction, because he recognizes that the penitent has a particular task, or when the penitent himself expresses the desire for such guidance, because he wants to get closer to the Lord but does not know how. In the second instance the confessor must first convince himself of the necessity of such direction. If it is urgent, the confessor will recognize it easily; the penitent is requesting only what God inspires him to request. Direction is almost always required when it is a matter of arranging an ordered, stable life of prayer and meditation. It is up to the confessor to choose the suitable means. He can concern himself more with the penitent during confession and above all during the exhortation, which he can expand and amplify by giving rules for behavior. He also can schedule the penitent to come at a different time in order to discuss important questions with him.

If the desire originates with the penitent himself, the confessor must make a thorough investigation of his motives and in so doing depend upon the Holy Spirit of confession in order to get a precise picture of those motives. There may be unhealthy, selfish desires hiding behind the main one. Perhaps the penitent merely wants to be more the center of attention or be more important. Perhaps he is living in a pathological disquietude and is seeking to use the spiritual director as a kind of psychiatrist. Or perhaps in a snobbish way he finds spiritual direction interesting for a time but wants to reserve for himself the decision regarding duration and intensity. It is not always easy to see through the motivating factors the first time, but the confessor should be able to achieve clarity after two or three meetings. If the penitent's wish is legitimate, it is

still up to the confessor to determine whether he should
lead this person to a harmonious development of his life of
faith without a particular task or apostolate, or whether perhaps subsequently a more specific mission will emerge; whether
everything should be cultivated at the beginning in order to be
selective later, or whether a particular path seems more urgent
right from the start.

To provide the right direction the confessor must extract as
much as possible from confession. He must guide the penitent
in a light that has its source essentially in confession; he
must concern himself intensively with the means whereby the
penitent can turn away from his sins, and suggest, introduce
and explain certain readings, spiritual exercises and meditations
on the Holy Scriptures. But the goal of spiritual direction is
always progress toward, not away from, something. Nowhere should a simple negative or a vacuum arise; the space of
sin should become an expanded space by means of God's
love. Simplifying matters, one might say that the task of the
confessor is above all to separate the sinner from his sin,
and that of the spiritual director is to introduce the person
receiving direction to a greater love of God. The ascertainable
step out and forward (pro-gress) would then be primarily in
confession, whereas the movement toward something new
would lie in humility, childlikeness and passivity to God's will
that could no longer be measured. In any case, all calculation is
useless. The person submits himself to God's own influence,
and all personal difficulties and successes that previously
served as signposts become secondary; he should speak about
them now only if the spiritual director expressly requests it.
All his energy is directed toward awakening the hunger for
God in his soul, allowing the Son's own attitude to influence
him ever more intensely and becoming more alert to the
demands of his discipleship and the inspiration of his Spirit.
The prerequisite is that his life become a consistent unity, that
his internal and external behavior be congruent and that his
behavior before the confessor coincide with that at home and

at work. Spiritual direction is meaningful only if the penitent is completely honest, and the confessor must be sure of this honesty.

Spiritual direction will always remain somewhat questionable, since many penitents—not to say most—do not attain this clarity and complete transparency, this unambiguously Christian attitude. The penitent should be totally taken into the Lord's own manner of thought, be surrounded completely by him. The more deeply he comes into the Lord's power, the more he will renounce his own overview of things; he loses the criteria of measurement. The confessor, however, must maintain this overview. A person needs a director precisely where he can or should no longer see. The necessity remains even if the direction can often be rather loose or the meetings rare. It is thus up to the confessor to determine when some form of more intensive direction is necessary. If he is convinced that it is necessary, he should proceed with the utmost tact; for if a penitent becomes prematurely aware that he might have a special mission or is being prepared for one, he might either withdraw or become arrogant, or he might be afraid of becoming arrogant. One should lead him to view this direction as something necessary for him at this time without his sensing anything distinctive or special in it. Although it sounds paradoxical, it is true: the more specific a penitent's path is, the more he should have the feeling of belonging to the whole. This is in fact correct, since the more specific and distinct a mission is, the more it reaches out to encompass the *communio sanctorum*. If the penitent notices that the confessor is undertaking some sort of direction, he may see a kind of "consecration" in it; but this must take place in such a way that his reflection is not nourished and so that he gets the feeling of being incapable of understanding the required service unaided, rather than the feeling of any sort of distinction. Somebody takes the broom out of his hand and shows him how to sweep the floor. He once thought he was able to master more delicate skills, and now he needs somebody to initiate him into the crude ones! It is like the washing of feet: a person probably has washed his face and hands, and now it turns out that his feet are dirty. Spiritual direction is a school of humility.

It is also such a school for the confessor, who now ceases "preaching on the mountain" and sets about the task of instructing the small group of disciples. For him, too, the Lord heightens the requirements and gives him sharper vision than the priest normally possesses. He must learn to submit himself to the Lord's own more intensive direction so that he himself will be capable of directing. Every person who comes closer to the Lord comes into truth and, viewed from a Christian perspective, under the demand of greater humility. The director and the one directed must become more humble together, which never means they should become unsure, but only more trusting, more childlike and more at peace.

The Prayers of Confession

The prayers spoken during the sacrament place the priest and the penitent together in the center of the Church. These words are immutably fixed and constitute a solid framework. In their particular sequence they constitute a whole; they effect what they express, and the Church both intends and guards their meaning. On the one hand they are like a final saving fence that makes all escape impossible, a guarantee for the correctness of what is happening without any consideration of either the individual confessor or the individual penitent, an expression of the official character of what happens. On the other hand they are splendid words containing complete fullness of life, words that gently surround the penitent and allow the confessor to give his utmost. They are a completely adequate expression of the truth. They do justice to every confessional situation and encompass both extremes, the depersonalized official element and the office that has become totally a person.

Dominus sit in corde tuo are the words spoken before the penitent begins. The Lord is to rule; the entire confession is his gift and his possession. He is acting in what is his most intensely personal concern. From the very beginning he should fill the penitent's heart and lips—let there be no distinction or tension between heart and lips!—so that the confession is proper and complete. And although it is the Lord's affair, it takes place in the name of the Father, the Son and the Holy Spirit. The Lord grants access and guarantee, but the actual realization comes about in the name of the triune God, as does everything that the incarnate Son does and institutes on earth.

Misereatur tui omnipotens Deus. After the exhortation, which leads away from sin and into new life, this prayer expresses the essential aspect of this sacrament: God is to be merciful. Confession, contrition and exhortation are meaningful only in view of God's mercy. What is said here is not a mere word, nor is it a mere wish; it is the Church's prayer for that which she requests in obedience to the Lord and which is granted her without fail: the absolution that is both offered and effected from the Cross. What the Church utters as a prayer the priest must also utter in the utmost prayerful seriousness. It is not a "formula", but rather the Church's dialogue with God. The priest's attitude should not be different from that of the Church. Neither should the priest's attitude while hearing confession, giving the exhortation or saying the prayers be any different; it all should issue from a single attitude of prayer. The penitent also has a right to this priestly prayer.

Absolution is a unity composed of various cooperating elements, both visible and invisible, natural and supernatural. In its innermost essence it is the evocation of the great absolution of the Cross in the case of this particular sinner. The Risen One has given the priest of his Church the full authority to bind and to loose, and this present absolution issues directly from the Easter situation. The pierced hand of the Crucified One, who is now transfigured, dispenses it. The priest is permitted to dispense it in the name of the Lord while both rejoicing at the transfiguration and remembering the price paid for it. It is an official act that he performs at the commission of the Lord, and which he knows contains the Lord's entire transfigured life. But it is also a part of the answer the priest gives to the Lord's invitation to discipleship, the fruit of his life as a disciple and a high point of his priestly efficacy. In absolution, the Lord, the priest and the penitent encounter one another in a communion otherwise unequalled. The Lord in his freedom has desired to join his grace to the priest's words of absolution, and the priest is permitted to disclose the source of heaven in an abundance incomprehensible both to him and to the penitent. It is objective grace, in its origin dependent only upon God himself and incapable of being coerced by any confession, contrition or ritual; yet it is immediately transformed into subjective grace and is then indivisibly both, for grace is always granted for a life in grace, though life always knows that it lives only from the grace of another who is independent.

The words of absolution draw their power from the Cross. Perhaps some scenes or situations in the life of the Lord gradually pale in the priest's reflection. Perhaps there comes a time when the small child in its mother's arms no longer means much to him, perhaps because of the saccharine pictures or because he has no real ties to small children. But he can never reflect enough on this transfer of the authority of absolution; he encounters it repeatedly in the confessional and experiences it either directly or indirectly in his encounters with people. It is the essence and summary of the Lord's life and contains the entire mystery that concerns him directly as a priest; the longer he reflects upon it, the less will he come to terms with it. Every time he speaks the words of absolution he feels himself invested anew with the authority that comes to him through all the centuries unbroken and directly from the Lord. He is now contemporaneous with the Lord, with the Cross and with Easter. The sinner's encounter with his Redeemer takes place now, and he, the confessor, is to serve as mediator between the two. As an unworthy vessel he speaks the *"ego te absolvo"*. At this moment nothing should be capable of distracting him from the necessity of uttering these words. His unworthiness plays no part whatever. He speaks the words as a commission; they are words of the Lord and are therefore the Lord himself.

Ego is a word that means the Lord and yet encompasses the priest as well; it means the office of the Lord that includes the priestly office, but also the Lord's love that includes the priest's love. The *ego* of the Lord includes the *ego* of the official priest who, out of love for the Lord, once chose to be his servant. Hence a certain relationship exists between the fruit of his previous priestly life and the dispensation of authority as the fruit of the Lord's life. It is the fruit of the priest's life, a life that is permitted to receive the fruit of the Lord and to pass it on as its own. The portion the priest takes is not that of a servant from a distance, but rather that of a friend in intimacy, a portion so intimate that the Lord not only lives in him but also says *ego* in him and draws him into his effective self. They are words of pure miracle, words of full explosive power, words that would be blasphemy and presumptuousness if separated even the smallest distance from the Lord. But because they are words of the Lord they can encompass the office of the Church and the person of the priest without distancing themselves from the true speaker. They can be spoken in complete simplicity; but how pregnant with mystery is this simplicity!

Ego TE *absolvo*. The *ego* absolves the Thou, the Thou that has just confessed and now may leave its sins behind because the Lord has given satisfaction for them. This Thou is present both as a totality and as an isolated individual who is striving to return to the totality of community, but it also comes from the totality of a community, the community between the Lord and the Church in the priest. In the *Dominus vobiscum—et cum spiritu tuo* of the Holy Mass the one primarily addressed is the unity of the congregation, and the priest stands before it as an individual. In confession the converting sinner is the individual who stands before the community of Lord and Church and through it is reintegrated into the communion of saints. He will not need to feel like a stranger in the community but rather will already be carrying the Lord's mark of honor when he returns and for that reason will be recognized as one who belongs. His temporary withdrawal has not made of him a second-class, suspect member; on the contrary, he has even come back equipped by the Lord with new gifts of grace. He also came to confession as a member of the community; the sinful member had isolated himself from the community through his own guilt, but the Lord grants him the harmony between person and community again.

Ego te ABSOLVO. The person is separated from sin; the bond between him and sin is severed. The sin can now go to hell; it is the shell that remains behind after its fruit has been removed. It collapses like a balloon without air. It has become insignificant, unimportant, null and void, meaningless. The person no longer drags it along with him. The Son who suffered takes it over. This is simply event, process, actuality. Whoever has confessed is the sheep that was lost and is now found again, found after all its straying through danger by the Cross and death. The newly found sheep is carried back to the flock. Through it the others learn what the Lord is prepared to do for them. If the shepherd has his hundred sheep before him, they are all equally dear to him. If he loses one, it is as dear to him as the other ninety-nine together. Afterward, he puts it back into the flock, and without loving it less he now finds that all are again equally dear to him. The one is not singled out; it does not keep the signs of having strayed, neither in the eyes of the others nor in the eyes of the Lord.

Absolvo. It is the Lord of life and death who says this, the one who brought back Lazarus from the community of the dead. Lazarus is absolved from his death; who can now address him as a dead person if he is living? Death has been cast off and replaced totally by life; no one can be alive and dead at the same time. In the same way, the sins of this penitent have been severed from him; life has replaced death. Yet when they were committed, when they were repented, they had such an enormous reality and belonged so clearly to the person who committed them!

When the Son is sent out from the Father in order to become a man among men, he maintains the vision of the Father, a vision that perhaps above all is knowledge. Yet what he then undertakes—existence as a human being—he undertakes totally. He does not intend to become a man only for a few moments at a time, and in the meantime to be a god. Nonetheless, he does remain the incarnate God. He requires something of this same totality of those who want to follow him, and he grants something of it to those who stay with him. He wants them not as half-sinners and half-saints but as total saints so that their relationship to him is undiminished; this is why he does not half-release them from their sins so that they must drag them around like chains. He steps between sinner and sin, severs the bond connecting them and alters the present reality according to his sovereign benevolence. Whoever has confessed may view his past sins in no light other than the one he is granted. An example is the Samaritan woman whom the Lord freed from her sins; she knows very well that she was a sinner, but she lives totally in the new grace. In everything that concerns faith and life in faith, there is a kind of analytical confrontation and recollection that is characterized much less by one's own personality than by the will of the Lord himself. If this were not the case, if we were left to ourselves, our prayers, for example, would quickly concern themselves only with our own affairs or would become like the preparation of an endless list of wishes. If we pray as God intends, however, our self-occupation grows weak and disappears more and more. This is the case with everything concerning faith. Once our sins have been confessed, they have sunk into insignificance and are worth mentioning only in relation to the grace that has been granted. If we pray properly—as far as we can—we become aware of the mystery of this free guidance by the Lord, and we should also entrust to this same guidance our awareness of our confessed sins. We can and will know something about them, but we should not seek to know something more or something different than the Lord shows us. He will determine the measure and manner of their subsequent effect; we ourselves may not fix the significance we will attribute from now on to these past sins in our life. A life of penance for earlier sins can at most give consideration to the extent of the sins' insult to God; but this can be done only in a form that becomes ever more objective. One's own sin can be an occasion and point of departure, but that is enough! It is not sin itself that carries the most weight, but God alone, the loving, offended God. In the end it no longer matters who offended him. A life of penance is an ecclesial life that performs penance for everything that displeases God. The illumination comes from the Lord; he may very well want us to look back sometime at our past sins and perform a personal "meditation on sin", but this ought to take place within an obedience of faith. We should not believe that the more we look at our sins and are disgusted, the more worthy we will become. It is absurd to seek to attain worthiness by considering one's own unworthiness! Even during the First Week of the thirty-day Spiritual Exercises one meditates in obedience, and the times and objects are determined and marked off by another. What is important is not sin, but conversion. It is important that the exercitant is brought into the proper attitude that he will need from the Second Week on. Of course, the opposite danger also exists, that of no longer wanting to have any connection with sinners. Meditation on sin can also serve to train us in the Christian awareness that we are, after all, sinners. Within this context, however, one should not forget that the thirty-day Spiritual Exercises are intended essentially to be made only once in a Christian's life, and that their First Week is intended above all to bring a person finally to a realization of what it means to confess.

Ex auctoritate ipsius. The power of the Lord is unbroken within the priest. He can employ it officially without having to come to terms with it anew each time. He has received it from the Lord once and for all for whatever situation is at hand. Whenever he absolves, he has it, and the personal decision to absolve or not lies in the priest's hands. He has it by virtue of his office, but it is not the "power of the office"; it is the power of the Lord.

Ab omni vinculo excommunicationis et interdicti. Everything that can stand as a hindrance between penitents and the Church is removed. The Church enumerates these hindrances and adds in the case of the priest-penitent the *suspensio*. The penitent is to return as a totally absolved and cleansed person, one newly obligated to the communion of saints. *Inquantum possum et tu indiges*, to the extent that the priest has received power from the Church to remit ecclesial punishments and to the extent that the penitent needs such remission. This limitation thwarts any misuse. For the Church bestows this authority of the Lord on the individual priest; even if the authority's power to bind and loose is complete, the individual priest cannot loose that which the Church wants bound and which she at the moment is not willing to loose. A country or city can be placed under interdict and with it individuals who themselves are not guilty, but who may nonetheless die under the interdict. The Lord will accept them, for his grace is not limited by ecclesial authority. It is also possible for a person to be excommunicated without knowing it. He, too, could be released from punishment, even if he did not know that he was excommunicated.

Passio Domini nostri Jesu Christi. The first thing mentioned after absolution is the Lord's Passion. Just as our guilt was the cause of the Lord's Cross, so also we owe it to the Cross that we are absolved from our guilt. Earlier, during our preparation and in confession, we were the guilty ones who had to stand before the Cross; now, liberated and rejoicing, we must enter our new life with the Cross. The merits of the Mother of God and of all the saints are mentioned in unity with the Passion. Earlier we were alone with the Holy Spirit; no accompaniment was mentioned. We stood like individual defendants before a court. Even though the priest prayed for us and helped us, we were alone. Now that we have been given back to the community, our view of all the Lord's saints is restored. Their merits are the fruit of his Passion, and in this way we, too, are placed together with them under the law of the Cross. The Cross is not just that which our guilt has caused, not just the Lord's own, lonely accomplishment; it is the community of all who live under the Cross. When the fruit of the Cross becomes available to us, the communion of saints also becomes available and with it the right to eternal life. If we were to remain the persons that absolution makes us, we would be certain of eternal life.

The absolved person is integrated into the community of those standing under the Cross in such a way that his merit, everything he undergoes and does in faith, is added to the totality of the work of salvation. He is once again a living member of the one, active and apostolic Church. No part of his life that was meaningful and fruitful for the Church can now be viewed as lost. His activity and suffering are valuable because through grace they are drawn into the merits of the Lord and his Mother. Hence his activity and suffering obligate him from now on. The priest, whose words will accompany him in the future, imposes this upon him in a double sense: he must do what is good, and he must not flee from what is difficult. For the Son perfectly fulfilled both the apostolic action commissioned by the Father and the apostolic suffering that was no less commissioned. The Lord mentioned only the Passion, but his image is what stands over everything the absolved person does, over both his actions and his passion. His activity will necessarily be accompanied by obedient passivity, and the Lord has a right to both, because he himself did both and because only both together create the balance of Christian life. Activity is not permitted to choke passivity. The Lord could not have balanced out or avoided his suffering by an excess of good works. Every absolution also contains a warning against activism.

Praised be Jesus Christ. This is how the penitent is dismissed, with this greeting in the vernacular. It is a praise of the Lord; it is the conclusion of confession and the beginning of new life. As a dismissal it is both end and new beginning. When the penitent answers "Now and forever, amen!" these are also the first words of his new life, a binding obligation to sing the praises of the Lord to the end and beyond into eternal life. He may no longer seek to separate himself from this praise; he takes it upon himself for his whole life, and life is now the unity of earthly and heavenly life, almost as if this dismissal from the confessional were a dismissal into eternal life, and that piece of earthly life still falling in between is only parenthetical and episodic. Every confession confronts us directly with eternity.

After Confession

The penitent takes up his daily life again. He ought to go about it in new freedom and new obligation. A complete realignment of priorities should have taken place for him. Even if his life remains externally unchanged, the spirit in which he forms it and comes to terms with it is new. Earlier, when guilt burdened him, his daily work did not go un-influenced by it. He and his work did not really fit together. Now that he begins anew, his relationship to his work—however secular it may be—should be a purified one. There is no longer reason to complain about the monotony and senselessness of life and no reason for melancholy and sulkiness. He has within himself a new power, which is capable of making his life into an expression of the word of God. The things he did under compulsion before, he now does as one who has been liberated, one accompanying the Lord and accompanied by him. His life is praise of Jesus Christ, and there is no reason for this praise to be feigned.

It is admittedly true that no sacrament that is taken seriously can tempt to resignation as can confession. We all know that we "fall short", that we who have just promised to praise God through all eternity nonetheless will fall prey to the world's temptations again. We are freed, to be sure, but we do not really believe in our freedom, and so we soon abandon it again and fall into the snares of sin. We are full of inner objections, and our entire person stands in its own way. We do not want to recognize the power the Lord has granted to us in confession. This power needs to be both exercised and practiced if it is not to grow lame. It remains alive only if it is able to manifest itself in our life.

The new power is a power of prayer and of the Christian attitude that the Lord gives us. No miracles or upheavals take place in our external lives. Grace is within us. It comes from the Lord and seeks to return to him. Its fruit belongs so completely to the Lord that perhaps it remains intangible to us and makes no impression on our surroundings; least of all does it bring about any changes in the external circumstances of our life. If this were its effect, we somehow would attribute it to our own proficiency; we would be successful in our own eyes and would have become zealots. We would have subordinated the power of absolution to finite goals and would not have had the right to say "Now and forever, amen!" Conversions are not something one can demonstrate to the astounded world by presenting one's moral successes from a stage. Admittedly, change is needed, even in the world around us, but the change should come about primarily through prayer and attitude.

These can exercise their effect in the world. But this is not what we strive for as our first goal; our primary goal is rather the nearness to the Lord, service of God, one that increasingly becomes a service unto eternity itself and is not something temporal, of today, or immediate. Just how the world is transformed through this service is primarily an affair of the Lord. We are no longer defenders of our own interests; we are defending those of the Lord.

When the priest leaves the confessional after having heard several or a great many confessions, he perhaps senses a new kind of loneliness. He has led all these people to a new life. He has absolved them under commission from the Lord, and this can elevate his spirits. He has tried, in a human way, to help people who are in difficult situations, and he hopes he has helped them out of these situations. He has seen the paths of unfailing temptation and sin, but the paths he has pointed out, ones that as such ought to be paths of grace, perhaps appear to be less unfailing. He must believe in spite of this, and must live more than ever from within a faith so strong and radiant that those he absolves are strengthened and accompanied by this faith. If he had had nothing to show them but paths of reason, he would now be a resigned person pure and simple. Yet even if he has heard confession in the power of the Lord and employed and demonstrated his own power as best he could, melancholy can still creep up on him. Perhaps his penitents included some he knew well whose situation had grown worse, others who appear to stay forever in the same place, and still others who apparently had not understood his exhortation or taken it to heart as he intended. Many merely wanted to receive absolution and be on their way as quickly as possible. In retrospect the priest perhaps will be inclined to view the institution of confession on the whole rather skeptically or to condemn as inadequate his own way of hearing confession and of giving the exhortation. Either the means or he himself is unsuitable. The effect of such a wonderful institution does not correspond to the effort expended. His mood is understandable, but he should not let it get the upper hand. He acts out of faith, and in his administration of the sacrament of confession he must become ever more believing and ever more trusting.

After administering the sacrament he must accompany the church of penitents in zealous prayer. The office of confessor is not over for him after absolution. He must remain in the power and weakness of the sacrament, which is the power and weakness of the Lord and his Church. It is the priest's consolation to consider that he is not dispensing his own power, but rather the power of the Lord, whose weakness is itself a form of power. At this point the priest should not calculate, but should reflect that through his office the Lord can help him far more than he suspects, and that his penitents oblige him to be as close as possible to the Lord. Just as he has released the penitent into eternal life, he may also believe that the penitent in his turn releases him into eternity and into the eternal power of the Lord.

Even while mutually releasing one another, confessor and penitent meet again in prayer. A sacrament is never concluded in an earthly, finite sense. It extends into eternal life, and the life of grace is also hidden eternal life. This life comes alive for us in prayer. In prayer each releases the other to God and in precisely that way maintains contact with the other; in prayer each binds the other more strongly to the communion of saints. Recommending the confessor to the power of God means making him more capable of carrying out his office and obtaining grace for him for subsequent confessions, one's own or someone else's. After all, one does not pray for oneself, but rather "into" the Church with the kind of selflessness that characterizes all ecclesial prayer.

Bound Sin

The Lord demonstrates the seriousness of sin and confession by holding open the possibility that a person's sins may be retained. The priest hearing confession employs the power of the Redeemer, and when drawing from this power he must act within the divine Spirit, must make distinctions and as far as possible have his own decisions approximate those of God. For it is revealed that God, too, makes distinctions and decisions in his judgment.

The Redeemer shows us the possibility that one's sins may be retained, but this possibility does not limit his love; it is included in the act of his love that institutes the sacrament of redemption. The retention of sins can and must count as just as much an expression of redemptive love as the forgiveness of sins. Both have the same goal: to guide a person back to the love of God. The sinner whose sins are retained is not for that reason an outcast, even if the path of absolution is made difficult for him; it is made difficult so that he may experience the greater love and become more capable of grasping it, and so that when he returns to the community he may bring to it a greater portion of love than he can now. The retention of sin may never be an act of anger; even if he whose sin is retained behaves in such a way that the confessor's personal anger seems justified, his anger must remain with God's own anger, and that anger is, from the perspective of the Cross, a form of his love. Under no circumstances should the retention of sin acquire the appearance of a break, particularly not of a final break. It is only there to clarify for the sinner in a more penetrating fashion the seriousness of his condition and also to point out how great the responsibility of both parties is, the penitent's as well as the confessor's. The latter should not let any aroused emotions misguide him, for in relation to the sinner he bears the responsibility of the Church as a whole, indeed that of God himself who gave him the power of absolution. The responsibility is so great that it ought to be shared by the entire community of those who confess. Every person whose sins were absolved should remember those whose sins were retained and carry them in prayer until absolution can be dispensed to them.

The exhortation in the case of retained sin must be given with particular care. The penitent would not be there if he had not hoped for absolution. He probably saw his own condition as less confused than it really is, and he did not expect the refusal of absolution but rather had hoped for absolution. The condition into which the penitent now falls is more humiliating than at the beginning of his confession. The exhortation must strengthen him, console him, give him more insight, bring him to the point where he can bear his penance with humility, and open up for him paths into the future which will lead ultimately to absolution. The blessing the priest gives him in place of absolution should be accompanied by an especially serious and penetrating prayer.

The Seal of Confession

Emerging from the mystery of Holy Saturday, the Lord institutes confession, which is totally enshrouded in this mystery. A person can imagine Good Friday; anyone can imagine the Cross and the physical pain accompanying it, the thirst and exhaustion that ultimately lead to death. He can remind himself of pain endured, of humiliation and anxiety, and can depict these for himself to a heightened degree. He can think, at least, that in this way he can comprehend something of the suffering of redemption.

But no experience can lead him into the mystery of Holy Saturday. Every natural power of imagination fails here. It is a most profound mystery between Son and Father. What we know of it through revelation is so little and so peripheral that no one can presume to have any real knowledge of it. Silence covers over the mystery of Holy Saturday, the silence of death, of the immeasurable abyss between dying and Resurrection, silence that no doubt says more than words because Father and Son are silent with one another in the most sublime intimacy, but silence, because the Son, returning from hell, says nothing about this mystery.

In silence over this mystery he institutes confession: the confession he suffered, but about which he was also silent in a mystery of silence with the Father, an ultimate mystery of night, of final intimacy as the final seal on the work of the Cross. Something of this silence clings to confession. The priest hears the penitent's sins according to their number, kind and circumstances. From the penitent's attitude the priest learns a great deal about the mystery of the penitent's existence in the Father and in the Church, of his dialogue with God and of the words and silence within this dialogue. He perceives something of the most intimate depths of this guilty person, something of which not even the person himself may be conscious and which lies beyond the boundaries of perception. He does not perceive all this separately from sin, but rather together with the confession of guilt, as does the Son on Holy Saturday. That is why the priest himself, who perceives the sinner's confession more through silence than through words, is himself obligated to silence. Although many other obvious reasons may be mentioned in addition, they are mentioned only in addition. The penitent should know he is protected against indiscretion and against any sort of misuse. He confesses to God so that God may absolve him, and God has decreed the intervention of the Church in order to make confession more human, more true and more Christ-like. The confessor is the concreteness both of God and of the Church for the sake of the penitent, and for that reason he may not constitute an interruption of intimacy.

When the priest dismisses the penitent, he dismisses him into the deeper silence of God and, in some sense, into Holy

Saturday, where the Son sounded out the ultimate mysterious depths of the grace of redemption. Therefore respect for the Son's mystery, and with it for the penitents themselves who have the courage to confess, respect for their attitude before God, obligates the priest to keep complete silence.

This maintenance of silence protects not only the individual who has just confessed; it also protects the entire ecclesial community, for which confession must remain the institution of redeeming grace to which one can entrust oneself without fear. If the priest were to speak about a confession he has heard, the sacrament would be devalued in the eyes of sinners, and devalued even more would be the Church that administers confession as a mystery of God that is to remain a mystery. The priest is not placed at the point where the sinner sins, but rather where he speaks, confessing, with God. If he confesses properly, he is so much in God's hands that God determines his attitude, and this divine effect is more noticeable than his own sinful personality. God allows the priest to see something of his activity by power of special grace, but he is not to see it for himself, but for God and the Church.

What the priest knows from confession is the object of his prayer, not of his conversation. It belongs to him only for the sake of enriching his office, not for the sake of satisfying human curiosity. It belongs to him for the sake of heightening his ability to perceive God in confessions. He need try neither to remember what he has heard nor to forget it; in this he should merely accept what God gives him. Of course, in his spiritual direction he must have a good memory and should not shy away from employing memory aids under certain circumstances for the more important things, but only for what is fruitful, for what brings the penitent closer to God and to the Church. He can drop and forget what is not fruitful in the Christian sense. In some instances it will be helpful and even necessary to ask the penitent for permission to speak with him about earlier confessions. Confessional responsibility itself may require this. The priest must have a general idea what has become of the more serious transgressions in earlier confessions of which nothing more is said—whether a person has forgotten them, views them differently, no longer takes them seriously or really has overcome them. Precisely here it makes a great deal of difference whether a penitent only comes to confession occasionally or is involved in ongoing direction.

11. THE CONFESSION OF THE SAINTS

Holiness is found at the Cross. It is actually the preeminent holiness, of which the dying Son of God offers a final, comprehensible proof. There he is both the God who left his own glory with the Father and the man whom God made holy in every respect. Every element of holiness comes from and is of the lineage of the Cross, even that of the untouched and innocent ones, the ones who, if it were possible, would have endured nothing of the Cross. All holiness comes from the Cross and returns to it—not to the empty Cross, but rather to the crucified Lord who on that Cross summarizes in himself his entire earthly life and everything constituting holiness and the life of faith of the Church.

Confession is the fruit of the Cross, and the moment this fruit becomes accessible to the Lord he passes it on. When he mandates confession he is pointing out his possession of this fruit that only now really has become his own, visible and tangible, as he distributes it. We can contemplate this fruit in confession just as we behold his flesh—indeed, himself—in the transformed Host. The difference is that we view the confessional fruit of the Cross not as something existing but as something to be accomplished. Though momentarily visible when Christ gave up his spirit, it remains comprehensible for us only in its application. Every saint will confess in the communion of all believers in order to receive a share in it—though the saint will perhaps do so not so much in order to hear the absolution of his own sins as to come to the place where the fruit of the Cross becomes visible. He confesses in order to reveal the form of grace, to lend that fruit greater

Editor's note: The few examples concluding the present book are continued in the author's work already mentioned, *Das Gebet der Heiligen*, in which she describes a large number of confessional attitudes of well-known and less well-known saints and ecclesial personalities.

visibility, to participate, indeed to share the burden of the Cross by means of his own confession, and by means of his own confession to let the Lord's word of grace become incarnate once more in the mystery of holiness he instituted. He confesses in a great nearness to communion; he actually confesses eucharistically.

The saint gives confession a certain quality that it receives only through him, a quality so precious that one might believe the Lord had precisely this quality in mind when he instituted confession. Precisely the saint who has sinned least could make the perfect confession: the confession of his distance from God, a confession that also includes all sinners. The confession of the saints, more than any other, is ecclesial and social. It is that confession in which the other sinners participate. It is a fruit so pure that it may not be consumed by one person alone.

We can differentiate three groups of saints: those who have sinned and know from experience what sin is; those who have not sinned and do not know from genuine experience what sin is; and those who have not sinned and yet know what sin is. As representatives we can list these three: Francis, the little Thérèse, and Aloysius.

Francis has sinned. He no longer views his sins individually; he views them as a sum of offenses to God. He loves the Lord ardently, ever more ardently. He is consumed by this love. The more truly, profoundly, penetratingly he loves, the more true, profound and penetrating his sensitivity becomes to the offense that sin causes the Lord. This holds true both for his own past sins and for all the others he comes to know. Whenever he hears that something evil has happened or that others have committed sins similar to those he once committed in the same mixture of knowledge and ignorance, whenever he sees how they prefer sin to love, he confesses, and his confession stands at the burning focal point of the offenses to the Lord; the more his love grows, the more burning this focal point becomes. It becomes the focal point of the focal point. Somehow he confesses in timelessness. The more his love consumes him, the more he senses how much more consuming it should be. In this heightening he also sees the offenses to God become heightened, and sin is subdivided for him into areas characterized by the sins he himself has committed. In one way or another he confesses distance from God, and every saint in this group does this. Although he no longer is deceitful, he loves truth too little. Although he no longer hurts his fellow human beings, he does not give them nearly as much as he could, as much as pure love wishes them to have. He confesses, as it were, a kind of reflection of his sins. Since he sees the offense to God better now, his earlier sin shows him how little his present virtue is actually fulfilled. He does not see it theoretically, but rather as a pure, pressing reality. He is the one who today has replaced his former sin with tepidity, the one who in spite of knowing better does not respond to the burning demand. Hence it seems as if he is always confessing his former sins, which appear in a continually new light the more he becomes aware of his responsibility. Precisely because he no longer is deceitful, he should possess a consuming love of truth. Every confession refines his insight and increases the feeling of his own unworthiness, but by no means drives him to despair; for he feels grace, and feels it all the more strongly the more unworthy he feels. God's mercy accepts this wretched sinner!

Little Thérèse possesses a peculiar manner of confessing, just as she has a peculiar knowledge of sin. Basically it never becomes clear to her what sin is. She learns by way of suggestion that people do things that offend God, and that those things have certain names which exhaustively define them—falsity, theft, murder, hatred, pride, self-love. But these things and their names have no essential relationship to her. Evil is for her simply the opposite of good, but this oppositional relationship remains somehow vague and abstract. Everything that is sin is somehow terrifying to her; she thinks about sin, she speaks about it, but in the way that one speaks about things which one really does not want to be explicit about. This relationship to sin is reflected clearly in her relationship to what has been called her "night". In her suffering she gets to the Mount of Olives; she also gets there with her insight, knowledge and burden of sin. Yet one really cannot know clearly and specifically what the suffering on the Mount of Olives is without knowing equally about the Cross of Golgotha. Hence Thérèse never gets beyond a kind of groping and furtive circling around sin. On the "Mount of Olives" one cannot evaluate fully just how sin offends God. Confession is a matter of Thérèse accusing herself of small and ever smaller things, but she never reaches the point at which Francis confesses. She is infinitely happy that she has not committed a mortal sin, but this knowledge inhibits her confession. It remains at the stage of preparation, just as the Mount of Olives is a preparation for the Cross. There are various beginnings, steps are made, but they never reach the end. There even occur a few excuses in the midst of her accusations. And yet she would be prepared to bear more and would be glad to be in the communion of those who confess. Here the accent on smallness can occasionally have a trivializing effect. Both her confession and her knowledge of sin lack full transparency, the light of day and realism. Saints in this group, too, could offer full confessions if the saint were seeking to be led all the way to the Cross, not by anticipating things the Lord does not give, but rather through a passivity that at the decisive moment not only passively forgets itself but also actively accepts what is revealed. Even he who has not committed sin should be familiar with it. It can be a matter of Christian courage that is not satisfied with what is vague, a courage that knows that after the "Mount of Olives", as painful as it may be, the real cross comes.

Aloysius is quite different; he is more like Catherine of Siena. He suffers from sin, and he does not withdraw from this suffering. He is able to view sin objectively and realistically. He has no share in it and is not bound to sin by sin, but he is familiar with it. He wants to know what it is, and what is unbearable for him passes over immediately into what is unbearable for the Lord. He is not bent on drawing and seeing his own boundaries or seeing to what extent he shares in it or does not. His past plays no great part. He is grateful to be allowed to do that which God expects of him right now. If he had committed a mortal sin, then he simply would have committed it; it would seem terrible to him, but he would confess and then carry on. If, on the other hand, he knew he had not committed one, perhaps he would quickly thank God, but he would not give the matter any lasting significance. He, too, confesses his distance from God, but without really concerning himself with the source of this distance. He looks closely at the Ever-More of God and his grace, and he confesses what he himself lacks. None of this is theoretical, and therein he resembles Francis. Neither does he develop any theology of the sins he sees others commit. In his opinion they are believers just as he is, even fellow religious, who do not love enough; but neither does he love enough. Hence, although he can identify their sins with certain suitable names, he is one with them in this lack of love. It is not important to him whether their lack of love occasions those specific sins, or, as in his case, hinders a more intense ardor. His contrition arises at the point where he recognizes his distance from the demands of love. Hence one cannot say that for him and those like him confession has no "content" and therefore no absolution. He senses the grace of absolution intensely, more than does little Thérèse. It gives him a new impulse for love.

The Mother of God does not feel excluded from the communion of those who confess, because she participates to the highest degree in her Son's confessional attitude. She participates in the confession of all sinners at the point where the Son as a man is completely transparent before the Father, where he lends his divine transparency to his own humanity. His Mother sees this infinite transparency, and in spite of her perfection she is always striving to attain that unattainable transparency. She strives without concerning herself with results. The essence of the confessional attitude for her is to become more like the Son. There is no absolution for her; instead, she enjoys the closest proximity to the Son as the Redeemer and purifier of all sinners, and she pours out this proximity in a eucharistic spirit.